Eastern cultures

A *Unesco Courier* anthology

Eastern cultures

A *Unesco Courier* anthology

Edited by Anila Graham

Longman

LONGMAN GROUP LIMITED
London
Associated companies, branches and representatives
throughout the world

First published 1971
ISBN 0 582 34101 9

Exclusive distributor in the U.S.: Unipub, Inc.,
New York
U.S. Library of Congress Catalog No 74-147794

Printed in Great Britain by William Clowes and Sons Ltd
London, Beccles and Colchester

This book is based largely on material which
originally appeared in the *Unesco Courier* (a monthly
illustrated magazine available on subscription from
Unesco headquarters in Paris).

Acknowledgements

We are grateful to the following for permission to reproduce and adapt copyright material:
George Allen and Unwin Limited and Harper & Row, Publishers, Inc. for an extract from *Part II:*
The Beginnings of Civilization by Sir Leonard Woolley in *History of Mankind* and *Prehistory and the*
Beginnings of Civilization by Jacquetta Hawkes and Sir Leonard Woolley, Copyright © 1963 by
UNESCO; Educational Productions Limited and World Confederation of Organisations of the
Teaching Profession for an extract from *Man Through His Art: Music* edited by Madame Anil de
Silva, Professor Otto von Simson, Dr Roger Hinks and Philip Troutman.

For permission to reproduce photographs, we are grateful to the following:
Paul Almasy, pages 36, 43, 125 *below*; Por-Olow Anderson, page 66; Ara Güler Collection,
page 112; Christine Bossenec, page 104; Bibliothèque Nationale, Paris, page 87; Serge Bourguy-
non, page 72; Camera Press, page 108 *below left* and *right**; Ceylon High Commission, page 108
*above left**; L. Cottrell, page 55; Dominique Darbois, page 51; Christiane Dessochs Noblecourt,
page 63 *below*; Egypt Exploration Society, from *Oxyrhynchus Papyri*, page 20; Gilbert Étienne, from
Inde Sacrée, Éditions Ides et Calendes, frontispiece; Hutchinson Publishing Group Limited, from
David Diringer, *The Alphabet*, pages 16, 17 and the cover picture; J. Van der Haagen, page 64
above left and right; India House, London, page 97*; Iwanami Films, Tokyo, page 40; Rex Keating,
page 64 *below*; Richard Lannoy, pages 38, 69; J. Lavaud, page 53; K. M. Lee, page 93*; Magnum,
pages 32, 56, 70, 77–80, 113; André Martin, page 73; Musée Guimet Archives, pages 37, 47, 54;
Nenadovic, page 67; Phaidon Press, from *Art of India*, Stella Kamrisch, page 50; P.I.C., page 39;
Albert Raccah, pages 62, 63 *above*; Radio Times Hulton Picture Library, page 109*; Sciroku Noma,
from *Japanese Sculpture—Archaic Period*, Bijutsu Shuppan-Sha, page 23; Skeel, pages 49, 52; University of Assiut, page 128; Victoria and Albert Museum, London, page 42; John Walsh, pages 95*
and 96*. Photographs not acknowledged here are reproduced from the *Unesco Courier*.

* Denotes photographs not originally appearing in the *Unesco Courier*.

Contents

Foreword

This book is an outcome of Unesco's major project on Mutual Appreciation of Eastern and Western Cultural Values. It has two purposes. One is to provide secondary school teachers and teacher trainees in Western countries with information about countries and cultures of Asia and the Near and Middle East which they can use to amplify and enrich their teaching about the Orient. The other is to serve the need of general readers everywhere for attractively presented but authoritative information which will help them to enlarge their knowledge and appreciation of Eastern cultures. Both purposes are spanned by Unesco's central aim of promoting better understanding between nations and peoples.

The book is an anthology of articles on a wide range of subjects drawn from issues of the *Unesco Courier,* the monthly illustrated periodical of the United Nations Educational, Scientific and Cultural Organization. The collection is indicative rather than exhaustive; it does not pretend to present a comprehensive and balanced picture of the regions or cultures concerned. One of the main difficulties has been to keep up with important developments which are taking place in the East today, for articles describing social and economic conditions written only a few years ago become rapidly out of date. However, where possible, the articles have been brought up to date with fresh material and they are linked by new texts prepared especially for this book. The manuscript has been prepared in consultation with authorities in the countries concerned. Views and opinions expressed are the responsibility of the authors and do not necessarily represent those of Unesco.

1 Points of view

Introduction

Nations see themselves as the hub of history and it is this that makes the study and appreciation of other peoples and cultures a difficult task. Each nation tends to consider that it is in the centre of the map and that all other cultures are peripheral. The same attitude applies whether we take the case of the ancient Chinese, who considered China the 'Middle Kingdom' or, at the other end of the world, the Western Europeans who believe that they are the centre of the world – a fallacy which the Mercator Map Projections do much to encourage!

The temptation to put not only one's own land in the centre of the map, but also one's own people in the centre of history seems to be universal. The story is often told of a small tribe whose word for 'mankind' was the name for the tribe itself. Other tribes were merely incidental in their picture of the world – perhaps not even fully human. Chinese, Hindus, Muslims and Westerners alike have smiled perhaps too quickly at the rather perilous naïveté of that small tribe, as one of the articles below shows.

During the past decade or so there has been an increasing awareness of the need for history of a world scope. But what goes by the name of 'world history' is still essentially Western history amplified by a few unrelated chapters on other parts of the world, notably India, China and Japan. In one of the articles which follow, the point is made that during the last three thousand years there has been one zone, the eastern hemisphere, in which various lands of urbanized literate civilizations have been in commercial and commonly in intellectual contact with each other. Today at least 90 per cent of the world's population now traces its history to some segment of this group of nations. A history of interregional developments among the civilizations of the eastern hemisphere, developments transcending cultural regions like Europe, the Middle East, India, China and the Far East, will go far towards meeting our needs for world history.

Peoples and cultures look very different when viewed from places as far apart as Washington, London, Paris, Cairo, Karachi, New Delhi, Tokyo or Djarkata. The tendency for most people is to look on other cultures as 'quaint' and to feel a certain smug superiority in their own cultural values. Perhaps Eastern cultures, more than any others, have been subject to many misrepresentations. To most Westerners the East is static and changeless and even well-intentioned school textbooks continue to portray ancient customs in their introductions to these countries – customs and conditions which no longer apply, as is shown in the article on textbooks on Japan – a dynamic country which is changing rapidly, but of which the average Western school-child is given a very distorted picture. And yet it is essential that young people of the rising generation should have the correct information to judge international affairs and to promote international understanding on the basis of an accurate appreciation of the mores and cultures of other lands.

In the centre of the map

Marshall G S Hodgson

In the sixteenth century the Italian missionary, Matteo Ricci, brought to China a European map of the world showing the new discoveries in America. The Chinese were glad to learn about America, but one point in the map offended them. Since it split the earth's surface down the Pacific, China appeared off at the righthand edge; whereas the Chinese thought of themselves as literally the 'Middle Kingdom', which should be in the centre of the map. Ricci pacified them by drawing another map, splitting the Atlantic instead, so that China appeared more central, and maps are still commonly drawn that way in that part of the world.

Europeans of course have clung to the first type of map, showing Europe in the upper centre; while the commonest maps in North America show the USA in that post of honour, even at the cost of splitting a continent in two.

ANCIENT CHINESE VIEW OF THE WORLD

Many Chinese used to suppose that the Temple of Heaven at the Emperor's capital, Peking, marked the exact centre of the earth's surface. To be sure, Chinese scholars even in the Middle Ages were aware that China could not be said to be mathematically central; they knew the general lay of Europe and Africa and the Indian Ocean, and a writer could remark that the 'centre' of the earth was along the equator. Nevertheless, even for sober historians, the pivotal fact of human history was the condition of the great Chinese empire, in which was concen-

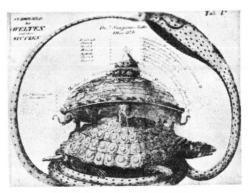

How ancient Hindus saw the universe. According to an ancient Hindu conception of the universe, the world was supported on the backs of several elephants, standing on a giant turtle. The cosmos is depicted here by a snake, the *Naga*

trated all the splendour of polished civilization.

It could in fact be claimed that for a time China was the wealthiest and most populous, the most aesthetically cultivated and even the most powerful state on the earth; but when this fact was made the basis for the Chinese picture of the world, the result was tragic miscalculation.

MEDIEVAL HINDU VIEW

For the medieval Hindu the world was a place for the purification of souls. Kings and their empires came and went, the gods themselves arose and perished – time was infinite, space immense, with unlimited opportunity for every soul to reap in birth after rebirth what it had sown. In much of the universe, indeed, souls dwelt in untroubled bliss; it was the distinction of our own toiling, earthy regions that here men could choose responsibly between good and evil and their consequences. Here life was arranged for the exercise of virtue, each caste of men having its own function in society; if a man fulfilled one role well, in another life he would have a higher role to play, and might eventually rise beyond the transient vicissitudes of existence altogether.

Accordingly, so far as history was significant, it was as ages varied in the degree to which society was well enough ordered to give virtue its due place. As a given cosmic cycle wore on, disorder increased and justice faded; only in the central parts of the earthly regions – in India, that is – was society still well ordered; there Brahmins still offered sacrifices and the other castes ruled or served according to their status.

As our degenerate age drew on, even

From the first known world atlas. The most important attempt of the ancient world to place the study of geography on a scientific basis was made by Claudius Ptolemy, celebrated mathematician, astronomer and geographer of Alexandria. His *Geographia*, written in Greek around AD 140 comprised eight books which included a general map of the known world and twenty-seven maps covering different countries. Ptolemy's original work written on papyrus has not survived but copies were made, the oldest dating from the thirteenth century. In 1886 a manuscript was discovered in the monastery at Mount Athos, Greece, which included a reproduction of Ptolemy's original world map. The section of this manuscript containing this map is now in the British Museum. The *Geographia* was printed for the first time in a Latin translation together with maps in Italy in the latter part of the fifteenth century. Its contents, however, had already become known in Western Europe through manuscript copies, and their study influenced map making in two ways. They led firstly to the addition of degree lines to maps and secondly to the compilation of new maps of countries which had been inadequately represented by Ptolemy

in India itself the social order was upset, rulers rose from the basest castes, and finally entered as conquerors—Muslims from the west, and even the remotest Europeans. Through all this outward humiliation, however, the Hindu could know that there in the central lands where the sacred Ganges flowed he could still live the way of truth and holiness—inaccessible to lesser breeds of men—and aspire to the highest degrees of rebirth.

THE VIEWPOINT
OF THE MEDIEVAL MUSLIM

To the medieval Muslim the world looked very different from what it did to his Chinese or to his Hindu contemporaries.

History was not a matter of the varying strength and weakness of an imperial centre of authority and civilization, nor was it a passing incident in an infinite succession of worlds. Rather it was the story of a single species created just some 5,000 years ago by God to do His will once for all. From Adam on, God had sent thousands of prophets to the various peoples, bringing to each its laws and sciences; at last He sent Mohammed, proclaiming the final law in which all earlier truth was perfected and which was gradually to prevail over the whole world, replacing all former laws.

Many Muslims believed that Mohammed's birthplace, Mecca, was the centre

of the earth's surface. To Mecca, men pilgrimaged yearly from the farthest parts of the earth, and it was supposed that in the heavens above it the angels themselves performed worship; here was the very throne of God, where heaven and earth were nearest. To be sure, scholars knew that the earth was a sphere, and God equally present everywhere in the hearts of the believers. But their more sober picture of the world was equally effective in supporting the eminence of Islam. They thought of the inhabited quarter of the globe as a land mass lying between the equator and the North Pole, and between the oceans to the west and to the east—roughly Eurasia and northern Africa.

This was divided into seven 'climes' from south to north, and from extreme heat to cold. Muslims writing in the latitude of Syria or Iran explained that in the hot south men grew lazy and so remained backward in civilization; and likewise in the far north where it was too cold—in northern Europe, for instance—men's skins were pallid and their minds sluggish. Hence it was that only in the central moderate climes, like the Mediterranean lands or Iran, were minds most active and civilization most advanced; from there the blessings of Islam were gradually being brought even to the remotest areas, among the Negroes in the hot south and the white men in the cold north.

MEDIEVAL WEST-EUROPEAN VIEW

The West-Europeans of the same age had many of the same ideas of history and geography as the Muslims, getting them from the same Greek and Hebrew sources; but their interpretation was very different. For them history was the story of God's progressive dispensations of law or of grace to His favoured people. Out of the descendants of Adam, God has first chosen the Hebrews, but with the coming of Christ it was a 'new Israel', the Christians, that received His favours.

Even among the Christians God had made a further selection—casting aside those of the Levant and Greece as heretics or schismatics, in favour of the West-Europeans under the Pope at Rome.

The West-Europeans allowed that the centre of the world's surface was Jerusalem (by exaggerating the length of the Mediterranean, their maps could show Spain and China as equally distant from it); but they assured themselves that, just as at the beginning of history Paradise was in the east where the sun rises, so in these latter days the centre of God's vicarship on earth was in the west, where the sun sets; henceforth Rome was the centre of all authority, spiritual and temporal.

THE MODERN VIEW OF THE WORLD

In modern times all these medieval pictures of the world have vanished, or been modified. With the discovery of America and the circumnavigation of the globe, the

---

One of the oldest Christian world-maps. This is how Beatus, a geographer and monk at the monastery of Valcavado, Spain, depicted the known world in AD 776. Considered to be one of the oldest Christian world-maps, it was attached to his *Commentaria in Apocalypsin* and was probably intended to illustrate the distribution of the apostolic missions throughout the world. It has survived only in ten copies, varying in date from the ninth to the thirteenth century. The one shown here, made at the monastery of St Sever in France around AD 1030, the most valuable, is now in the collection of the Bibliotheque Nationale, in Paris. The earthly paradise is shown at the east of the known world (right of the map). The adjoining inscription *Gens Seres* (the silk people), is Beatus's description for the Chinese. Beatus has represented mountain chains by markings with saw-like edges. Like earlier geographers he sees the world as an island in a circumfluous ocean filled with fishes and islands

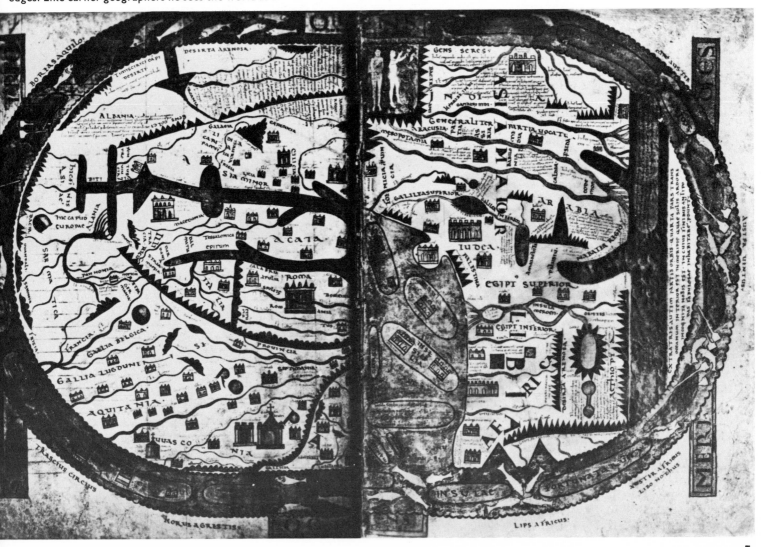

discovery that Earth is a tiny planet in an immensity of space, that mankind has been upon it hundreds of thousands of years and is still a newcomer, we have had to rethink our situation.

The West-Europeans were the first to be really faced with the new discoveries and have consequently led the way toward creating a new picture of the world. But they have not yet escaped the temptation to make geography and history centre upon themselves.

EXAGGERATION OF EUROPE'S SIZE

The map of the world is constructed accordingly; Westerners distinguish five or six 'continents': Africa, Asia, North and South America – and Europe. It is sometimes ingenuously remarked how much smaller Europe is than the 'other continents' – yet in political discussions, in grouping statistics, or in historical comparisons these divisions repeatedly recur as if fixed by nature.

In European 'world atlases' each European country has its own map, with the rest of the world in a few pages at the end. The map ordinarily selected to show the world as a whole is ideally suited to reinforce this way of seeing mankind. On the Mercator world map not only is Europe in the upper centre: it is represented as a good deal larger than the other great culture areas. Most of these lie south of the fortieth parallel, while Europe is almost wholly north of it, where Mercator's projection begins to exaggerate the size of things enormously.

Accordingly even on the world map, which ought to provide a sense of proportion, there is space to name a great many places in Europe, while in other populous centres like India or China, shown on a much smaller scale, only a few chief places need be indicated. Although equal-area projections of the world have long been available, in which shapes as well as sizes are much less distorted, Westerners understandably cling to a projection which so markedly flatters them. They explain (as if they were engaged in nothing but sailing) that the true angles given on the Mercator map are of convenience to navigators; and in atlases and wall-maps, in books of reference and in newspapers, when Westerners turn to see what the world looks like as a whole their preconceptions are authoritatively gratified.

In Western thinking – and this thinking still dominates too greatly other parts of the world as well – the West was the centre of the world; and the world at large was to be regarded, historically most especially, in the light of its effect upon and contributions to the modern West.

All too often men of other regions also have tacitly accepted the Western criterion, trying to show the supremacy of their own region by showing how much it helped to form or is worthy to alter, the West. Such an explicit orientation is now being sloughed off; but it has left innumerable traces in our thinking which do not disappear so easily.

A peculiarly important example of the results of this attitude is the concept of 'the Orient'.

The root fallacy is to take 'Orient' and 'Occident' for two equal halves of the world. A Mercator projection map of the world, which frankly exaggerates the Western countries in comparison to more southerly lands like India, may encourage this. But the new global maps, as well as the briefest study of linguistic and historical variation, will remind us that the West is historically simply one among several regions in the eastern hemisphere, each of the same order as itself in size, populousness and cultural wealth.

Even today it is very hard to persuade a historian of 'world literature' that it is misleading to give a chapter to each of the little literatures of Europe, and then one chapter to that of 'India' – as if he shared the supposition so often found among the uninformed that one should learn 'Indian' before going to live there. If it is worthwhile treating world literature at all, then Tamil and Bengali and Maratha should have chapters as distinct from Sanskrit as are the Italian and German from the Latin.

But in any case, for the purposes of comparison and of perspective, it would reflect the position of India as an understandably complex subcontinent, not as one incomprehensibly vast 'country' in 'Asia' roughly answering to Italy in the more comprehensible Europe. Throughout the serious work of scholars we find 'international' affairs in Europe treated as matters of world import, while relations between parts of Africa or even between India and China come under the head of regional studies; a war among Western powers is a world war, while one between China and Japan is 'localized'.

Judging all the world by its effect on the West, Western history used to set about tracing civilization from its earliest times in Egypt and Babylon only up to a point – only so long as these lands remained the nearest direct antecedents of the modern West. We ceased tracing civilization in those countries almost as soon as Greece and Rome came to have a literate history. As soon as north-western Europe came to have an independent story, all lands east of the Adriatic dropped from sight, and the very words we used suggested that henceforth the West was the world.

The whole story commonly ran as if (as Westerners have indeed actually believed) civilization itself had been moving steadily west. From this false impression of the story's continuity arose a number of illusions, which continue.

First, it came to be supposed that after the early years the more eastern nations had in fact little significant history. This impression was early extended from Egypt and Iraq to other lands; reinforced by a number of accidents, including the habits of Indians and Chinese of glorifying and exaggerating the antiquity of their institutions. A variant of the same notion, encouraged by the speed of changes in the modern West, and by illusions of distance, was that of the static, changeless East.

Second, a different and more persistent illusion produced by the pattern was that of historical discontinuity – recurrent degeneration, followed by a new start.

The famous fall of the Roman Empire seems to be the kernel from which such conceptions have grown. Spengler decried a West-centred history, yet accepted the limitations imposed by the westward pattern, allowing no history to India or China in the last two millennia. Toynbee is anxious to recognize the continuing evolution of the non-Western nations; yet he seems to have used the 'Fall of Rome' as his starting point, and hence involved himself in a system of distinct societies, definitively rising and falling, which naturally bristles with fundamental anomalies. Thus the distortion has infected his work, even though he guarded explicitly against the illusion of the 'static East'.

Some will have the impression that in advocating an interregional history of the eastern hemisphere, I am advocating not world-oriented history, but just Oriental history. Not quite: a history of 'Asia' without Europe could conceivably resemble a history of Western art or letters without France.

Japan misrepresented

A LOOK AT FOREIGN TEXTBOOKS
Tatsumi Shimada

From *Japanese Family* (England 1950)

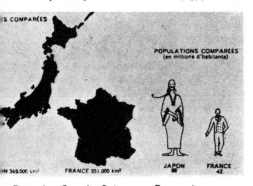

From a primary school text book (Egypt 1957)

From *Les Grandes Puissances Economiques* (France 1957)

POPULATIONS COMPAREES
(en millions d'habitants)

JAPON 88   FRANCE 43

FRANCE 551.000 km²

From *Over Land and Sea* (England 1956)

The point is that from a world-historical point of view, what is important is not European history in itself, however important that be for us all; but its role in interregional history. This role has latterly been momentous; but our very concentration on internal Western history has commonly obscured our view of the West as one dynamic region among others in the wider world.

Today, when the other side of the moon is visible to us through photographs, one would expect people on one side of our own globe to be well acquainted with the opposite side. In fact, though, there is a surprising lack of accurate knowledge. With countries like those of Western Europe, which are extremely close to each other, and where travel is unhampered even by the necessity for visas, understanding between nations can be hoped for.

However, greater distance – not to mention differences in ways of life, religion and cultural forms – soon reduces this understanding to a far from satisfactory level. Even in such cases, a constant supply of accurate information, together with efforts toward comprehension by both sides, ought to make it possible to maintain a satisfactory degree of understanding. In fact, however, things do not work out this way.

People tend to have preconceived ideas about distant countries. In particular, inhabitants of far-off Europe and America who have never seen Japan seem to include such preconceived ideas in the image they cherish of this country. The unsavoury picture of Japan as a country of militarists doubtless still persists, and, along with it, the romantic ideas associated with Madame Butterfly.

Not infrequently, Japanese who happened to be travelling in foreign parts have been taken by surprise by the questions put by the local inhabitants. These range from specialized queries on, say, 'the role of Shintoism' to elementary ones such as 'does Japan have trains and street-cars?'

In the case of Japan, about which accurate knowledge tends to be very rare and misapprehension common, the question of what practical steps can be taken to improve this situation is a matter of serious concern. A small number of enthusiasts, therefore, recently made a start – albeit a very unspectacular one – toward remedying the situation, by making a thorough investigation of inaccurate accounts of Japan in school textbooks in use in foreign countries.

Textbooks, unlike specialist works, are compulsory reading for schoolchildren and students. This means that when they misrepresent the truth about Japan their harmful influence is extremely pervasive. Once errors have occurred in the basic facts given to children in primary and middle schools, it is wellnigh impossible to erase these first impressions. Yet a survey of textbooks collected from thirty-one countries, which was begun in 1948, shocked those responsible by the depressingly large number of distorted views of Japan it revealed.

The more their investigation proceeds, the more apparent becomes the large number of inaccuracies and outright errors in the contents of the articles on Japan. Many cases have also been discovered where very old photographs and illustrations depicting Japan in the Meiji or Taisho Period are presented as if they showed modern conditions.

The photographs are generally extremely old and many of the illustrations show strange people and ways of life which suggest a mixture of Japanese and Chinese cultures without representing either of them accurately.

The early Meiji Period – roughly from the 1870s into the 1890s – saw work started on the Panama Canal in the New World (1881) and on the Trans-Siberian Railway in the Old, while in Asia Burma was annexed by Britain in 1886. If, in the case of any other country, street scenes or local manners of this period were represented as those of today, it would cause no little surprise. In most countries there are even considerable differences between ways of life before and after the Second World War. This being so, it would be a shock to anyone, let alone the Japanese, to find children being shown without any explanation conditions as they existed nearly a century ago.

In the case of Japan, however, modernization started late, and astonishing changes occurred even within fifty years. The large towns change in appearance from year to year, and even in country towns and villages a constant transformation is in progress. All this is ignored in many foreign textbooks, however; children are presented with any material that comes to hand, however old, and told, 'This is Japan'.

One example is an English textbook called *Japanese Family*. Though published in 1950 the Japanese family life shown is a most peculiar mixture of Chinese and Japanese styles, and of the old-fashioned. The illustrations, for instance, show father and daughter riding in a rickshaw – a thing one would have difficulty in finding in Japan today – while a family like something out of a fairy tale is shown gazing over the sea wondering whether there will be an earthquake or not!

One shudders to think of English children getting the idea that the 'quaint Japanese' are like this, but what is still worse is that the writer of the textbook seems to be unaware that such things never existed at any period in Japan. I am not, of course, picking out this English textbook for particular criticism. Endless examples of much the same kind of error can be found in those of other countries.

Some of the incorrect accounts of Japan deal with things which, though not completely unknown in Japan, are by now far from common sights. For example, in an Italian geography textbook for readers at secondary school level there appears a photograph of a Japanese woman with her back covered all over with tattooing, over the caption: 'In Japan there is a general tendency for women also to tattoo themselves.' Not only is this astonishing in a textbook published in 1957, but it will certainly make Italian children start off from the first year of secondary education with the impression that Japan must be a very savage country. There would be no objection if it were used in a book with some such title as 'Believe it or not', but a school textbook about a country should stick to the customs prevailing among the larger part of its population.

In practice, though, the compilers tend to pick out only the odd and peculiar customs in order to stimulate the curiosity of the reader. This is true not only of books on Japan: it is a point on which all the nations of the world should exercise care, for each others' sakes.

The compilers of textbooks should realize the importance of their mission in promoting mutual understanding among the younger generation in different countries, and work harder to present the true rather than merely the curious.

Gradually to reduce the number of such errors on all sides would help greatly in supplying the young who will form the next generation with the correct information necessary for judging international affairs, and for this, international cooperation on a wide scale is most desirable.

The West has much to learn from Asia

Claude Lévi-Strauss

If there is one notion that a European seeking to understand the problem of South Asia must banish from his mind, it is that of the 'exotic'. Contrary to what so many suggestions in literature and travellers' experiences may imply, the civilizations of the East are, in essence, no different from those of the West.

Let us take a look at the bare remains that the passage of the centuries, sand, floods, saltpetre, rot and the Aryan invasions have left of the oldest culture of the East—the sites in the Indus valley, Mohenjodaro, Harappa, 4,000 to 5,000 years old. What a disconcerting experience! Streets straight as a bowstring, intersecting each other at right angles; workers' quarters with houses of dreary, unvarying design; industrial workshops for the milling of flour, the casting and chasing of metals, or the mass production of those cheap goblets whose remains still litter the ground; municipal granaries occupying (to use a modern term) several 'blocks'; public baths, drains and sewers; residential quarters providing comfortable yet graceless homes designed more for a whole society that lived in comfort than for a minority of the well-to-do and powerful—all this can hardly fail to suggest to the visitor the glamour and blemishes of a great modern city, even in their most advanced form as Western civilization knows it, and as presented to Europe today, as a model, by the United States of America.

One would imagine that, over four or five thousand years of history, the wheel had come full circle—that the urban, industrial, lower middle-class civilization of the towns of the Indus valley was not so basically different (except of course as regards size) from that which was destined, after its long European incubation, to reach full development only on the other side of the Atlantic.

Thus, even in their earliest days, the most ancient civilizations of the Old World were giving the New World its lineaments. Admittedly, this twilight of an ancient history of uniform design marked the dawn of other, heterogeneous histories. But the divergence was never more than occasional.

From the days of prehistory down to those of modern times, East and West have constantly striven to re-establish that unity which diverging lines of development have undermined. But even when they seemed to diverge, the systematic nature of their opposition—the placing at each extreme, geographically and one might say even morally, of the most

ancient and the most recent scene, India on the one hand, America on the other—would supply additional proof, if such proof were necessary, of the solidarity of the whole.

TWO CONFLICTING THEORIES

Between these two extremes Europe occupies an intermediate position, a modest position, no doubt, but one she strives to make worthy by criticizing what she regards as excesses in the two extremes— the paramount attachment, in America, to things material, and the exaggerated concentration, in the East, on things spiritual; wealth on the one hand, poverty on the other.

When, having spent long years in both the Americas, the writer received, from a Keeper of Bengali manuscripts, his first lesson in Asian philosophy, he might have been enticed into an oversimplified thesis. The picture was this: against the Amazon region of America, a poor and tropical but underpopulated area, was set South Asia, again a poor and tropical, but this time overpopulated area, in the same way that, of the regions with temperate climates, North America, with vast resources and a relatively small population, was a counterpart of Europe, with comparatively small resources but a large population.

When, however, the picture was shifted from the economic to the moral and psychological plane, these contrasts became more complex. For nothing seemed further from the American pattern than the style of life of this sage, whose pride lay in walking barefoot and having, as his sole earthly possessions, three cotton tunics which he washed and mended himself, and who thought he had solved the social problem by cooking his food on a fire of dead leaves, collected and ground up with his own hands.

From the material point of view, at least, one seems to be the 'reverse side' of the other; one has always been the winner, the other the loser, as if in a given enterprise (begun as we have said, jointly) one had secured all the advantages and the other all the embarrassments.

In one case an expansion of population has paved the way for agricultural and industrial progress, so that resources have increased more quickly than the number of people consuming them; in the other, the same phenomenon has, since the beginning of the eighteenth century, assumed the form of a constant lowering of the amount taken by each individual from a common pool that has remained more or less stationary.

It is to the birth and development of urban life that Europe has come to attach its highest material and spiritual values. But the incredibly rapid rate of urban development in the East (for example, in Calcutta, where the population has increased from 2 to 5½ million in the space of a few years), has merely had the effect of concentrating, in the poverty-stricken areas, such misery and tragedy as have never made their appearance in Europe except as a counterpart to advances in other directions.

As recently as the seventeenth and eighteenth centuries—thanks no doubt, very largely, to the Mogul emperors, who were admirable administrators—the population of South Asia was not overnumerous, and there was an abundance of agricultural and manufactured products. European travellers who saw bazaars extending from fifteen to twenty miles into the country (as, for instance, from Agra to Fatipur Sikhri) and selling goods at what seemed to them ridiculously cheap prices, were not sure whether or not they had arrived in the 'land of milk and honey'. It can never be stated often enough that it was Europe which, by forcibly incorporating the still primitive Asia in a world economic system that was solely concerned to exploit raw materials, manpower and the possibility of new markets, brought about a crisis which, today, it is its duty to remedy.

Comparing itself with America, Europe acknowledges its own less favourable position as regards natural wealth, population pressure, individual output and the average level of consumption; rightly or wrongly, on the other hand, it takes pride in the greater attention it pays to spiritual values. It must be admitted, *mutatis mutandis*, that Asia could reason similarly in regard to Europe, whose modest prosperity represents, for her, the most unwarranted luxury. In a sense, Europe is Asia's 'America'. It is therefore not in the least surprising that this Asia with less riches and more population, lacking the necessary capital and technicians for its industrialization, and seeing its soil and its livestock deteriorating daily while its population increases at an unprecedented rate, is constantly inclined to remind Europe of the two continents' common origin and of their unequal situation in regard to their exploitation of a common heritage.

Europe must reconcile herself to the fact that Asia has the same material and moral claims upon her that Europe often asserts she herself has upon the United States. If Europe considers she has rights *vis-à-vis* the New World whose civilization comes from hers, she should never forget that those rights can only be based on historical and moral foundations which create for her, in return, very heavy duties towards a world from which she herself was born.

INSEPARABLE WORLDS

Preoccupied as it has been, and for too long, with the economic aspect of the relations between the two worlds, the West has possibly overlooked a number of lessons it can learn from Asia, and which it is not too late to ask for now. Despite the interest evinced by scholars and the remarkable work accomplished by Orientalists in the nineteenth and twentieth centuries, the mind of the West has not, as a whole, been very open to the messages of Asian thought.

All Western civilization has tended to separate corporeal from spiritual activities as completely as possible, or rather to treat them as two uncommunicating worlds. This is reflected in its philosophical, moral and religious ideas, and in the forms taken by its techniques and everyday life. Only recently, with the development of psychiatry, psychoanalysis and psychosomatic medicine, has the West really begun to grasp the inseparability of the two worlds. This key, which is new to it and which it handles so clumsily Asia has long known how to use for purposes which, it is true, are not exactly the same. For the West, which for three centuries has concentrated mainly on developing mechanical processes, has forgotten (or rather has never tried to develop) those processes of the body which can produce in that instrument—the only natural and also the most universal one at man's disposal—effects whose diversity and accuracy are generally unknown.

This rediscovery of man's body, in which Asia could be a guide to humanity, would also be a rediscovery of his mind, since it would (as in yoga and other similar systems) bring to light a network of actions and symbols, mental experiments and physical processes which, unless they were known would probably prevent the psychological and philosophical thought of the East from being, for the West, anything more than a series of empty formulae.

PEACEFUL CO-EXISTENCE

This keen feeling, found in Asia of the *interdependence* of aspects of life which elsewhere one tried to isolate and close off from each other and of the *compatibility* of values sometimes considered to be incompatible, is also to be found in the sphere of political and social thought. The finest illustration of this is in the field of religion. From Buddhism to Islam, proceeding by way of the various forms of Hinduism, the religions of South Asia have shown that they were able to live together with very different forms of belief. These irreconcilable yet at the same time definitely complementary forms of human faith could exist peaceably together. From the days of the Indian Emperor Asoka who attained to the concept of a universal comity seeking good of all created things to that of Gandhi the ideal that was sought was that of peaceful brotherhood. This ideal is particularly evident in the political and aesthetic achievements of the Emperor Asoka whose ruined palaces—a combination of the Persian, Hindu and European styles side by side—affirm the will and the possibility that different races, beliefs and civilizations should live together in harmony.

2 Languages

Introduction

In no other field of culture is the spiritual unity of man so clearly manifest as in the field of language. In the early endeavour where speech could not serve to form a method of communication between individuals, in the effort throughout the ages to perfect such a method, an effort in which so many peoples have taken part, irrespective of age or clime, race, creed or form of speech, we see at work something more than a great cooperative principle. There is something which forms a basis for mutual respect between peoples.

Mankind everywhere has developed communication skills, and the articles in this section show how specific languages have emerged in different places and at different times. As modern research deciphers ancient hieroglyphs and forms of writing, a fascinating insight is gained into the daily life of ancient peoples, with an intimacy and a poignancy that annihilates the passing of two thousand years. Man has used all kinds of methods and devices for the transmission of thought—images, symbols or arbitrary signs. The most convenient and adaptable system of writing used by man is the alphabet. The development of writing is described later in this chapter.

Language can play a key role in the integration of a nation, as the experience of Israel shows. Immigrants came from more than sixty countries speaking more than seventy languages and dialects, but the Hebrew language was not submerged under the influx of new arrivals. The first objective of the adult education programme, which is highly developed over the country, is to teach Hebrew to the newcomers.

Yet the existence of a variety of languages can act as a bar to communication and some idea of the trials and tribulations of trying to learn a foreign language are shown in the experience of a language student in Thailand.

The map on pp 12 and 13 shows the diversity of the world's language families. With the growth of new independent nation states in Asia and the Middle East, ancient tongues are being moulded to meet the challenge of today.

Old languages find new jobs

Our planet is a veritable jigsaw puzzle when it comes to languages, with the pieces shifting and moving about, growing smaller or larger or splitting off into new bits with the passing of time. In Asia and the Middle East the puzzle is particularly 'jigged'.

This is not at all surprising when we remember that Asia is the most densely populated area of the globe, and that a huge portion of it—South and South-east Asia—is still more thickly populated than Asia as a whole.

In the postwar period the jigsaw language pattern of Asia has been made even more complicated by a new factor: a great upsurge of nationalism—similar to the one which swept through Europe in the nineteenth century, upsetting the language pattern—that has been rolling across Asia and producing major changes in the world language map.

The Philippines, Burma, Pakistan, India, Ceylon, Indonesia and Israel are new-born states, and all of them have adopted new official national languages. Their educational problems are now very closely linked with linguistic problems.

India, where some hundred different languages are spoken, has chosen Hindi as its official federal language. But at the same time others are recognized as official regional languages. For all official business and for education, English (the official language during British rule) is being kept for some years so that the change to Hindi may take place gradually.

If you were born on one of the thousands of islands which make up the Indonesian Archipelago at the extreme southeast tip of Asia, your mother tongue would be one of 200 languages and dialects spoken by 80 million fellow Indonesians. Most people, though, speak one of the four main languages: Javanese (40 million), Sundanese (12 million), Madurese (6 million) or Malay (4 million).

Malay, spoken by the smallest of these four groups, and renamed 'Bahasa Indonesia' is now the official language of the Indonesian Republic. Today, most Indonesians, young and old alike, are therefore having to set to work and study their new national tongue.

Several thousand miles away, at the far western tip of Asia, the state of Israel presents a completely different linguistic problem: that of a dead language suddenly brought back to life and rejuvenated to serve the needs of a modern world. For a thousand years ancient Hebrew had ceased to be a living language. It existed only in holy books and in prayers. Its resurrection and modernization presented an enormous problem.

Politically, Israel and the Arab-speaking countries may not be on the friendliest terms, but linguistically they are brothers under the skin, and both offer remarkable examples of how a classical language can be revitalized to meet the needs of the modern world. Among the peoples of ancient civilization who, from the Pacific to the Mediterranean now face new linguistic problems, it is those of the Arab world who have probably had the longest experience in adapting their language to the impact of the West.

Theirs is the story of a community which, after enjoying a high standard of culture, went through a period of political, economic and cultural decline. Arab civilization almost died when Baghdad fell to the Tartar invaders in 1258 but it was saved by a handful of scholars who fled to the Nile valley. It flourished again until the sixteenth century when the Turks invaded Egypt and made Turkish the official language. Arabic then deteriorated and lost its vigour. Only a part remained in use: the rest stayed in the 'cold storage' of old books and records.

The linguistic renaissance of Arabic really began, interestingly enough, when Napoleon landed in Egypt in 1798. He brought with him many scientists and scholars interested in the people, their language and their past. He founded the Institut d'Egypte and opened the door to cultural contacts between Egypt and Europe. The French stayed in Egypt only three years but their influence was enormous and they opened the minds of the people to the possibility of a new and fascinating world.

As a result, Egypt took the lead in modernizing Arabic. Western culture came to Syria at a later date and to the other Arab countries of the East much later still.

In 1932 the Arabic Language Royal Academy was founded with Egyptian and other Arab state members. Its purpose was to create or standardize technical and scientific terminology and generally to modernize Arabic.

However, because of the Academy's heavy concentration on scientific terminology, terms of a general nature have tended to be neglected. Newspapers, periodicals and the public must shift for themselves and this has often led to the creation of a score of words for one

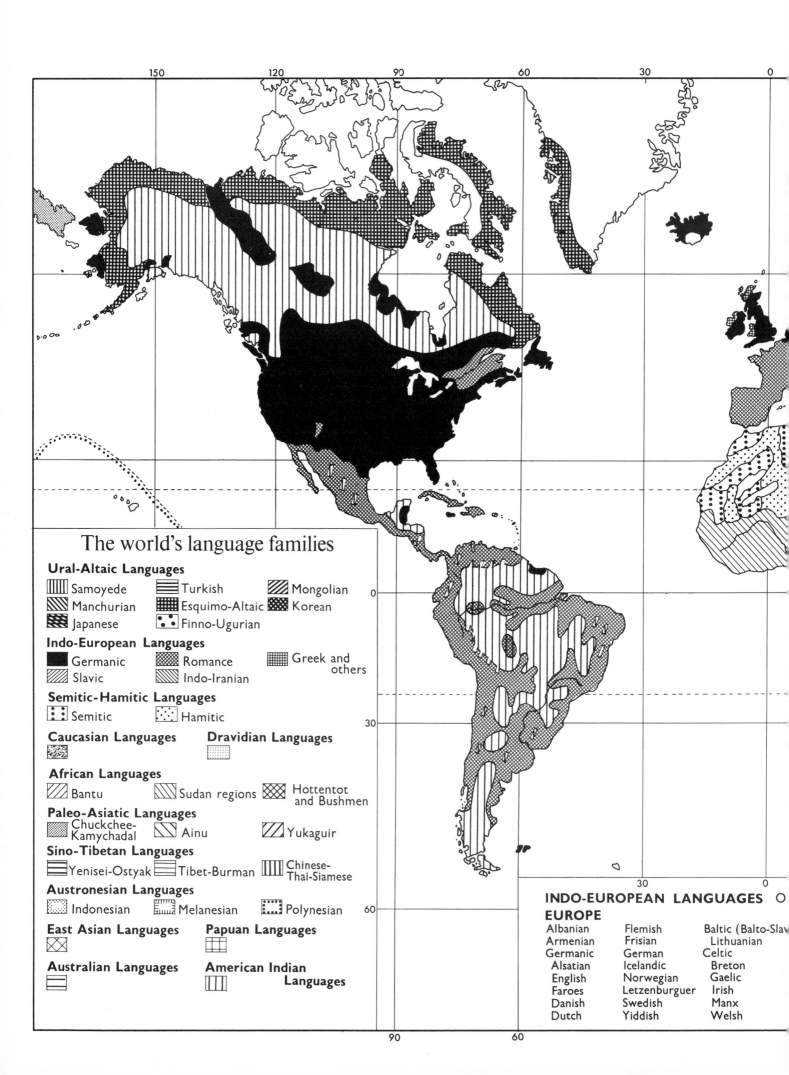

The world's language families

Ural-Altaic Languages

Samoyede	Turkish	Mongolian	
Manchurian	Esquimo-Altaic	Korean	
Japanese	Finno-Ugurian		

Indo-European Languages

Germanic	Romance	Greek and others
Slavic	Indo-Iranian	

Semitic-Hamitic Languages

Semitic	Hamitic

Caucasian Languages   Dravidian Languages

African Languages

Bantu	Sudan regions	Hottentot and Bushmen

Paleo-Asiatic Languages

Chuckchee-Kamychadal	Ainu	Yukaguir

Sino-Tibetan Languages

Yenisei-Ostyak	Tibet-Burman	Chinese-Thai-Siamese

Austronesian Languages

Indonesian	Melanesian	Polynesian

East Asian Languages   Papuan Languages

Australian Languages   American Indian Languages

INDO-EUROPEAN LANGUAGES O

EUROPE

Albanian	Flemish	Baltic (Balto-Slav
Armenian	Frisian	Lithuanian
Germanic	German	Celtic
Alsatian	Icelandic	Breton
English	Norwegian	Gaelic
Faroes	Letzenburguer	Irish
Danish	Swedish	Manx
Dutch	Yiddish	Welsh

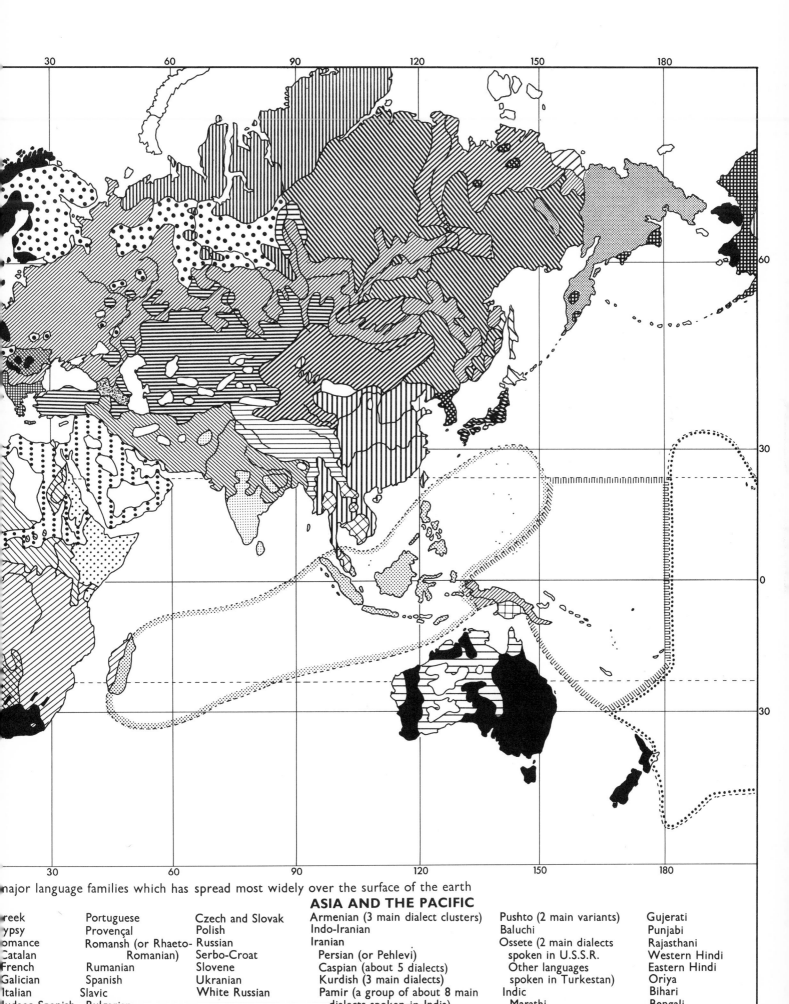

major language families which has spread most widely over the surface of the earth

ASIA AND THE PACIFIC

Greek	Portuguese	Czech and Slovak	Armenian (3 main dialect clusters)	Pushto (2 main variants)	Gujerati
Gypsy	Provençal	Polish	Indo-Iranian	Baluchi	Punjabi
Romance	Romansh (or Rhaeto-	Russian	Iranian	Ossete (2 main dialects	Rajasthani
Catalan	Romanian)	Serbo-Croat	Persian (or Pehlevi)	spoken in U.S.S.R.	Western Hindi
French	Rumanian	Slovene	Caspian (about 5 dialects)	Other languages	Eastern Hindi
Galician	Spanish	Ukranian	Kurdish (3 main dialects)	spoken in Turkestan)	Oriya
Italian	Slavic	White Russian	Pamir (a group of about 8 main	Indic	Bihari
Judaeo-Spanish	Bulgarian		dialects spoken in India)	Marathi	Bengali

modern expression. A jet plane, for example, is sometimes called 'naffatha', from a verb meaning 'to spit out with blowing', and sometimes 'nafouria' meaning 'fountain-like'.

The art of writing

CHAMPOLLION, CLEOPATRA AND PTOLEMY

On 22 September 1822 a young French scholar who was passionately interested in Egyptology burst into the room in the French National Institute, in Paris, where his brother was working. He had hardly the time to cry out 'Je tiens l'affaire' (I've got it) before he collapsed in a dead faint. Jean-François Champollion, poor and exhausted by overwork, had just solved the riddle of Egyptian hieroglyphic writing. Although eight years earlier, an Englishman, Thomas Young, had managed to recognize the cartouche with the name of Ptolemy in hieroglyphics on the trilingual Rosetta Stone, no further progress had since been made.

In 1821 Champollion made a capital discovery. Counting the hieroglyphic signs on the Rosetta Stone and the words of the corresponding Greek text, he found the hieroglyphics outnumbered the Greek words three to one; thus it took several hieroglyphs to form a single word. Using a demotic script written on papyrus, he confirmed the hieroglyphic form of the name Ptolemy and, in 1822, succeeded in deducing and writing with almost perfect accuracy the name of Cleopatra. He now had eleven letters as a basis for future decipherment. His findings were confirmed when he deciphered the name Thutmesis and he thus opened the way for a complete understanding of hieroglyphs – the key to ancient Egyptian history which had been lost for 1,500 years.

For the Egyptians, pictures and hieroglyphs continued to be closely associated even after the hieroglyphic script had become syllabic and its signs given phonetic value regardless of their original meaning. For three thousand years hieroglyphs remained the basis of monumental writing because of their inherent artistic qualities.

The engraving of characters on scarabs used as seals was one of the very earliest uses of writing, to judge by remains from civilizations like that of the Indus Valley cities, roughly contemporary with the earliest Egyptian kingdoms, and where the only objects found bearing writing (in a script which has not yet been deciphered) are seals.

CUNEIFORM WRITING— BORN FROM THE POINT OF A REED

The Sumerians in Lower Mesopotamia rank with the Egyptians, the Cretans and the Chinese as the earliest inventors of an efficient system of writing. They took the first step from the pictographic to the syllabic system and thus helped to develop writing as we know it today. About 3000 BC, the Sumerians made seals, used as property marks, and then employed word signs picturing the object referred to. These original 'pictographs' were then given phonetic values resulting in a greater descriptive precision. This was now a

From the family of Asian scripts. *Above:* an eighteenth-century manuscript in Gujarati which began to be widely used in India from the eleventh century AD. *Below:* manuscript in Mongolian script which is read downwards and from left to right. Top line is written in Tibetan script. Mongolian script is derived, with various additions, from the writings of the Uighurs, a Turkic people

'rebus-writing', a word that was difficult to render pictorially being shown by the sign for another word with the same or similar sound. It thus became possible to write almost any combination of spoken words. By 2500 BC the writing had evolved into a few wedge-shaped strokes from which the name 'cuneiform' is taken. It was written on tablets of damp clay with a stylus, often the sharpened point of a reed. The Babylonians and Assyrians—and later the Hittites and Persians—took over the cuneiform script from the Sumerians and adapted it to their own languages. Sometimes an explanatory picture was included with the writing to guide the illiterate. But pictures and script now had no need of each other. Reading and writing began to spread throughout Mesopotamia.

In the Aegean Islands, Crete and Cyprus, distinctive civilizations developed whose writing also began with a hieroglyphic stage.

We do not know exactly how or where the alphabet originated on the Eastern shores of the Mediterranean. Like other scripts, it was probably pictographic in origin. What is certain, however, is that in the region of the main scripts of the Near Eastern civilizations, and 2,000 years after them, the alphabet was invented only once, so far as we know, in the form of a phonetic system of writing, based on the smallest components of words. It thus consisted of very few characters (hardly more than twenty) with simple outlines not representing any object. This ushered in the reign of sound signs or letters.

The characters which were to develop into our alphabet made their appearance in Phoenicia and the neighbouring regions, in the case of both Canaanite and Aramaic, at least as early as 1000 BC (some archaeologists say 1300 BC in the case of certain Phoenician monuments). This alphabet had twenty-two letters, all consonants.

The adoption of the consonantal Semitic alphabet by the Greeks, possibly about 1000 BC, either by direct borrowing from the Phoenicians or by some channel of propagation in Asia Minor, had far-reaching consequences.

The first was the completion of the alphabetic system by the addition of letters denoting consonants and vowels. As regards the actual writing, the direction, after some hesitation, became established from left to right.

Writing must have made its appearance in India somewhere about the fifth century BC. Although it was almost certainly borrowed from the consonantal Semitic alphabet, the shapes used from the beginning for the majority of the letters differed sufficiently to throw some doubt on this theory. What is certain is that a system of vowel-notation grew up differing greatly from that of the Greeks and leading to the formation of a syllabary alphabet.

There is not just one Indian system of writing, but a variety of different scripts, with different forms of calligraphy, the writing running from left to right.

It was not only the Canaanite and Aramaic branches which derived from the early Semitic prototype; a southern branch is represented mainly by the South Arabian inscriptions, with symmetrical characters (probably influenced by Greek); and the practice of writing alternate lines from right to left and from left to right, which is often found in large monumental inscriptions, is an aid to continuity for anyone looking up at a façade. The Ethiopian writing derived from this branch runs from left to right.

As an offshoot towards the West we have the Libyan-Berber script, not used over a wide area, which also had symmetrical characters of distinctive appearance, arranged in columns on ancient stelae and read upwards.

In the Semitic area Aramaic writing developed differently into various distinctive forms read from right to left. One was the 'square Hebrew', which is now the official script of the state of Israel; others were the Syriac of the minor state of Edessa, which still survives as a religious script, and the Palmyrene of another little state, Palmyra, which soon disappeared after providing the first examples of letters joined together.

Outside the Semitic area, Aramaic writing was carried northwards into much of Asia, among Iranian, Turkish and Mongolian-speaking peoples.

In the south of the Semitic area itself, the Bedouin of Arabia borrowed their writing from the Nabataeans. With the rise of Islam this innovation was to have enormous consequences for writing. The Arabic script lent itself to all sorts of calligraphic exercises and refinements, in which some stylization was used, but it was also widely employed ornamentally on both objects and monuments, particularly on sections of ornamental stucco. Being used by Muslims other than Arabs, it spread through near and central Asia, through parts of India and of the Malay archipelago and in various regions of Africa.

The Indian scripts covered the area in which Indo-Aryan languages are spoken, reaching as far as Nepal, and the area in which the Dravidian languages are used, to the south; but, following Buddhism (which was not to survive in India itself), they reached Tibet in the north and part of Indo-China and most of the Malay archipelago in the south-east. The letters which form these different scripts represent syllables, and the variations between the scripts, unlike the slight differences to be found in Arabic-type alphabets, are such that each one is quite distinct from the other.

With the spread of Christianity, Greek script was used in Africa for Coptic and for the language of the Nuba people. For a time, to the north of the Black Sea, it was used to write the Germanic language of the Goths.

Greek script then took the form still used for the Slavonic languages—the Cyrillic alphabet, with its distinctive but very similar characters—as it followed the path of the Eastern Church (Greece itself being an exception). Aberrant imitations, incorporating elements from a different source, were used for the Armenian and Georgian languages. The Soviet Union is now extending the use of the Cyrillic alphabet, to many of the regional languages, including Finno-Ugrian, Turkic and Mongolian, replacing Arabic characters in some cases.

Westwards, alphabetic writing spread in antiquity as the result of cultural influences and apparently without any particular religious implications. It did so above all in Italy, both among the Etruscans, whose mysterious language has still to be deciphered, and, either through the Etruscans or by some other means, among the Italic speakers of Indo-European languages, especially the Latins.

A northern variety, in the Alps, apparently gave rise to the runes, the characters used in the ancient Germanic and Scandinavian alphabets, which in the Scandinavian countries had a certain magical significance.

The characters of the Latin capital-letter script, like the Greek, were largely symmetrical in shape and very clear. This script was thus well suited for monumental inscriptions; when need arose the characters could be made large enough to be read from a distance. For everyday use and the writing of books all sorts of different forms were adopted; these have their own distinct history in which aesthetic tastes and the practical need for reconciling speed and legibility both played a part.

In the sixteenth century came the Gothic book hand, then the humanistic script, on which our printed characters are still based.

The Latin script spread throughout Europe, first with the Roman administration and later on, with the gradual extension of the Roman Church, as far as the frontiers of the Cyrillic script. Thereafter, with European navigation and colonization, it reached much of the rest of the world, including the Americas. It is now by far the most widely spread script.

A museum of the alphabet

David Diringer

Writing is so much a part and parcel of our lives today that it is difficult to imagine a world in which writing is unknown. Yet for by far the greater part of his immense past man was without writing. Nor is it easy to realize in these days of popular education, that for a great part of the time since its invention, writing has been the prerogative of a few.

Ancient peoples held writing in such awe that its invention was frequently attributed to leading divinities. The ancient Egyptians assigned it to Thoth or Isis; the Babylonians to Nebo, son of Marduk, who was also the God of man's destiny; the ancient Chinese to the dragon-faced Ts'ang Chien; the ancient Greeks to Hermes and others of the Olympians; the Romans to Mercury.

The Teuton god Odin or Wotan was credited with the invention of the runes; the Celtic god Ogmios with the invention of the Oghams. The Aztecs attributed their writing to Quetzalcoatl; the ancient Indians to Brahma. Even amongst the Jews there was a tradition that considered Moses the inventor of the Hebrew script.

The development of writing forms the subject of the Alphabet Museum in Cambridge, England. As will have been gathered, the field is vast. The endeavour has been to cover all ages and all lands. The story, however, is more than the story of writing. It is a story which, it is thought, gives some insight into the history of man's social and spiritual development; for writing, especially under the dominion of the alphabet, is probably the greatest instrument which has helped man in his upward struggle from a more or less tribal state.

In this broad picture, the alphabet has a special place. It is often a matter of great surprise to learn that the alphabetic system is distinguishable from writing in

In the history of writing there have been various scripts called ideographic which are a developed form of picture writing. Some have disappeared but among those that are still known is the script used by the Na-Khi, a people who lived an independent existence within the frontiers of China until the eighteenth century. No-one knows when and how the script originated, but it is believed to have been created by Tombas or medicine men. This is the first page of an illustrated Na-Khi manuscript

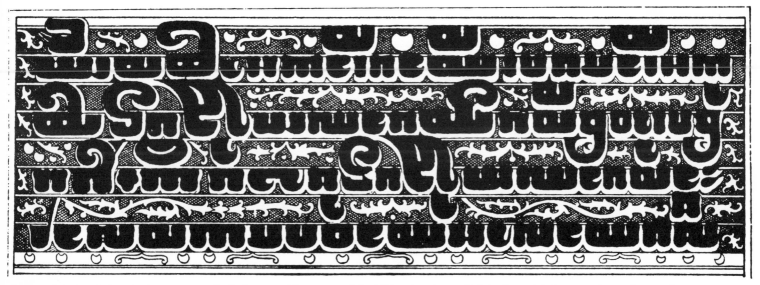

Square alphabet. Pali is the language in which the sacred literature of Buddhism is written. Originally oral, it began to be put into written form in the fifth century BC. The script employed for writing these books is not easily readable. The letters were painted with a broad brush and were correspondingly thick. This is Pali script from the sacred book *Kammuwa*

general. Indeed, for long the two were regarded as one and the same. The truth is that the alphabet was invented long after the dawn of writing—roughly about the eighteenth century BC.

Its great virtue, due to its intrinsic phonetic principle, is its value in simplifying writing, reducing the number of symbols or letters to small compass—usually between twenty-five and forty-five letters. So by lightening in no small degree the task of teaching and learning, in itself an immeasurable gain, it opened more and more widely the doors of education.

Not least of the merits of the system is its easy adaptability; so that it has, in fact, been adopted for almost every important language of the world. Even the Chinese have now officially adopted it.

Great thinkers such as Kant, Mirabeau, Carlyle, reflecting on human progress, have referred to the invention of writing as the real beginning of civilization. Today, writing—and in this context we include such secondary forms as printing—has entered into the whole fabric of our civilization. Almost without our realizing it, it has become an indispensable part of our whole system. Yet, astonishing though it may seem, the history of writing is the true Cinderella with learned men and laymen alike.

The Alphabet Museum was formally opened by Sir James Pitman, MP on 8 June 1959; it assembles the results of many years' research by the present writer and provides an archive more comprehensive than any so far attempted

in this field. Indeed, as a 'documentary' on the development of script, it is, I think, unique in the world.

The large collection includes original inscriptions on stone and clay, casts of inscriptions, original manuscripts, photographs of many more, charts and maps, and lantern slides. The items are drawn from the world over, from north-east Siberia to central Africa and Peru, from the Pacific Islands through Indonesia, India and central Asia, through Europe to North America; and the age ranges from prehistoric times to the present day.

Its main interest for the West European student will doubtless be the wealth of material on the development of the Greek and Roman and related alphabets; for the East-European student, the abundant material on the development of the Cyrillic alphabets and their adaptation to dozens of other alphabets including Finnish, Turkish and Iranian.

For the Far Eastern student, there is material on the development of the Chinese, Japanese, Korean, Mongolian and other scripts. The Indian and Indonesian student will find much on the development of the numerous branches of the Indian and Further-Indian scripts.

The Islamic student will find explanations of the origin and development of the numerous Arabic scripts, the Jewish and Old Testament student, on the development of the Early Hebrew and Square Hebrew scripts, and the central African student, on the interesting memory-aid devices and the adaptation of the Latin alphabet to very different languages.

It is of no small help to see these numerous scripts in their appropriate places in the general picture of the development of writing. On entering the Museum, a visitor first sees a striking wall-chart, painted in colour, the Alphabet Tree.

An interesting point, sometimes causing great surprise, is clearly evident from the chart: all alphabets, however widely separated geographically, even alphabets long abandoned, are probably descended from a common ancestor, the North-Semitic. They are the non-alphabetic systems (scientifically known as 'analytic', but generally though wrongly called 'ideographic') of the ancient Egyptians, the Mesopotamian peoples, the Hittites, the ancient Cretans, the Chinese, the Mayas, the Aztecs, and so on.

The syllabic scripts also claim attention, particularly those of the Japanese and the ancient Cypriotes.

The Alphabet Museum seeks to illustrate the underlying unity of mankind in his search for means of communication between individuals.

The influence of Chinese ideograms

Nearly one-quarter of the world's population still uses a form of writing which originated in China over 3,000 years ago. Chinese writing is in a class on its own. It is not an alphabetic script and each character represents an idea and often a complete word. As a symbol and as an image, each character also has artistic and philosophical significance.

Because of its graphic wealth and its stylized forms, writing quickly gave birth to a new form of art, calligraphy. As an early Chinese author wrote: 'Speech expresses what is in the mind, and writing portrays it.' It was this principle which guided the calligrapher in his aim of combining the strokes of a character into a complete and harmonious whole.

Many peoples in the Far East adopted the Chinese characters in whole or in part, or drew upon them in evolving their own script. The Japanese may have adopted them as early as the fourth century AD, but the first known example of Japanese writing dates from AD 712. This is the Kojiki, the oldest Japanese historical work. Because of the polysyllabic structure of the Japanese language syllabic characters had to be added to indicate grammatical inflexions phonetically. The first attempt in this direction was made in the eighth century.

In the following century the Japanese adapted from Chinese characters a set of phonetic syllables for inflexions. The Koreans also tried to use the Chinese characters phonetically and this led to the invention of the Idu script of which very few traces remain. In the fifteenth century a phonetic alphabet covering all the sounds in the language was invented.

But even earlier in 1403, the Koreans had already invented printing with movable type. (Gutenberg, the 'father' of printing in Europe was only a few years old at the time.)

Chinese gets a Latin alphabet

Chou You-Kuang

In 1957 China started on a big programme to change her written language from a set of ideographs to one in which words are 'spelled out' in letters denoting sounds. Some fifty million children in China's primary schools started learning a new phonetic alphabet using Latin letters. They will not stop learning the traditional

Calligraphy, in the eyes of the Chinese, is just as much a fine art as painting. Writing is so close to painting that many Chinese artists are also authors. Text and image are often combined to form a single work of art. This is the text and figurative drawing on the page of a manuscript by Tsen Yen-tung

Evolution of the Chinese character *ma* meaning horse

characters. For the time being both will be taught simultaneously.

Up till now students of Chinese have faced the task of mastering over 3,500 separate characters before they could read a newspaper or a simple novel. To reach university level, it has been necessary to acquire at least five or six thousand such symbols. Even this is not a sufficient key to the great treasure-house of China's classical literature – to understand the writing of the past, a scholar may need to recognize at least 10,000 characters.

The need for a reform has long been recognized. To transform China from a backward country into an advanced industrialized one demands the rapid education of the whole people, and the wiping out of illiteracy. At present, simply to learn to read takes months or years of time.

The characters also run counter to the needs of modern techniques and communication.

For the last sixty years, Chinese scholars have tried to devise and promote new systems of writing. The adoption of the new alphabet by the State Council was preceded by a whole year of public discussion of a draft scheme, prepared by the Committee for Reforming the Chinese Script.

Why was the Latin alphabet preferred to others? The reason was that, though not entirely appropriate for reproducing all Chinese sounds, it is the most widely known one in the world. More than sixty countries now use it, including the majority of those in Europe, the Americas and South-east Asia. Its letters are internationally employed as symbols in mathematics and natural science. Mastery of it will permit Chinese people to learn other languages more easily. Its use will make Chinese more accessible to foreigners. Moreover, attempts to use the Latin script to write Chinese have a long history.

The most successful and vigorous efforts to introduce a phonetic alphabet began in the late 1930s. Impressed by the successful use of such scripts to provide written languages and wipe out illiteracy among some of the minorities in the Soviet Union, a group of Chinese revolutionaries, led by the Communist writer Chu Chiu-pai, set to work in 1928 to devise a phonetic system for China. This was introduced in 1933 under the name of Latinxua Sin Wenz (New Latinized Writing).

But even with the Latin alphabet there is still a lot to be done before it becomes a workable method of writing Chinese. One necessary step – already under way for some time – is to popularize what is called 'the common speech', the standard Peking pronunciation. China has a number of dialects and people from different areas often find it difficult to communicate with one another orally, though they use the same written language. To help them learn a common language in addition to their own dialect is desirable in itself; it is essential if a phonetic language is to succeed. Primary school teachers and workers in other educational fields all over the country are now studying the standard pronunciation. Radio, theatre and cinema are popularizing it among the people at large.

Another question is how to put words together. Each Chinese character represents a separate syllable and may stand by itself or be combined with one or several others to form a word.

These and similar problems, such as the writing of Chinese versions of foreign place names, will be settled through study and trial. Only when all are solved and the new practice has won the assent of the public will it be possible to say that a new phonetic written language actually exists. Only then will the new script be recognized as a standard method of writing, alongside the old character-method.

Even after the phonetic language becomes universal for ordinary purposes, middle school and university students will continue to study the traditional Chinese characters, just as some in Britain and France study Latin and Greek. At present most students who have reached university level can only read works in the modern literary style, or *pai hua* – common speech. Those specializing in history, the Chinese language, and literature will continue to study *wen yen*, or the classical style, which is widely different.

At the same time the classics will be translated into plain modern language. This is already being done, and later they will be transliterated in the phonetic alphabet. So China's ancient culture will not be buried. On the contrary it will be brought within reach of the whole people for the first time in our history.

Desert wastepaper baskets

CITY LIFE 2,000 YEARS AGO
E G Turner

Supposing the contents of your waste paper basket were by some miracle to be preserved for two thousand years, generations of the future would have the most exciting material from which to construct a picture of your daily life. Yet that is almost exactly what has happened in some of the cities in which the Greeks and Romans lived in Egypt two millennia ago. The dry climate has preserved those everyday writings and notices that are usually the first victims of time.

Turn over casually the pages of a catalogue of papers from these cities and you find here an invitation 'Theon, Origens' son, invites you to his sister's wedding tomorrow, 9th Tybi, 2 o'clock', here a shopping reminder 'to get olive kernels', here again a duplicate of the form you put in at the local town hall to register yourself and your family in the census.

The material principally in use for writing 2,000 years ago was papyrus (it is the same actual word as paper). It was manufactured by cutting the stem of the papyrus plant into fine vertical sections with a sharp knife, and laying these pithy ribbons across each other in two layers placed at right angles. Skilful ancient craftsmen turned out a smooth surface which had the colour and expectation of

19

Tattered text unearthed from the sands of Egypt is one of papyrus fragments from which the daily life of Greeks and Romans living in the Valley of the Nile two thousand years ago can be reconstructed. This text, dating from the third century, contains illustrated verses on the Labours of Hercules (Heracles). The only Labour illustrated on this fragment is the killing of the Nemean Lion and is from the beginning of a roll

life of good handmade paper. For writing, a reed pen and carbon ink (lamp-black and gum) were employed.

It is only in the last hundred years that these papyrus texts have begun to re-emerge from the sands in which they have slept, and to speak to us again. The systematic exploration of the better preserved cities like Oxyrhynchus by men like Grenfell and Hunt resulted in the publication of their findings in *The Oxyrhynchus Papyri*. But we learn to know the place best of all from the allusions contained in letters and papers found on the spot.

Childhood treasures of a little boy named Theon were found among ruins of houses at Oxyrhynchus. They include a rag doll, a wooden horse and spoon and a papyrus rosette.

Trades carried on and different classes of inhabitants are reflected in the names given to the various districts of the town— the Shepherds' or Gooseherds' Quarter, the Cobblers' Market Quarter, the Cretan or Jewish Quarter.

The economic position of the inhabitants can be measured by what they leave in their wills or what they deposit with the pawnbroker.

Theophanes, a civil servant who went on an official trip to Antioch has left us his laundry list: 'Fine tunics 2, self-colour 1, Dalmatics 2, self-colour 1, other wraps 2, birruses 2, chlamys 1, Ditto linen: Tunics 4, Dalmatics 4, mantles 3, face-cloth 1, scarf 1, bath-towels 4, face towel 1, linen squares 4, Romans' 2, counterpane 1, dressing-gown 1, bolsters 2, breeches 2,

boots 1, felt slippers 1, rug-cushion 1, small rug 1, carpet-bag, ground-sheet, small pillow etc.' These were clothes intended to last for a trip of some five months in summer time. Some of them seem to have gone missing for there is a query mark against them.

Among his miscellaneous papers Theophanes kept a few sheets that stimulated a father's pride—the letters sent to him by his schoolboy sons. They are beautifully written and spelt, and of impeccable sentiments, no doubt put together under a tutor's eye. So other schoolboys write formally to their parents, occasionally relaxing with a postscript: 'Please feed my pigeons.'

Some fathers, however, failed to gain such respect from their children. Here is how little Theon writes to his father:

'That was a fine thing not to take me with you to town. If you won't take me with you to Alexandria, I won't write you a letter, I won't speak to you, I won't talk to you. And if you go to Alexandria, I won't ever take your hand or ever greet you again. That's what happens if you don't take me with you. In future send for me, please do. If you don't send I won't eat, I won't drink, so there.'

It is, however, not only in their joys but in their sorrows too that we can share. A friend writes to comfort one whose son has died young:

'The gods are my witness that when I

heard of my master, our son, I was as distressed and mourned as if he were my own child—yes, for he was winsome. When I was eager to rush to you, Pinoution held me back, saying that you, my lord Apollonianus, had instructed him I was not to come up since you were gone to the Arsinoite home. But bear it nobly. This, too, is what the gods have in store.'

Two thousand years are annihilated by the poignancy of this distress.

'I speak English snake snake fish fish'

THE TRIALS AND TRIBULATIONS OF A LANGUAGE STUDENT IN THAILAND

Manich Jumsai

I was born in a typical provincial village in Thailand far from modern civilization. From my early childhood I was eager to learn English and dreamt of strange lands where lived those funny white-faced people (of whom we sometimes heard) with blond hair, who spoke in a strange tongue and had strange customs. I had never met any one of these people. Why should I, when even my provincial teacher had never seen one of them, and our grim-looking, strict headmaster, most learned of the village people, did not know them?

One day, my curiosity getting the better of me, I asked my master, and he in turn asked the headmaster, the name of the capital city of these strange white people who spoke the foreign language we now had to learn in all secondary schools, even in the remotest village. But neither of them could give me an answer. Such were the conditions in Thailand when I started to learn English fifty years ago.

Of what use to us then were the direct method theories? My teacher did not speak English, he only read and translated words from the blackboard, together with their meanings, so that we could learn them by heart. At the next English lesson we had to tell him the meanings of the various words. As to writing, the teacher would avoid it very carefully so that, during my childhood, I did not have much chance of writing anything other than translations of sentences from English into Thai or Thai into English, usually from books.

As for the meaning of words, there was

no distinction in our minds between apples, pears, peaches, cherries, grapes, strawberries or raspberries, however large or small, whatever their colour, whether grown on vines or on trees. All we knew was that they were 'a kind of fruit', the teacher said so. We had never seen them, and neither had the teacher. They were English fruits which could not be grown in a hot country like Thailand. They were strange fruits which puzzled our minds and our imaginations.

As to trees, flowers, animals, insects, etc., while learning English at school I had stored away in my mind many strange names for each of them, but they were all the same to me—a kind of tree, a kind of flower, a kind of animal, which the English people had but we did not have.

I would therefore repudiate a list of basic words, if it contained words like 'bread', 'apple', etc. instead of words appropriate to the food grown in the country where English was being taught. I consider that such a list should contain words which have a real meaning for the child because he sees and uses the articles described in his everyday life.

When it comes to English spelling and pronunciation, we people of Thailand find that the words are never pronounced the way they are spelt. It is of no use to learn any rules, but only exceptions. 'Ou', for instance is usually pronounced as in 'cloud', but in 'through' it is 'oo', in 'though' it is 'oh'; and in 'tough', it is 'uf'. Then comes a new invention: the international phonetic script. This is a device whereby we can see how the various peculiar English words are pronounced; but then we are introduced to new signs and symbols. This, again, is like learning a new language. Is not English difficult enough that we must now read a new language?

Even this phonetic system is not a satisfactory solution to our problem. Whatever signs and symbols are invented for us, we do not pronounce them in that way since our own language is so different. We don't sound the endings of our words as do the English, we don't twist and roll our tongue to sound an 'l', or an 'r', we do not make sounds through our teeth like 'th', we do not have hissing sounds like 's' and 'ss'. These are only English idiosyncrasies to make things harder than they look. The Thai and English languages are fundamentally different, having absolutely nothing in common. The two

peoples lived in worlds far apart, each developing their own language to suit their different needs without ever having the opportunity to discuss what they should say for certain things, or how they should express certain feelings or ideas.

Therefore, a Thai student starting to learn English would say: 'I speak English snake snake fish fish.' This does not mean anything to an Englishman, but it means everything to the Thai student. When a person knows only a few odd words of a language, such as snake or fish, and has to use those same words all the time because he knows no other, it is obvious to a Thai mind that he really knows very little of that language. On the other hand, when he knows so much of the language that the words flow from his mouth without hesitation, like water flowing from a spout, he will say: 'I speak English like water.' He understands this clearly, although it will not be understood by an Englishman.

Look at these phrases which are perfectly obvious and clear to a Thai: 'I have ox two body'; 'He woman have son ox two body'. Why should one say: 'I have two oxen'; 'she has two young oxen', etc.? Why should the language be made more difficult by using 'has' on one occasion and 'have' on another? Why should the words be changed to plural when singular can mean the same object? Why should one use a new word 'she', when one can say 'a female he' or 'he woman'? Why should one say 'young oxen' when they are really 'sons or daughters of oxen', and so on?

There are instances when a Thai would say 'yes' and an Englishman 'no', and yet both expressions have the same meaning. Here are some typical comparisons:

Englishman: Q. Have you never been to England? A. No. (I have never been.)
Thai: Q. Have you never been to England? A. Yes. (The fact that I have never been there is 'yes' in this case.)

The Thai language has no tenses, no feminine nouns, no comparative and superlative adjectives and adverbs, no plurals. It is quite straightforward. English grammar is perhaps one of the most difficult in the world to learn, owing to the number of tenses and irregular verbs.

As far as Thailand is concerned, I do not know of a single book which has been written by any of the eminent exponents

of a number of accepted methods of teaching English which would be perfectly satisfactory and thoroughly understood by the pupils. English is made infinitely more difficult by the fact that the books are written about things which the indigenous child has never seen or heard of during the whole of his short life.

A Thai child starts to learn English at the age of eleven plus, by which time his mind is fully developed. He is a big boy or a young man—no longer a child. He has a thirst for true stories, for adventure, for culture, for his own social inheritance—something which is no longer childish, but which will fill his mind with future ambitions, aspirations, adventures and heroism. He is not a fool who can be easily led to believe things which are untrue, such as fairy tales, spirits, goblins that inhabit the forests, and animals that talk. English primers written for children of lower age level are therefore not suitable for him.

Those who attempt to improve the teaching of English in Thailand should make a complete analysis of the Thai and English languages to see where lie the parities, similarities and discrepancies in both languages. When this has been done they will then be able to understand the mind of the child who is struggling to understand a foreign language like English. So far, no such analysis has been made.

3 Architecture, sculpture and painting

Introduction

Many peoples have contributed to the rich and varied storehouse of art treasures to be found in the East. This chapter deals with art forms (particularly architecture, sculpture and paintings) many of them arising in the mists of antiquity, and covers countries stretching from Egypt right through to China. It should, however, be emphasized that although this chapter has concentrated on the past, this does not mean that the artistic tradition is dead. Far from it; there has been a great artistic revival in the East. For reasons of space it has not been possible to deal here with the significant emergence of contemporary art in the East where the twentieth century has made its own impact. One has only to name such Indian painters as Jamini Roy (the pioneer of modern art in India whose understanding of the significance of folk art is a real contribution to contemporary Indian art), the late Amrita Shergil (who while trained in European techniques discovered the Indian mode of sensibility), Y F Hussein (whose works, like those of Jamini Roy, have been exhibited in the West and figure in private collections), Francis Souza, Avinash Chandra or the Sinhalese painter George Keyt, whose painting is a successful fusion of inherited style and certain twentieth-century French developments. Chapter 5 deals with the inspiration provided by Buddhism in the masterpieces of sculpture, architecture and painting to be found in Asian countries like India, China, Japan, Ceylon, Burma, Indonesia, Nepal and Tibet. The articles which follow show, among other things, the influence on art of the religious beliefs of Egypt, Islam and Christianity.

A great civilization with its own artistic and intellectual tradition, was built around the Muslim faith, and when the Caliphate broke up in the tenth century, the civilization remained to be carried round the world and enriched by the various Islamic peoples. The glory of its literature, especially its poetry, is well known. The subtlety of Arabic verse and the sweetness of the Persian poets have inspired local literature wherever Islam has gone. More accessible to outsiders have been the splendours of its visual arts. In painting and architecture were mingled the tradition of pre-Islamic Iran—going back to ancient Mesopotamia—and those of the Greco-Roman world. The lovely miniatures of Persia and India owe much of their grace to the further addition of a

Below: Dancers in the moonlight. Arranged in circles around the burial mounds which began to be erected in Japan in the third century AD, archaeologists have found clay sculpture in the form of human figures, animals and objects. Named *haniwa* from *wa* (a circle) and *hani* (clay) this ancient sculpture has chiefly come to light in western Japan. Largest in number among the Haniwa figures are men and women, some in armour, others dancing and singing. Those shown here are Haniwa dancers, the larger one (thought to represent a woman) being 18 inches high and the smaller (a man) 11 inches. The tops of these cylindrical figures are modelled into faces with large eyes and noses, and despite their simplicity the figures have a lively, joyous air. Looking at them, says Seiroku Noma, one might well imagine men and women of antiquity dancing in some moonlit field

Chinese influence. The architecture has owed much, here or there, to Byzantine or Hindu example. But above all in architecture, the strength and precision of Islamic art, its delicacy combined with uncompromising orderliness, are fully its own.

In the early days, paintings and sculpture simply embodied in a visual form, suited to yet untutored minds, truths now accessible to all, thanks to the increase in the number of printed books. They filled the place in instruction that films and television are tending to take at the present time, a process which may one day end in their ousting the book and replacing the civilization of the printed word by that of the visual image. A curious repetition of history by which man is placed in the same situation as his distant ancestors.

Japan

MASTERWORKS OF JAPAN'S STONE AGE ART

Seiroku Noma
The history of Japanese art stretches far back into the mists of antiquity, possibly some 6,000 years. Clay figurines or human figures of the Stone Age are the oldest existing works of sculptural art in Japan, and together with the later Haniwa figures, form the two characteristic kinds of sculpture of Japan's pre-Buddhist period. The embryo of sculpture has always been bizarre, and the clay figurines of early Stone Age Japan, with their squat bodies and flattened heads, are no exception to this rule. They have been found all over Japan, especially in great numbers in the central and northern districts. These figures began to be made in the early Jomon period which stretches roughly 5,000 years before the Christian era, to the first or second century BC.

Why did these ancient people make such figurines? Like the many primitive figurines of similar fantastic shape which have been excavated in central Europe and Siberia, many of the Japanese figurines represent pregnant women with swollen breasts and bellies. It is therefore presumed that men prayed to these symbols of fertility that their families might multiply and prosper. The clay figurines were a kind of icon, but most likely they were not for community use, but were worshipped in houses by individual families. They must have been hung, for they are unstable in shape.

Following the clay figurines in ancient Japanese sculpture come the Haniwa, quite different from the figurines in age and location. Produced in about the fourth century AD these belong to a different culture. The Haniwa figures were set up in a circle on the slopes of burial mounds which began to be built in Japan in about the fourth century AD, a custom which continued until the second half of the sixth century, when the introduction of Buddhism brought the cremation system. These are sometimes interpreted to have been part of the funeral procession. Haniwa figures were made for the huge tombs of men of rank from the fourth to the sixth century. On the death of one of these men, the work of 'mass producing' the Haniwa began, the greatest number required being cylinders to surround the burial mound. They were erected in many circles so that hundreds, and sometimes thousands, were needed. They were made rapidly by clay workers normally engaged in making earthenware vessels. Haniwa figures were not made by sculptors working intently from models, but by craftsmen reproducing forms they carried in their minds.

The clay figurines of the Jomon Period and the Haniwa figures which have come to light only recently, after being hidden underground for many centuries, have a remarkable freshness.

China

THEY PAINTED WITH KNIFE AND BRUSH

Chou Ling
Two thousand years ago, the Chinese developed an unusual form of art. They engraved paintings directly on stone. From this ancient art another evolved, called stone 'rubbings' which achieved exquisite, highly delicate results on paper and silk. The Chinese have, from the earliest times, been charmed by pictorial art. Painting has an extraordinary power of suggestion and description. Form and movement can be expressed in a few firm, lively strokes. To depict the three-dimensional world on a flat surface is no matter of accident either – it is merely one of those human possibilities which the Chinese regard as a kind of discovery, and the secret of which they long kept to themselves.

The considerable pictorial skill among the Chinese is provided by an important

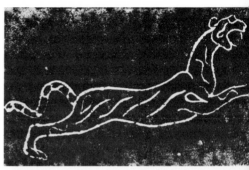

Tiger and leopard: carved stone rubbings dating from the Han period, discovered at the beginning of the twentieth century

group of engraved stones belonging to the Han period (206 BC–AD 220). These are tombstones or funerary monuments, and the process is a kind of engraved painting. They are not bas-reliefs as might be supposed; they are real paintings, in which the feeling for composition and pictorial sense are fully evident. Only instead of using a brush, the Chinese of that period preferred to engrave their compositions directly on the stone with a knife.

Later on, a method of 'pressing' was invented in China, making it possible to take a kind of rubbing of these sculptural compositions and transfer them direct on to paper or silk. As a result, these engraved paintings reached a wide public as the centuries went by, and had an undoubted influence on painting itself.

These engraved stones deal with a variety of subjects, and throughout the different regions and epochs, preserved a most remarkable similarity of style. The earliest actual paintings which have come down to us date from the fourth century AD.

In the Sung period (960–1276) China began to work out its own laws of beauty. This period produced many admirable works in Chinese ink touched up with gouache – misty landscapes, restrained and rapidly executed portraits, and delicate, elegant, thought-provoking drawings.

Lakeshore in winter. Painting on silk by an unknown master typical of the Sung dynasty (twelfth–thirteenth century) which produced one of the greatest landscape schools the world has ever known. Artists sought only essentials in landscapes, discarding all trivial and accidental effects. This masterpiece, measuring 4½ feet by 3¼ feet, is now in the British Museum

It was at this juncture that Chinese painting took the final form which it retained for nearly a thousand years until modern times. It is notable for its lyricism, naturalistic style and quality of line. It also reveals a unique concept of painting; volume being rendered solely by means of very firm outline, with no shadows to destroy the ethereal effect of the painted surface. In the Yuan Period (1276–1308) China, under Mongol domination, developed a keen interest in hunting scenes and the beauty of horses; in the subsequent Ming Period (1386–1644) there was a deliberate return to the strictly Chinese manner and the earlier highly stylized and calligraphic form of beauty.

Through all the stimulating variations of its 2,000 year history, China has preserved a unity of style and an aesthetic aim which is peculiar to the Chinese people.

Egypt

SCENES OF A HAPPY AFTER-LIFE

Jacques Vandier

The Egyptians were not only architects, sculptors and craftsmen of genius; they were also painters who were aware from the beginning of the extent to which a drawing or a carving in relief could be improved by colour. The artists of the Nile Valley made use of colour in every field of art—even in goldsmith's work, where pigments were replaced by semi-precious stones or fragments of coloured glass. Statues and architectural motifs, too, were painted. In speaking of painting, however, it is natural to confine onself to the bright coloured scenes which decorate the walls of Egyptian temples and tombs. These were carved either in relief or in hollow relief before being coloured; but wall painting was also used at all periods in the decoration of tombs. Under the New Empire (1580–1090 BC) in the famous metropolis at Thebes, capital of the Empire, this process predominated.

Apart from black and white, the Egyptians used only four colours—yellow, red, blue and green—which could of course be mixed if desired. Egyptian art is governed by a number of conventions which often disturb the uninitiated, though specialists, through familiarity, hardly notice them. They seem to have felt that the profile was more typical of the individual than the full face. The details of the profile are depicted

The god Khonsu offers a king of the nineteenth dynasty the emblem of life. Painting from the Temple of Seti I

realistically, except for the eyes, which are shown more or less as though seen from the front. Complications did not arise except where the whole body was shown.

At the beginning of the Old Kingdom (3200–2300 BC) the scenes themselves were very simple. With a few exceptions, the best known of which are in the Meidum necropolis, in northern Egypt, the only portion to be decorated was the stele used to simulate the door separating the world of the living from that of the dead. From the Fifth Dynasty onwards (2750–2625 BC), in the mastaba tombs of important officials, the chapel walls were entirely covered with illustrations. This type of decoration originated in a belief which persisted until the end of the Eighteenth Dynasty (1580–1350 BC) that the after-life was modelled on life in this

In the tomb of King Seti I, Isis, consort of Osiris, king of the dead, stretches out her winged arms in a protective gesture

world, that the dead had the same desires and needs as the living. In the Eighteenth Dynasty a great change took place and the official aspect of the dead man's existence is regularly illustrated, side by side with more pleasurable scenes taken over from previous epochs.

Another great change took place under the Nineteenth Dynasty (1350–1205 BC) when secular scenes were no longer depicted in the tombs. The decoration was confined almost entirely to religious and funerary themes drawn chiefly from large mythological compositions illustrating the ritual of the dead. The royal tombs, like the temples, showed a god conferring life, stability and strength upon the king, or the goddess Isis (consort of Osiris, King of the Dead) spreading her wings protectively over the dead sovereign, or, kneeling on the emblem of gold asking protection for him from Gheb, the Earth-God.

All the scenes found in the tombs, varied as they are, reveal one and the same concern—that of a happy after-life. From the earliest epoch until the end of the Eighteenth Dynasty, the attempt was made to beguile fate by depicting that life was a pleasurable affair and thus, by means of imitative magic, to achieve eternal felicity. From the Nineteenth Dynasty onwards the same purpose was pursued solely by means of the performance of religious rites and strict obedience to the divine decrees.

Iran

THE TREASURES OF THE PAST

Geographically, Persia (the Iran of today), was situated in the centre of the ancient world. Historically, a distinctly Persian civilization goes back as much as twenty-five centuries when the great Persian Empire stretched westwards to the Danube and south to the Nile Valley. Culturally, it is one of the few countries which can still claim a continuous tradition in literature, art and philosophy, going far back into the pre-Christian world.

Because of Persia's geographical situation, one of the chief characteristics of Persian art was its extraordinary power of assimilating foreign influences such as Greek, Egyptian, Islamic and Chinese, and of combining them with others to create an original and homogeneous style. This is specially true in painting.

Art under the Achaemenid kings enhanced and adorned the public life of the court from the sixth to the fourth centuries BC. The twin capitals of Susa and Persepolis were unmistakably royal with their friezes of attendants, guards and tribute bearers sharply cut out in stone, or brightly coloured in the equally clear and hard tiled faces. This was the art proper to an open-air court ceremonial.

The splendour and magnificence of Persepolis astounded Alexander the Great and the victorious Greeks who captured and burned it about 331 BC. The regal city with its portals, royal quarters and audience halls, was built by Darius, third ruler of the Achaemenid dynasty, who came to the throne in 521 BC and by his son, Xerxes I. It was constructed on a great rectangular terrace, jutting out from cliffs, on which remain the ruins of colossal buildings of dark grey marble from the nearby mountain and hundreds of bas-reliefs. The Great Apadana, or audience hall, built by Xerxes I is approached by a double stair whose sides are lined with two groups of figures cut in low relief on the stone masonry. The vast interior hall of the Apadana, about 200 feet on each side, contained six rows of six columns, sixty-five feet in height. The most striking of the audience halls at Persepolis was the famous 'Hall of a hundred columns', several of which still remain standing. Workmen and materials were brought to the site of the new Persian capital from all over the Empire and the style of the architectural details and the carved reliefs is a composite of the arts of Egypt, Babylonia and Asia Minor.

The period of Hellenistic dominion after the conquest of the Persian Empire by Alexander the Great, saw the introduction of a less priestly, more human art followed by a return to national ideals and a deliberate revival of the monumental rock carving of earlier Achaemenid times. Then in AD 639 came the invasion of Islam, changing the Persian mood and spirit.

In Persia, painting developed at a comparatively late stage. Only when a site was unsuitable for carving was there recourse to painting as a substitute. Islam had always had a great respect for calligraphy since it was a way of preserving the inspired words of the prophet so that painting, when associated with calligraphy, was always considered as subordinate. Well before the rise of Islam, the Persians had enjoyed depicting heroic scenes and pastimes of the nobles, such as hunting and feasting. The new Islamic rulers, the Caliphs, revived the tradition, but for this work, which Islam regarded as unorthodox, they employed foreign artists.

The Mongols who invaded Persia at the beginning of the thirteenth century, paid no heed to the prohibitions of Islam (which forbade the decoration of religious works with human forms) though they became Muslims later. Worshippers of the Heavens and the infinity of Space, they brought in their train painters and decorative artists from China and the Far Eastern influence became the dominant one.

At the end of the fourteenth century Iran was once more ravaged by a conqueror from the Steppe—Timur the Lame—the world conqueror Tamerlane. Yet despite these events, Iranian culture showed astonishing vitality. Poetry, philosophy and history flourished; architecture put on the most splendid robe of brilliant faience; and metalwork continued the great tradition of bronze casting which had been one of the glories of Iran, since the late twelfth century.

The earliest illuminated Iranian manuscripts which survive are from the time of the Mongol invasion. The Chinese influence radically affected the whole composition. For the moment colour almost disappeared. The drawing became nervous and calligraphic; and above all, the attempt was made to set figures in a landscape. In the next generation, this style seems to have been further absorbed into the Iranian tradition.

In the arts of the book, the later fourteenth century saw the birth of a new style that was to persist in its main characteristics for three hundred years and is one of the great gifts of Iran to the world. Of this period Basil Gray has written 'craftsmanship went hand in hand with invention. Craftsmanship supplied superlative materials: paper, mineral pigments, gilding, and the skill to use them in calligraphy, illumination and painting. The splendours of carpet and tile revetment were transferred to the page in these glowing miniatures and in that setting stood the cyprus-like figures of lovers sung by poets, while overhead moved the birds pouring out their song to the air scented by unfading blossoms. The nearest that Western art has approached to this in feeling and richness is in French tapestry

Exploits of heroes and
the romance of chivalry
are given expression
in the *Shahnameh* in
the setting of the
Iranian spring, when
the bare hills are
dotted with flowers
for a few weeks and the
foliage is fresh. Here,
one of the heroes of the
Shahnameh, Isfandiyar,
kills two wolves—one
of a series of deeds
which he, and a rival
hero, Rustam, must
perform to prove their
courage

of the fourteenth century; and in pure colour in some Sienese panel-painting, nearly contemporary with them.'

Perhaps the most beautiful of Persia's miniatures are in the remarkable collection preserved in the Gulistan Imperial Library at Teheran. These were almost completely unknown to the world until the Library sent them for exhibition in London in 1931 and later in Leningrad. The collection includes the manuscript of the Iranian epic the *Shahnameh*, or Book of Kings, completed by the poet Firdausi in the early eleventh century and copied about 1330. It contains twenty large miniatures and a double-page frontispiece. Another manuscript in the Library is the *Kalila* and *Dimna*, a collection of animal fables. These miniatures show a sensibility and intimacy with the natural world missing from the more formal epic scenes. These Indian fables were also partially translated into French in the seventeenth century. La Fontaine learned of them through François Bernier, a French doctor who came across them while in Asia, and used some of them in writing his own fables. There is also a copy of an album of miniatures bound together in a luxurious volume by the Moghul Emperor Jehangir in the early seventeenth century. The most famous miniature of this album, the *Muraqqa Gulshan*, or Flower Garden Album, probably dates from about 1480 and is by Bihzad, hailed as the greatest master of Persian painting and the foremost of the few Persian painters whose names are known today. He was a reformer in the treatment of landscape which appears more realistically in his pages than in those of his forerunners. Moreover, he revolted against the dictation of the calligraphers and admitted at best, only a few lines of text in the pages he illustrated.

At the end of the sixteenth century, all the artistic forces in Persia were being concentrated at the new capital, Isfahan, under the impulse of Shah Abbas the Great. The sixteenth century was a wonderful epoch alike in Europe and Asia, an epoch of great rulers like Charles V, Elizabeth of England, Suleiman the Great of Turkey and the Great Moghul Akbar and the Iranian Shah Abbas I, who came to the throne in 1587. In 1598 he made his capital at Isfahan which he turned into one of the architectural wonders of the world with several magnificent palaces, monuments and gardens which still exist

today. It was built on the banks of the Zenderhud on a plateau over 5,300 feet above sea-level. The waters of the river are distributed among the palaces, gardens and avenues in an endless series of reservoirs, fountains and cascades. Isfahan is approached by stately bridges which lead past the luxurious gardens of courtiers to the Great Imperial Square—the Maidan-i-Shah, 560 yards long by 174 yards wide, bordered by buildings of recessed arches or arcades. On the far side of the Square is the Masjid-Shah or Royal Mosque, completed in 1612 and completely covered with enamelled bricks of great brilliancy. It is still one of the most beautiful buildings in the world.

Isfahan's epoch of splendour lasted nearly a century and a half until it was partially destroyed when Iran was invaded in the eighteenth century. In 1788 the capital was moved to Teheran.

Parallel to the developments taking place in Persia under Shah Abbas, a new development was taking place at the court of the Moghul emperors in India. One of them, Humayun, visited Persia half way through the sixteenth century, and returned to India with two Iranian painters who became heads of the new painting workshop he established in his royal library. This patronage of the arts was continued, and a new style of painting was born, owing academic discipline and technical knowledge to the Iranian tradition, but informed with quite another spirit. This Moghul art is at its most characteristic in depicting historical events and in portraiture. In their wish to record, Akbar and his son and successor Jehangir, found the European science of picture-making with perspective and chiaroscuro interesting, and for a time the influence of Flemish and German line engraving is clearly visible in Moghul painting.

Turkey

LIFE OF COURT AND PEOPLE IN ANCIENT TURKISH ART

The splendid achievements of Turkey in the field of architecture, carpet weaving, pottery and tile-making have been universally recognized. Yet of all the schools of painting which existed in the Near and Middle East during the Islamic period, that of Turkey is least known. One of the reasons is that very little of this art ever left Turkey, and even in Turkey itself it remained almost inaccessible, being

housed in the palace libraries of the sultans. Only since the establishment of the Republic under Ataturk have manuscripts and paintings become more readily available.

The Turkish miniaturist can be distinguished from his better-known counterpart of the Iranian school by his choice of subject matter. He prefers the market place swarming with people, rather than a fairylike garden of some Prince Charming. Though a 'courtly style' of painting existed and was used to depict incidents in the lives of the great sultans, even this was latterly combined in the same painting with the 'popular style' which showed episodes in everyday life and crowds with their noise and gossip, which even went as far as the grotesque. This documentary approach makes many a Turkish painting a valuable historical record.

The splendour of Turkish art

Georges Fradier

European travellers returning from Turkey in the sixteenth and seventeenth centuries had many tales to tell of the marvels they had seen at the court of the sultan—carpets of a quality unknown in Europe, brilliantly executed designs in ceramics and tapestry, and exquisitely worked metal objects decorated with ivory, silver, enamel and precious stones.

The Turks were long practised in the working of metals—armour, silver inlaid helmets, swords with inscriptions in gold, coats of mail, daggers and pistols adorned with ivory, silver, enamel and precious stones. Turkish carpets have, of course, long been world renowned. For 400 years, in every city of Europe, they have symbolized the wealth of Turkey. From Smyrna (Izmir) they were shipped to Venice or Bruges, and Flemish and Italian and other European artists vied with each other in reproducing their colouring and designs. They succeeded so well that their paintings often afford a clue to the date of the carpets themselves, some of which—the Uchak carpets, for instance—are named after Hans Holbein.

As early as the thirteenth century the workshops of Anatolia were turning out masterpieces whose praises Marco Polo sang after he returned from his epic journey through Asia. The imperial factories went on to introduce one refinement after another in the art of carpet

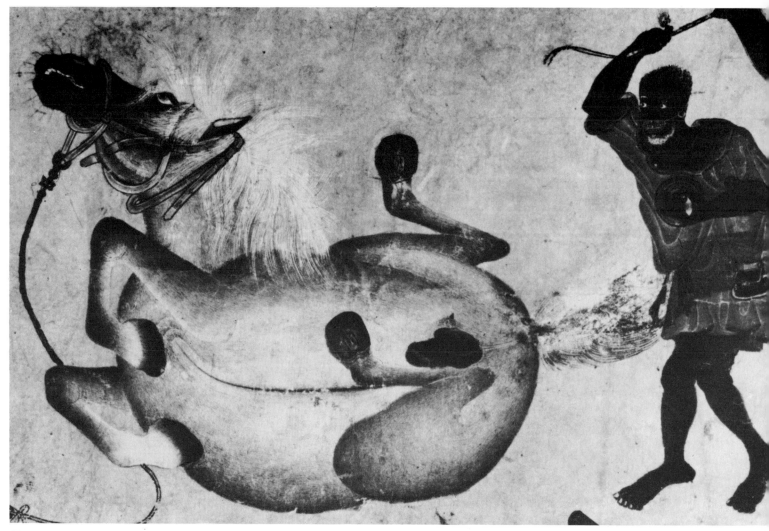

This drawing of horse training is by Mehmed Siyah Kalem, a remarkable fifteenth-century artist whose works figure in the *Album of the Conqueror* – three volumes of drawings, miniatures and specimens of handwriting by Chinese, Uighur, Seljuk and Ottoman masters of the fourteenth and fifteenth centuries. Siyah Kalem never depicts the settled life of the towns. His subjects – travellers and animals chiefly – come from the highways, and he may well have been the painter of a nomad people.

Two examples of ancient Turkish calligraphy – a distinctive field of the country's decorative art

making. In West and East alike, they exerted a very real influence, just as did the weavers and needlewomen of Brusa, Konia and Scutari, through their celebrated fabrics. Some of their finest works which date from the sixteenth century have been piously preserved.

Turkish supremacy in the art of working wool and silk must not blind us to the brilliance of Turkish ceramics which are just as important. The earthenware tiles, originally designed for use on outside walls and later for interior adornment of mosques and palaces, are typical of Turkish decorative art. And while it was from the Moors that the Spaniards learnt the technique of ceramics, it was through the Turks that faience, which perhaps had its birthplace in Turkestan, was introduced into Italy and then spread to the rest of Europe.

The artists of Asia Minor always remained faithful to the complex heritage they owed to their Byzantine, Mongol, Tartar, Persian or Arabic origin. But they made it unmistakably their own and the four symbolic flowers—hyacinth, carnation, tulip and briar-rose, woven, carved or painted, became their stamp, their hallmark. Another motif is the cyprus, a privileged tree which symbolizes the soul rising to heaven, in death or contemplation.

Turkish painters were long subject to Chinese, Persian and Italian influences, which they had welcomed enthusiastically. Yet they were hampered by extremely rigid religious scruples in a society which forbade the hanging of any portraits on walls, and they had to confine their essays in portraiture to the pages of albums and the illustration of poetic or official work. These limitations did not prevent the emergence of a remarkable school of miniaturists dating from the fifteenth century. The miniatures at the Topkapu palace, painted in the eighteenth century by Levni, are intact and as fresh as the day they were painted. They are also first rate documentary material and recall the delights of a legendary yet true to life Istanbul, with its officers, dignitaries, musicians and dancers and the splendour of its court.

Turkish calligraphy is also famous. Every cultured Muslim has dreamed of copying the Koran in a writing worthy of the divine words, and the Turkish calligraphers pursued this dream with passion, mindful of the saying that 'in the last judgment the ink of writers will be valued as highly as the martyrs' blood'. Calligraphy was used not only for the adornment of books and mosques, but in furniture and rooms of any household rich enough to afford a beautiful plate inscribed with a verse from the scriptures or some philosophical maxim.

A note of austerity is found in all products of Turkish culture. The finest carpets are those made for prayer. The loveliest faience is that intended for mosques; and among similar oriental work they are distinguished for their sobriety and purity of line. The architecture of Anatolia, impressive and rough hewn, was that of a people both religious and warlike, and later, at Brusa and Istanbul, expanded to opulence; but its mosques were never gaudy or pretentious. It is perhaps the strength of this art and its seriousness that should be emphasized.

Nemrud Dagh

Pauline Bentley
One of the great monuments of antiquity, over 2,000 years old, stands at Nemrud Dagh, the mount of Nimrod. It was raised in the first century of our era by Antiochus I, King of Commagene in the Anti-Taurus Mountains of present-day Turkey to be a 'Holy common room of all the Gods' and a palace of pilgrimage for his people.

Because of its geographical position, the differing cultures of Persia and Greece poured into Commagene to mingle with the richness of Anatolian history. The capital city, Samsat, the Samosata of today, commanded one of the epic crossing points of the Euphrates; the whole kingdom lay astride the ancient trade route of the Orient and the West, among lands, bearing two of the world's seven wonders—the Temple to Diana at Ephesus and the Fort of Helicarnassus built in memory of the Anatolian ruler Mausolus—whence came the word mausoleum. In these regions Xenophon led his ten thousand to their fatal meeting with the Persians, and the Apostle Paul trod his dusty way from Tarsus.

It was not until 1882 and 1883 that Nemrud Dagh first fell to the archaeologist. Reports written then on the sanctuary by Turkish and German archaeologists in turn fired the enthusiasm of an American woman geologist, Teresa Goell. After fourteen years of research work and two preliminary visits, she led her first expedition there in 1953.

Far from being the crude product of some semi-barbarian monarch as had been suggested, the beauty of the shrine established it as one of the glories of the Hellenistic world. Hewn from the mountain rock, the sanctuary consists of three terraces levelled on the summit and decorated with mighty statues of the king and his gods which tower on their bases to the height of a five-storey building.

The ceremonial heart of the shrine is the Persian fire altar on the East Terrace. Majestically facing the fire altar there still sit, though shaken and dismembered by earth tremors, most of them decapitated, an imposing array of 25 to 29 foot high statues of Antiochus and the deities worshipped by his Greek and Persian ancestors. They reflect the hybrid culture from which they spring—the Sun God Apollo-Mithra-Helios-Hermes; the Commagene Fertility Goddess Fortuna; Father of the Gods, the 'Thunder Shaker', Ahura-Mazda-Zeus. Next to him sits Antiochus I, himself flanked by the Hero God of strength, Herakles-Artagne-Ares. The sculptured head of Antiochus, some 16 feet high, was found lying on the West Terrace. It is of calm and striking beauty and bears a strong likeness to Alexander the Great from whom Antiochus claimed descent on his mother's side. The head wears a Persian headdress to remind us that he also claimed descent from the Achaemenid dynasty of Persia through his father. Not only the sculptured figures of Antiochus and his gods with their attendant eagles and lions, but also their sandstone relief portraits cut into the walls running the length of the East and West terraces show the purity of form and line of the great classical tradition. Nemrud Dagh is a sanctuary which by its beauty outstandingly exemplified the amalgam of East and West of Persian, Greek and Anatolian cultures.

Cappadocia

COUNTRY OF THE CONE DWELLERS

In the centre of the Cappadocian plateau of Turkey stands the town of Urgup in the heart of a country of volcanic towers, a fabulous land of some two or three hundred thousand stone cones. Melting snows, rains and winds took a part in sculpting the weirdest landscape the human eye has ever seen outside the moon. Pyramids, towers, spires, cones, minarets and needles of rock in a brilliant phantasmagoria of colours ranging from blinding white to bright yellows and softest rose were left jutting skywards in haphazard confusion.

Sometime about the fourth century AD, a community of Cenobite monks discovered the advantages offered by this rock land for the preservation of the seclusion demanded by their order. Side by side with the humble farmers who tilled the valleys, they established themselves in one of the cone villages a few miles from Urgup. With considerable ingenuity they dug out living quarters, sometimes at ten different levels in the same cone reaching the entrances by ropeladder or by a central inside chimney niched to provide hand and foot hold. Ground-level doorways they sealed with large stone wheels which rolled on carefully cut grooves. These monks left a rich heritage for the archaeologists. They built dozens of small chapels in the cones, mainly following the Byzantine form of architectural construction, and covered the walls and ceilings with brilliant paintings depicting the iconography of the Christ, Mary and the Saints. In the earlier chapels, probably built about AD 400, the paintings were done in simple wash on the stone face. More elaborate work was done from the eighth to eleventh centuries when artists had learnt the art of using tempera which is more resistant to the ravages of time.

The departure of the monks following the decline in the Christian monastic communities in the fourteenth century, brought another era to the rock country. The villagers were not slow to put the former chapels and living quarters to practical use. Cells became store-rooms and not to be outdone by the monks in artistic effort, the villagers decorated the outside of crofts and barns with figures of animals and geometric patterns.

Even today changes have come slowly to this outlandish place. Though the richer members of the community sometimes build house fronts and install wooden doors to give the appearance of ordinary dwellings, they show no desire to alter the caves behind, and a step over the threshold is a step back across the centuries.

Strangely shaped rock towers and pinnacles stud the countryside around Mount Argaeus, Asia Minor's highest peak, which rises 12,848 feet on the Cappadocian Plateau of Central Turkey. In prehistoric times, the mountain erupted, spewing ash and lava hundreds of feet deep across the land. Rains and melting snows created valleys and riverbeds, and wind and water slowly carved the volcanic debris into thousands of pyramids and cones. For thousands of years men have made their homes in these rock shapes. Macan is one of half-a-dozen villages half-hidden in this lunar landscape. The first cone dwellers hacked out homes from the soft rock. Many carved entrances high above the ground to protect themselves from attack. The double towered cone shown here, no longer inhabited, has many rooms on different levels

Samarkand the fabulous

It was to Tamerlane, whose empire finally spread from northern India to Asia Minor, that Samarkand, capital of the kingdom of Transoxiana owed its legendary splendour. Tamerlane whose ruthless cruelty became a black legend recounted down the centuries and who devastated entire regions during his thirty-five year reign (1370–1405) embellished his capital with care and affection. His son Shah Rukh and his grandson, Ulug Beg, as pacific as he himself had been warlike, in their turn made Samarkand a brilliant centre of Persian culture. It was already a very ancient city, for its name first appears in accounts of Alexander the Great's expedition. After the Islamic conquest it became a metropolis famous for its gardens, canals and fountains. It was well known as a centre of paper-making. In AD 1220 it was sacked by Ghengis Khan. Ulug Beg, a patron of science and the arts, was passionately interested in astronomy and built an observatory on a hilltop close to his capital. His measurements of the astronomical year made in the fifteenth century are said to differ only by one minute from the calculations made four centuries later.

Capped with a bright blue-green tiled cupola, the Gur Emir is one of the most striking monuments of Samarkand renowned for the beautiful architectural and decorative treasures of the fourteenth and fifteenth centuries. Tamerlane and Ulug Beg are buried within this Gur Emir. Tamerlane's tomb was opened for the first time in 1941 and examination of his skeleton proved that, as it had been told, he was lame.

Mount Sinai

THE MONASTERY
OF THE BURNING BUSH

Albert Raccah

In the first century of the Christian era, the Sinai Peninsula became a centre of refuge for monks and anchorites (the early Christian recluses and hermits). About the beginning of the fourth century they sent a delegation to St Helena, mother of Constantine the Great, asking her protection. She ordered the erection of a small fortress with a church built inside.

On the accession of the Emperor Justinian in AD 527, these monks who were living on the reputed site of the Burning Bush (where, according to the Bible, God appeared to Moses), asked the ruler to build them a monastery behind whose walls they would be safe from bandits and other marauders. Justinian agreed, and on his orders, the present monastery was built. With its towers and high walls, it was more like a castle than a home of monks. The monastery gained its name from the fact that relics of St Catherine of Alexandria, found on the Sinai Peninsula, were brought there and may still be seen by pilgrims. Entering the fortress-monastery by the three successive gates is like stepping into the past, into a fortified castle of the Middle Ages.

Despite all the sieges and pillaging, the treasures which have accumulated there during fourteen centuries are considered priceless. The walls of the Basilica are covered with ancient icons of great artistic value. On each side of the altar are two reliquaries—offerings to St Catherine—decorated with precious stones. One, dating from the eighteenth century, was the gift of the Russian Empress Catherine the Great.

The pride of the monastery is the library which today is housed in a new building. With around 3,500 Byzantine, Greek, Arab and Russian documents, it is regarded as the second most important collection of manuscripts in the world. (The most important is in the Vatican.) St Catherine's has also a number of gospel books, some of them bound and others illuminated with delightful miniatures.

4 Music, minor arts and astronomy

Introduction

Art is that area of human experience which encompasses expressive activity. Story-telling, celebrating, acting, singing, painting and dancing are the fruits of man's need for expressive activity. One of the distinguishing features of the human spirit is the need to record personal and group experience. The finger tracings, drawings, engravings, bas-reliefs and paintings on the walls of caves inhabited by earliest man tell us a clear and distinct story about the dawn of human history. With the greater ease we now have in making contacts across frontiers, we are gradually coming to know more about the ideas and art forms of other people. We thereby lose any feeling of uniqueness or superiority and this, for all of us, is a great gain.

This chapter seeks to show how different art forms have developed in different countries and also draws attention to the pioneering work in the field of technology undertaken in countries of the East. It deals with Chinese opera and the influence this has come to have on Western stage production; puppet theatres throughout Asia, and Indian dancing, which through the pioneering work of such artists as Uday Shanker, and more particularly, Ram Gopal, have come to be better appreciated in the West. To do justice to the extensive literary heritage of the East is not possible in the confines of this anthology; a brief reference is made to the writings of the Chinese sage, Confucius and the less well known religious writings of the Sikhs of India.

Since modern Indian languages are little known internationally there is a prevailing ignorance abroad about Indian writers. Yet modern Indian literature ranges from purely socialist fiction to novels of the stream-of-consciousness technique and even of the anti-novel school, from surrealist to beatnik poetry or literature that is pronouncedly existentialist in content. There are many little magazines in India which are exclusively devoted to poetry.

It has not been possible to deal with the tremendous strides that have been made in the modern cinema in Japan and India where vast numbers of films are produced every year. The cinema is probably the chief form of mass entertainment in India. In Japan, on the other hand, as in many countries in the West, television has begun to undermine the power of the cinema industry. The Japanese director Ahira Kurosawa's film *Rashomon* in 1950

first opened the eyes of the West to the importance of Japanese films. In this film he broke all the conventions of the historical film and concentrated on the psychological conflicts between the characters. The film won the Golden Lion at Venice. Before the 1956 Cannes Festival, the Indian cinema was as unknown in the West as the Japanese had been prior to *Rashomon*. Then with *Pather Panchali* the Indian director Satyajit Ray placed India on the international film map. His subsequent work has lived up to the high standards of his first film. Ray has been greatly influenced by the works of Eisenstein and Pudovkin and particularly de Sica, yet his films retain an essentially Indian character. There are, of course, other well-known Japanese and Indian directors whose films have come to and been appreciated in the West.

While painting and sculpture are easy to understand (and are dealt with in some detail in Chapters 3, 5 and 6), the music of the Orient has, till fairly recently, been less well appreciated in the West. The music of Asia is principally melodic; even the percussion is melodic as the drummer subtly alters the pitch and texture of his sound. As Yehudi Menuhin has pointed out, Western music and indeed Western civilization, is by comparison with Asia and Africa, a recent upstart, in the same way as Western science. It should not be forgotten that Chinese, Indian and Arabic science was well developed long before Western science began its momentous development in the past few centuries. Western music has, however, shown a tremendous open-mindedness and as it has absorbed influences in growing measure from all parts of the world, it has developed an enormous vitality. Though Western music may originally have come from India, it met, at the Balkans (the cross roads of the Near East) Mongol influences from Asia. It absorbed the haunting monodic improvization from the Middle East through the great Muslim civilization which extended into Spain all the way from Indonesia. Still more recently in the Americas it added the African to the Western European. And now, back in full circle, Western music is drawing on India and the Far East again. Musicians like Ravi Shankar and Ali Akbar Khan are now well known in the West and Indian musical instruments like the *sitar* are even being incorporated in the music of the 'popular' groups in the West.

Music of the Orient

A NEW LANGUAGE FOR WESTERN EARS
Alain Danielou

The general Western view is to think of 'music' exclusively in terms of occidental forms and traditions which seem to reduce anything else to a kind of folk music which, however charming and attractive it might be, could not be regarded as anything more than a simple and unsophisticated musical form surviving among peoples who had still not attained the level of polyphonic maturity.

The music of the Orient has the power to move immense numbers of peoples, it lends itself to grandiose and complex melodic structures and is perhaps even more suited than Western music to express human emotions at their most subtle or their most intense—those, in fact, of humanity in general, and not simply the people of the Orient.

We quickly see the absurdity of a supercilious attitude when we are dealing with monuments, architectural masterpieces or examples of the graphic and plastic arts which need to be saved from damage or destruction. But the problems become far less straightforward when it is a question of the living arts and, in particular, music.

When we hear a language being spoken which we do not understand, we readily admit our ignorance. Curiously enough, this does not seem to be the case with music. Even when we hear a musical language whose syntax and vocabulary are completely different from what we are used to, we believe we have understood it all, and at once feel confident to express our views on it, more often than not basing them on a few inferior examples of the music in question.

Already audiences in America, Great Britain and Germany, and to a lesser degree in France and Italy, have had the chance to hear great musicians from countries like India, Iran and Japan, as well as orchestras from Indonesia. But the musical impression left by such performances is transitory, thus making it difficult for Western audiences to analyse a work or to understand the outlines of a musical system. Unesco is producing a musical anthology on record of Asian music which should open up a larger place for the great Asian musicians in international musical life by providing fine works of music taken in their purest and most original state from the musical treasuries of countries with highly developed cultures, and particularly those

Richly garbed musicians of a Japanese orchestra perform the classical Gagaku court music whose history goes back over ten centuries. From left to right: flutes, oboes and a mouth organ with vertical pipes. The orchestra also uses a kind of horizontal harp and percussion instruments

of Asia. These records should create a greater measure of mutual comprehension for we can never hope really to know another people unless we understand the kind of music which moves and stirs them.

Man through his art: music

Roger Hinks
The distinction in kind between music and the visual arts—the one art existing in time, the other in space—is a fundamental one and is valid in any time or place.

Asian music being purely melodic and free in rhythm, can be suggested by the flowing, swaying lines of the design, and the tonality may be implied by the chromatic range of the whole composition. Here at least, the European is at a disadvantage. He has lost the power to respond emotionally to any modes but the major and the minor which he still equates with 'cheerful' and 'sad' moods.

On the other hand, the European does respond very readily to the clear and singing colour of a Persian miniature, to the voluptuous movement of an Indian sculptured frieze or fresco, to the rhythmic

calligraphy of a Chinese scroll, even if he knows he is missing all the overtones and associations that make them precious to the Asian mind and eye. And he knows that the richness and variety of his own musical and pictorial tradition has been purchased by the sacrifice of purity, clarity and directness.

By comparison with the art of Asia his own art has shown a certain evasiveness, a certain tendency to obliqueness in its musical analogies. But when in recent years the European artist has wished to create a permanent image of movement in time, he is forced (like Matisse) to rely

36

This sculptured group of celestial musicians from the great Buddhist temple of Borobudor, Java, is a detail from a frieze which forms part of a series of reliefs depicting the life of the Buddha. The frieze shows the Buddha in heaven before he descends to earth in human form. The group is diverse, yet in complete harmony; each face and figure is like a note of music forming a melody. The figures have a gentle grace that flows like the music they are making. The relief is typical of the delicacy and tranquillity of the art of central Java between the eighth and tenth centuries AD, which was closely linked with everyday life. In many parts of present day Indonesia music permeates life to a remarkable degree, and religious ceremonies and theatrical performances alike take place to the sound of the Gamelan orchestra.

upon the intermediate art of the dance, where alone music becomes visible, but whose effect is of its very nature as evanescent as music itself.

Dance

KALAKSHETRA–TEMPLE OF BEAUTY

In 1936 an Indian dancer, Madame Rukmini Devi, founded in Madras a school called Kalakshetra—temple of beauty, consecrated to art. Although at first glance Kalakshetra seems just another school offering courses in the dance, music, painting and sculpture, it is less interested in producing professionals and artists than in producing men and women whose lives are rounded and complete, whose entire personality, mental, moral and physical, blends into a harmonious whole. Madame Rukmini Devi sought to show the underlying harmony uniting all the arts; the vital importance to progress in its many individual, national, religious and international forms; and at the same time how the dance could serve the cause of peace through an understanding of the art and culture of all peoples. Kalakshetra soon became known as a *conservatoire* and international cultural centre, and a school where more than 600 children were educated by the most modern methods. Madame Maria Montessori travelled half way round the globe to meet her, and for many years collaborated with the Indian dancer in her work at Madras.

Kalakshetra's primary aim is to help every pupil give full expression to his artistic and creative ability. Therefore in the different courses of instruction open to the children at Kalakshetra as much time and importance is devoted to the arts as is given to textbooks and scientific training in other schools. Though all the arts are called to play their role in education the greatest emphasis is placed on music and dancing.

Many Western teachers, too, would like to give more prominence to dancing in their educational programmes. It is unfortunate therefore that folk dancing, figure dances and modern rhythmics lack the powerful historical and religious force of *Bharata Natyam* with its wealth of tradition dating back two or three thousand years. India's rich heritage of dances ranges from religious and traditional temple dances (*Bharata Natyam*) and dance dramas (*Kathakali*) down to simple folk dances.

The gestures, rhythms and postures

used in the Indian dance and mime have their fixed symbolic values which blend harmoniously one into the other. The hands alone employ a whole vocabulary of signs or *mudras* – capable of expressing or evoking the most imaginative stories. This gesture language of the fingers follows rules that are as strict as they are subtle. These gestures through which the audience follows the story narrated by the dance, offer to the performers a means of expression as eloquent as the spoken word. Nowhere is this more fully shown than in the sacrificial dance where every type of rhythmic expression is conveyed, from the lift of an eyebrow to a curve of the fingertips, from a twist of the neck and shoulders to the smallest movement of the feet. The purpose of the dance at all times is to stir the emotions, and if it is an 'expression' dance, also to reveal *satyam*, *shivam*, *sundaram* – the true, the beautiful and the good. As Madame Rukmini Devi has said, 'To bring the young to appreciate beauty and therefore to live it, is one of our greatest tasks.'

Chinese opera

Balwant Gargi

The classical Chinese opera differs from the occidental in many ways. Eastern music is not polyphonic in form. In Chinese music, as in Indian, strength and charm lie in subtle nuances and variations of the same melody. It creates a mood, a feeling.

Dance in both India and China has a highly evolved language of gesture which can convey anything and everything. It is so perfect in mime that an expert in Kathakali dance can deliver even a highly political speech. Stylized dance gestures which describe songs must be exact and perfect. Dance, both classical and folk, has always been accompanied by vocal songs and percussion instruments. A song is a running commentary unfolding a story which is enacted in dance. Music and dance have walked hand in hand and given and taken much from each other.

In occidental opera and theatre, the recent trends to experiment in mixing songs and poetry with realistic acting (in the manner of Berthold Brecht), and combining action and mime in opera owe much to the Chinese. Born in Peking, the seat of ancient kings and courts around which all the arts flourished, the Chinese opera assimilated the best traditions of theatre, music, modes of singing, mime and dance. In the nineteenth century, artists like Tcheng, Tchang-Keng, and in our own times Mei Lang-Fan and Chou Sing Fan, by their brilliant performances have carried forward and contributed to the tradition. Chinese opera is a synthesis of dance, music and mime, and reveals the effect of concentration and stylized gesture, retaining always the essential of realism. The accompaniment by percussion instruments underlines and reinforces the rhythms.

Chinese opera does away with most of the decor. Chinese theatre and opera do not strive to give an illusion of reality. They break 'the illusion of reality' and create in turn a world of their own. The Chinese opera player, like the Kathakali dancer in India, uses pure gesture to create palaces, chariots, houses, rivers, forests, streets, boats, cars, light and darkness, everything required for his own actions. Masks and costumes are designed to express particular characters. Different colours signify different people. Style of beard, cut of moustache, angle of the eye, curves and lines of make-up and dress have meaning. The flapping and fluttering of long open double sleeves, which unsophisticated audiences in the West may ignore as a natural flourish of the costume, is in fact a highly skilled manipulation by the actor. The dropping of the sleeve, the backward and forward toss, the ripple and tremor, circling and billowing, all denote a change of mood. These conventions and their symbolic significance are known to all Chinese audiences, as opera has been a popular medium since its inception.

The choreography which makes one's head spin in its complex patterns has been evolved through hundreds of years of tradition and training, has been worked by ancient masters, perfected and matured through the ages. The performances do not seem to have been rehearsed in theatre halls at scheduled times, but through centuries, through generations.

I do not know any theatre which requires less knowledge of the spoken word than the Chinese opera.

The simplification of form in Chinese opera does not rise out of a primitive or naïve folk quality, but from a highly

Peking opera star

evolved technique, the product of centuries of strenuous search. Its simplicity has the conscious master's hand behind it, the craftsmanship of the super-painter who with a few strokes of his brush sketches a human figure, a scene of battle or a running horse.

In the creation of new opera China has borrowed much from the West. *The White Haired Girl* and *The Butterflies*, and more recent operas are a blend of Western realism with native traditions, using harmonic music patterns and symphonic orchestration as a background to solo music.

Asian puppetry
A VANISHING ART
Roshan Dhunjibhoy

It has been said that puppetry is universal and as old as civilization itself. Nowhere is this more true than in Asia, where the origins of the puppet play are buried deep in the mists of antiquity. Writing one thousand years before the birth of Christ, the Chinese chronicler Let-Tse tells us how the puppets of that epoch were made and how the puppet plays were performed. In the East the stories of the puppet plays have been handed down from generation to generation, and many old legends and traditions have been kept alive.

In Asian eyes, the puppet is not simply a doll-like figure portraying a story, it is a living ancestral symbol and an intrinsic part of each country's religious life. The puppet drama remains to this day in Asia as a true People's theatre presenting in vivid form and colour old folklore and legends in a manner easily understood by all.

INDIA
There are many and varied allusions to puppets and animated figures in the legends of Indian literature. In the puppet plays performed today in south and north India, the whole cavalcade of Indian history and mythology marches past in an endless procession of amazing scenes. Episodes taken from the great Hindu classics the *Ramayana* and the *Mahabharata* are the classic themes for south Indian showmen. For generations, puppet dramas of this nature have been enacted before village audiences throughout India. Today, however, the Indian peasants have increasingly been brought under the spell of the cinema and ancient arts are losing their hold on the people.

CEYLON
This is also true of Ceylon, where the puppet theatre is now confined to a single coastal town in the south of the island. Ceylon probably inherited her puppet art from India, and references to methods of manipulating puppets are found in ancient literary works written in the days of the island's kings. Although there is no record of a continued tradition, or even patronage, puppetry in Ceylon still exists in its primitive form and the reason for its survival probably lies in its traditional and folk connections.

JAVA
In the seventh century AD the shadow theatre in Java was already a well established art form and this early tradition can still be seen in the Wayang puppet plays.

In Java and Bali, the development of the art of puppetry has been complex. There are no fewer than five different types of Wayang puppets, each with its own individual method of colouring, carving and dressing the figures. The Wayang Poerwa, one of the five types, was originally used as a rite to communicate with the dead. Although much of the religious significance has been lost, puppet plays are

39

Bunraku puppets

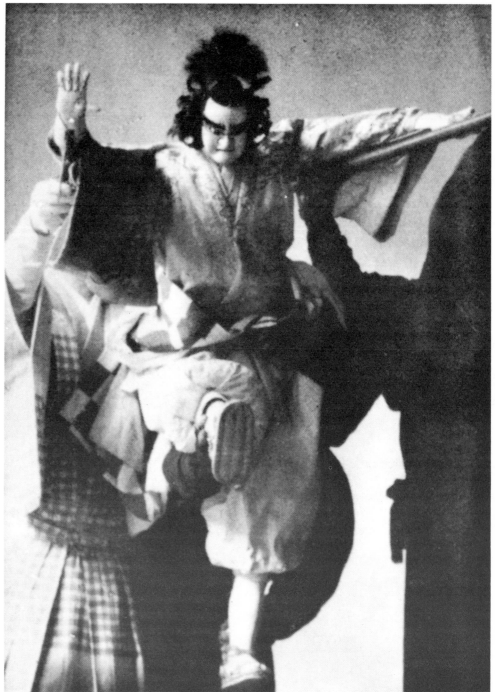

usually performed on marriages and ceremonies to celebrate pregnancy or circumcision. Good and refined characters have long thin features, evil puppets have huge bulbous noses and fat bodies. Men have privileged places and watch actual puppets; women sit behind screens and see puppets as shadow shows. Plays begin after sundown, and long complicated plots are acted out until morning.

CHINA

As long ago as a thousand years before the birth of Christ, puppets were as popular in China as the cinema is today. Even today shadow plays are performed all over China. The tradition of the puppet theatre has been preserved intact, and to old folktales and legends have been added adaptations of Chinese plays and translations of foreign works.

The making of shadow puppets in China is a special craft. The figures, cut by scissors, are individually styled. Openwork and embroideries are indicated by delicate traceries. Tinted in rich translucent colours, the puppets have a decorative appeal which fascinates the audience. The travelling puppeteer is his own theatre as he carries his stage on his head and manipulates the puppets from underneath his voluminous robe. In the 1939–45 war, the

Chinese puppet theatre was used as an effective method of anti-Japanese propaganda—a good indication of the profound influence of puppetry on the modern Chinese peasant.

JAPAN

The growth of puppetry in Japan was comparatively recent; by the mid-eighteenth century the Japanese puppet theatre had become the most lavish in the world. Through the rivalry of two puppet companies, drama reached such heights that it outshone the traditional Japanese Kabuki theatre. Human actors watched the puppets to learn the niceties of acting; the greatest Japanese playwright of his day, Chikamatsu, found greater freedom in writing plays for inanimate actors.

Following this apex of Japanese puppetry, a decline set in and it was not until 1872 that a puppet company in Osaka, brought new life to the art. From Osaka, the new form of puppetry spread to Kyoto and thence throughout the length and breadth of the country. The name of this Osaka company, Bunraku has since become synonymous with the classical puppet theatre.

Centuries of lifetime devotion and painstaking study by generations of artists have gone into the development of Bunraku, Japan's unique form of puppetry. What makes Bunraku really different is that the puppets are two-thirds life size and are manipulated on a stage in full view of the audience. It takes three persons to manipulate a Bunraku puppet: the chief puppeteer, garbed in an ancient ceremonial robe, works the head and the right arm, with two assistants, one to work the left arm and the other, the feet. The assistants whose presence on the stage is supposed to be unnoticed, are clad in black robes and hoods which signify 'nothingness'. Once the Bunraku play has started, the audience is no longer conscious that the puppeteers exist. It sees only the graceful or forceful 'actors' whose every gesture is perfectly timed to the accompaniment of samisen music and the joruri singers reciting the theme of the play and speaking the lines. Japanese consider that perfection comes after thirty years of training and experience.

Foreigners witnessing a Bunraku performance are invariably impressed with the harmony of the performance and are curious to know how three men moving one puppet can read each other's minds so perfectly. This harmony is achieved only by assiduous practice. It has long been an established rule among Japanese puppeteers that it takes ten years to handle the feet properly, ten more to control the left hand and another ten to control the central movements.

The first thing that strikes the visitor to the puppet chamber of a Bunraku theatre, is the disharmony in the features of the puppets, the eyes, eyebrows and mouths being wholly out of proportion, and even the left and right features being dissimilar. The reason is that exaggeration is an important trait of the puppet which otherwise would lose much of its dramatic effectiveness at a distance. And it is amazing to observe how from a distance the expression of a Bunraku puppet can be discerned on an oversized stage. The theme of the puppet plays has always remained the same—the triumph of justice and the struggle of good against evil.

BURMA

In contrast with the high moral tone of the Japanese puppet plays, the Burmese puppeteer gives his performance with the primary purpose of entertaining his audience, and many of his puppets are lively, laughable figures of fun. However, in common with Japan, music plays its part on the Burmese puppet stage. The true Burmese puppet play is more often than not concerned with events in the lives of former Burmese kings.

Puppetry in Burma now is a declining art and the spirit of the puppet theatre is largely kept alive here, as in India and Ceylon, by the itinerant puppeteer wandering from village to village and fair to fair playing to those audiences who still remain out of touch with the cinema—particularly true in Burma where the cinema has not spread to the same degree as in other Asian countries. The simple dedicated artists have most probably been given the secrets of their calling by their fathers as the art of the puppeteer tends to run in families.

Asia still has its puppet theatre, but the art of puppetry is fast disappearing in the face of the ever increasing advance of the travelling cinema and the radio.

Confucius
'THE MOST SAGELY ANCIENT TEACHER'

Cheng Chi-Pao

Confucius, the great Chinese sage, born 2,500 years ago, is one of the few men who have continued down the centuries to

Ten-headed king: in ancient Indian epic, the *Ramayana* Hindu God Sri Rama slays the ten-headed King Ravana of Lanka. Gandhi often referred to the reign of Rama as India's Golden Age

exercise a profound influence on the thoughts and actions of many millions of people.

The basis of Confucianism rests mainly on three great books, all of which were edited by his disciples. To these, the *Great Learning*, *The Doctrine of the Golden Mean* and *The Confucian Analects*, must be added a fourth book, the work of Mencius, who lived one hundred years after Confucius and was one of the chief expounders of Confucian philosophy.

The *Great Learning* embodies psychology, education, science and political philosophy. It begins with the development of personal mind and virtues, through the cultivation of man's social relations, and ends with training for government leading to the final achievement of the ideal of a world commonwealth.

The Doctrine of the Golden Mean is a great book on the exposition of the 'natural way'. It can be summed up in one sentence: 'In everything, the Golden Mean is the best.'

Confucius himself said: 'What Heaven ordains is called Nature. What conforms to Nature is called the Natural Way. What regulates Nature is called Instruction.' Man's duty was to discover the way of nature and thus avoid being swayed by doctrines and dogmas. In this way would he accord with the natural motion of the universe and be able to live in serenity.

Confucianism is not a religion. Confucius believed that man's attitude towards the Supreme Being should be one of deep reverence, but he was not interested in such problems as the soul or the nature of God. Speculation about such matters was to him a waste of time.

Confucius emphasized particularly the development of personal virtues. He believed that the nature of man is essentially good, but that contact with the everyday world often brings about its degeneration. The well-being of society depends on the right relations of men.

'The wise man regards the moral worth of a man, a fool only his position; a wise man expects justice, a fool, favour.'

But it is on the practical side of life that Confucius has made the real contribution not only to China, but also to the entire world. Living in a time of great political confusion, he was primarily interested in politics. Not satisfied with existing conditions, he held up as a pattern for his and succeeding generations, the model of a Golden Age. 'Devote yourself patiently to the theory and conscientiously to the practice of government. Without the confidence of the people no government can stand very long. Government is good when it makes happy those who live under it and attracts those who live far away.'

Confucius was a great teacher—an educator in the modern sense of the word. He gave us principles of education which are as sound today as they were in his time. Students, he maintained, should be both diffusers of knowledge and discoverers of new truth.

Confucian philosophy is essentially the study of how men can best be helped to live together in harmony.

Sacred writings of a warrior race

Khushwant Singh

Most people are inclined to regard the Sikhs of India as a martial race and do not realize that they have produced a body of religious literature which is amongst the best in India. In 1954 Unesco undertook to translate selections from the Sikh sacred writings, the *Granth*, for the benefit of the English-speaking world.

The compilation of the *Granth* was largely the work of Arjun (1563–1606), the fifth of the ten Sikh Gurus or teacher prophets. He collected the writings of the four preceding Gurus and the writings of Hindu and Muslim divines from all over India. The tenth Guru, Govind (1666–1708) pronounced that after him there would be no more Gurus and that the *Granth* was to be regarded as the living symbol of all ten prophets. Today the *Granth* is the object of worship in all Sikh homes and temples. It forms an integral part of Sikh life. Passages from it are read every day, and on special occasions it is read non-stop from cover to cover by a relay of worshippers. (It takes two days and nights to recite its five thousand verses.)

Apart from the sanctity accorded to it by more than six million people, there are other things which make the *Granth* a very remarkable piece of work. It is perhaps the only scripture in the world which could be described as truly secular in the sense that it does not propagate the tenets of any one creed. It contains the writings of all religious groups in India at the time, and is in the nature of an anthology of religious poetry representing the blending of Hinduism and Islam. This makes it a unique historical document as well. It has preserved the writings of medieval saints, some of which describe events of the time, such as conquests, social conditions and religious controversies. The *Granth* has also saved the traditional form of Indian music from corruption. Its 5,000 verses are set to measure—according to thirty-one ragas or modes—of Indian music, for all the hymns of the *Granth* are meant to be sung, and professional singers render them today as they were rendered three hundred years ago.

Three thousand years of glass-making

Anita Engle

The first recorded reference to glass-making was on the Phoenician coast in the fifteenth century BC; the ancient industry was brought to an end in the fifteenth century AD by the Mongol invasion which destroyed the ancient pattern of life all over the Middle East.

The origins of glass-making are tied up with the beginnings of metallurgy. From 2600 BC onwards, the narrow strip of Canaan, known as Phoenicia, was acting as a long bridge between Mesopotamia, the cradle of technology, and Egypt, the ever-open market for goods, ideas and craftsmen.

The oldest traditions of glass-making that have come down to us are centred on the mysterious little river Belus, today

A rare example of the early glassmaker's art, this second or third century miniature portrait is engraved or stippled through gold-leaf and backed by blue glass

In a workshop in El Khalil (formerly Hebron), a master craftsman keeps a watchful eye on the molten glass in his ancient brick furnace. Today, as in past centuries, this city of western Jordan is famed throughout the Middle East for its glass production. Using techniques unchanged by time, its craftsmen make jewellery of translucent glass with a predominantly blue-green tint. Ancient Hebron ranks among those of the world's oldest cities that are still inhabited

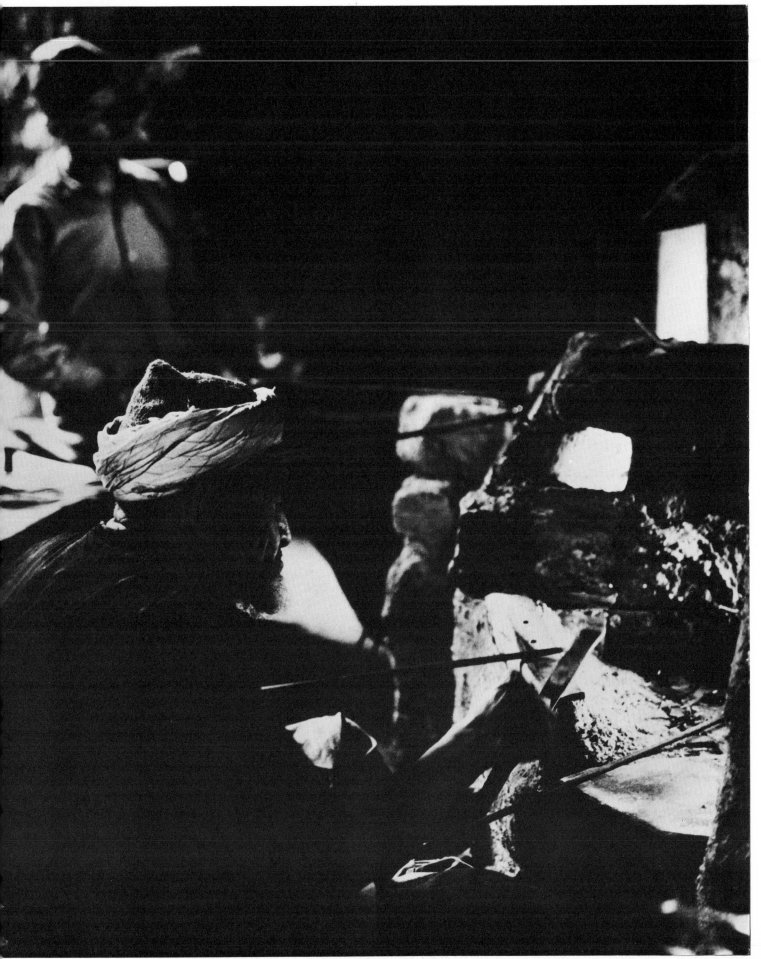

called Naaman, in western Galilee. The classic association of the river Belus with glass-making is to be found in Pliny's *Natural History*. Pliny relates how some merchants encamped on the sands of the river Belus, placed their cooking pots on blocks of soda, and that the heat from the fires fused the sand and the soda to form glass. Whether this story is true or not, it remains a fact that ancient Syrian glass-makers found the sands in this area ideal for their work. It is from Egyptian sources that we have the first documented indications of glass-making on the Phoenician coast.

The earliest vessels of glass known to us, the beautifully coloured little cosmetic jars of Egypt, only begin to make their appearance after Tuthmosis III conquered Phoenicia and Syria.

Like the other imported treasures, the glass, in whatever form it came, and the enslaved artificers, would be sent to the temple of the god, or to the mortuary temple of the Pharaoh himself. There would be small workshops attached to the temples, for we find the high priest of Memphis bearing the title 'director of the glass factory'.

Glass-making was one of the industries of the prosperous Israelites at the time when the Northern Kingdom was finally absorbed by the Assyrians in 721 BC. Glass-makers would be among the varieties of craftsmen taken into exile to enhance the splendour of the Assyrian capitals.

Assurbanipal (668–626) one of the last of the great Assyrian kings, caused to be collected in his capital copies and translations of every important book (clay tablet) to be found in the temple cities of Mesopotamia. Some of these tablets are the earliest literary record of the plant and processes of glass-making. As they are copies, they probably date back much earlier. They reveal a highly developed and unsuspected glass industry in Mesopotamia in the seventh century BC, some 400 years after Egypt had faded out of glass history. In Mesopotamia we find the origin of the reverbatory furnace which is the precondition of glass-blowing. The final development of the Babylonian glass furnaces must have taken place somewhere on the Phoenician coast, for it is here, some 500 years later, that the history of glass-blowing begins. The time lag fits in well with the fact that in the pre-scientific age, the average time-span for

new technological developments was about 500 years.

Harbours along the Phoenician coast took on new life after the Persian conquest, and so did glass-blowing. The type of many-coloured unguentaria or perfume bottle which is characteristic of the Persian period was widely distributed by Greek traders, together with their Attic pottery. Later, they distributed the mould-pressed lathe-turned vessels which were found in the most far-flung areas of the ancient world during the Hellenistic period.

By the time the Romans came to the Middle East–around 63 BC–Phoenicia was widely famed for its glass and glass-makers. But the Alexandrian glass-makers were producing the most beautiful glass–the rich gem-like pastes, the vessels carved like rock crystal, and the millefioris. This profitable trade in imitation of the fabulous precious and semi-precious stones of India and the nearer East which reached the Roman market via Alexandria, kept the Egyptian glass-makers tied to their static cutting and moulding processes.

The glass-makers of the Phoenician coast followed their markets to Italy and Gaul, laying the foundation of a European glass industry which bore the marks of their ancient origins right into the sixteenth century. These glass-makers spread throughout Asia as well. All traditions associated with glass-making in the countries of the East, including India and China, claim 'Syrian' origins.

By the twelfth century, Damascus had become the centre of a new development in the Eastern glass industry, the richly enamelled Saracen glass beakers and mosque lamps.

The Venetians who provided shipping, services and supplies for the Crusades, in return secured special privileges and quarters on the East Mediterranean coast. By 1124, at the height of Crusading success, they were firmly established in Jerusalem, Acre, Sidon and particularly in Tyre. Raw materials, together with craftsmen, were exported to Venice, and as early as 1224 there was a glass-blowers' guild there. When Tamerlane took Damascus in 1401 and virtually extinguished the Syrian glass industry by deporting its craftsmen to Samarkand, Venice replaced the East as the world's centre of fine glass-making, although it was some two centuries before Venice could begin to rival the wares of Syria.

The first astronomers of China and Babylon

Sir Leonard Woolley

Popular opinion has mistakenly ascribed to the Mesopotamians and, still more to the Egyptians, a profound understanding of astronomical phenomena. Although it is true that from a very early time the heavenly bodies and their movements were observed and recorded, this is not the same as saying that astronomy begins early; men's interest in the celestial bodies was calendral on the one side and astrological on the other. Professor Neugebauer has said:

'Astronomy does not originate with the recognition of irregular configurations of stars or the invention of celestial or astral deities. Scientific astronomy does not begin until an attempt is made to predict, however crudely, astronomical phenomena such as the phases of the moon.'

Only in the course of the first millennium BC did Babylonian astronomers succeed in *predicting* the lengths of lunar months and it was only from Babylon that the Egyptians subsequently acquired such knowledge.

The advance from observation to prediction was really made impossible for the Egyptian by the elementary character of his mathematical system which could not cope with the elaborate calculations demanded by astronomy. It would appear that having once obtained, by very simple observations, the agricultural and ritual data necessary to an ordered life, he had no urge to pursue the matter further. Thus we find in the Egyptian texts no reference at all to lunar eclipses.

From China, on the other hand, we have in one Anyang bone inscription a very early record of an eclipse which took place 'on the fifteenth day of the twelfth moon on the twenty-ninth year of King Wu-Ting', i.e. on 23 November 1311 BC, which shows an interest, and possibly a knowledge, antedating anything of the sort in Egypt. Thus, as early as the twelfth century BC, Chinese astronomers were able to calculate the lunar eclipses in advance, and with such confidence that an error of twenty-four hours was enough to alarm the authorities, for we are told that in 1137 BC the Chou ruler Chou-wen-sung ordered a sacrifice to be offered because 'the eclipse happened not on the right day'.

The Babylonians, possessing a mathematical basis for astronomical calculations much superior to that of the Egyptians, made far greater progress in the astronomical field, and started at quite an early date to amass a *corpus* of information which would ultimately supply the material for science. The earliest computations were concerned with (*a*) the duration of the day and night in different seasons, (*b*) the rising and the setting of the moon and (*c*) the appearance and disappearance of Venus.

From the time of the Third Dynasty of Ur (2100 BC) onwards the omen texts, which combine astrological forecasts with astronomical observations, prove the careful attention paid to astral phenomena. Thus, by 1200 BC in Babylonia, the foundations of real astronomical research as defined by Professor Neugebauer, had been well and truly laid. Further, it appears likely, though it cannot be definitely affirmed, that already the first tentative steps had been taken in the direction of scientific thinking over the data which careful observation had amassed, and that certain rather crude and elementary results had been achieved which in the course of the following millennium would be developed into the astronomical science inherited by the Greeks.

Eighteenth-century observatories in India

Francis Brunel
Early in the eighteenth century, an Indian Prince, Jai Singh-Maharajah of Amber, conceived and carried out a plan to erect a series of observatories unparalleled in his time. Even today the purity of line and abstract form of the structures he built, offer one of the most remarkable examples of astronomical architecture. Mathematics, astronomy and architecture were his greatest interests, and in these fields he was regarded as one of the most talented men of his day.

Prince Jai Singh considered available astronomical data of his time inadequate. Even the famous tables of the Sultan Mirsa Ulug Beg of Samarkand, he felt, were out of date. So he decided to draw up new and more accurate ones.

Between 1710 and 1730 he ordered the construction of five observatories—at Jaipur, Delhi, Mathura, Benares and Ujjain, a town situated on the main meridian of India, on the Tropic of Cancer—so that observations and calculations made by his astronomers and mathematicians could be verified and corroborated.

Today in Jaipur City, which Prince Jai Singh founded in 1728, the remarkable structures which made up one of these five open-air observatories, provide a record in stone of the scientific progress for which this mathematician and astronomer is famous. When he ordered the building of the observatories, Prince Jai Singh planned to use types of apparatus made of metal, but finding these unsatisfactory, he had huge new instruments constructed in stone. The size of these was intended to facilitate more accurate studies and readings of stellar space and time.

Some of the structures such as the Samyat Yantra 'the emperor of instruments' are as much as 65 feet high, run 130 feet in length from north to south and are proportionately wide from east to west. One instrument, the Rama Yantra, consists of two partitioned cylindrical structures, which make possible the observations required at that time for the revision of Ulug Beg's tables of altitude and azimuth of heavenly bodies.

Besides these instruments, and pointing into space, are a series of other complicated instruments—evidence of the spirit of research which since ancient times has urged man to extend the field of his knowledge and to explore and understand the great universe.

They call their telescope 'Bima Sakti'

Victor H Blanco
A unique institution in South-east Asia is the Bosscha Astronomical Observatory in Indonesia. On the western hills of the Island of Java, amidst meticulously kept gardens, rises a monumental dome-shaped building housing two of the largest refracting telescopes of the world. The principal instruments at this observatory were installed in 1928 and 1929, and from its founding up to World War II, several distinguished Dutch astronomers worked there. The war and subsequent conflicts were disastrous to the observatory, but rehabilitation work started in 1949. In 1950 Unesco joined the Indonesian Government in the acquisition of a new telescope for the Bosscha Observatory. Today the telescopes at the observatory are manned by young Indonesian scientists and are actively helping to widen man's scientific horizons. The publications of the

Observatory are read and collected in hundreds of scientific centres throughout the world. The Bosscha Observatory is a symbol of the opportunities that the Republic envisages for its young scientists.

The geographic position of the observatory, seven degrees south of the equator, is important from the astronomical point of view. Bosscha's telescopes can sweep across some of the most important constellations in the sky. The nucleus of our galaxy or Milky Way, for example, lies in Sagittarius, a constellation that cannot be observed to advantage from the northern hemisphere where most of the large telescopes are concentrated.

The new telescope has been named 'Bima Sakti'—one of the heroes of the Javanese wayang or puppet plays, based on the Hindu epic *Mahabharata*. In Javanese mythology, Bima Sakti is so tall that he straddled the Milky Way. The name of this ancient hero is thus particularly appropriate for a telescope that will be devoted to Milky Way observations.

5 The impact of Buddhism

Introduction

No account of Eastern masterpieces of sculpture, architecture and painting would be complete without an analysis of the impact of Buddhism which spread along the ancient trading caravan routes of Asia from its birthplace in India. The world in which 2,500 years ago Buddhism was born and spread was a world of vast movements of men and ideas. In this world India was geographically the crossroads between Western and Far Eastern civilization.

The coming of Buddhism, coinciding as it did with increased trade and intercourse between Asian countries, resulted in a period of intense intellectual life. The message of the brotherhood of man stimulated a resurgence of popular feeling, just as Christ's message did in Rome in early Christian times. The richly human content of the Buddhist message was the spiritual basis of an art which overrode the frontiers of artistic expression, revitalized local traditions, making them truly Buddhist and at the same time free expressions of national character. It was a message of hope and a message of peace. And these two important factors helped the development and maturity of a noble art that has enriched the artistic traditions of the world.

Buddhist art is essentially religious, but the arts of Egypt, of medieval Europe, of Negro Africa and the ancient Mayas, were religious too. Are we to say that no attempt to grasp the beauty of Luxor, or Chartres can be made without a fine knowledge of their religious portent?

In early Buddhist art, Buddha was portrayed *symbolically*. For example, a riderless horse symbolized the 'Great Departure' when Buddha left his home, wife and family. A tree with an empty seat stood for the attainment of Supreme Wisdom (Buddha sat in meditation under the sacred Bodhi tree when he achieved enlightenment). Buddha's first sermon is represented by a wheel—the Wheel of Life. It is significant that early Christian art also expressed itself in symbols, the Fish, the Dove and the Cross, while Christ on the Cross was only seen much later.

About the second century AD these symbols were replaced by images of Buddha himself. The first images of Buddha were made independently by the sculptors of Mathura and Gandhara. Mathura was the great trading centre where Buddhist images were made to be sold all over Asia, and the Mathura artists

First portrayals of Buddha as a man rather than as a symbol are accredited to the Gandhara school whose images reveal its debt to Greco-Roman art in the first century. The resemblance of some of the Buddha heads to the Apollo Belvedere is apparent. Buddha's cranial protuberance has been disguised by the adaptation of the top-knot of the Greek sun-god, though the other marks of greatness are in the Indian tradition

used the earlier 'Yaksha' statue of pre-Buddhist cults as their model. The sculptors of Gandhara and Taxila in the northwest (Afghanistan and Pakistan) used Greco-Roman models of Apollo for their first Buddha.

In order to standardize the Buddha's image to make it easily recognizable, the artists, basing themselves on legends that Buddha was born with certain signs of greatness, depicted him with a protuberance on the skull, a tuft of hair between the eyebrows and long ear lobes. Right down to the present time, images of Buddha have borne these unmistakable characteristics. The ancient Buddhist artists also depicted particular moods, such as tenderness and compassion which characterize the Buddha. Unlike the later Christian artists who portrayed Christ undergoing human suffering on the Cross, they present the Buddha as one completely detached from human pain, looking with compassion on all humanity. Most frequently the Buddha is shown seated on a lotus throne. Buddha's image is conveyed through graceful gestures or *mudras* (derived from earlier gesture lan-

guage in common use in ancient India and from which the elaborate Indian classical dance *mudras* are developed) expressing a state of illumination, meditation, preaching, the act of giving or charity, fearlessness or reassurance, or setting the Wheel of the Law in motion.

At the death of the Buddha his ashes were divided up into eight parts; these were put in jewelled caskets and enshrined in eight *stupas*. (A stupa is a sacred shrine built as an enormous dome mounted on a pedestal with a stylized umbrella, symbol of royalty, on top.) Around the main Buddhist stupas containing important relics of the Buddha or his disciples, there are often smaller ones containing other reminders such as images, sacred writings and prayers.

The first stupas gave birth to a million others. Down the centuries the stupa modified its form, and in each country in Asia it took on distinct national characteristics. The great stupa of Borobudur in Java has been described as 'a ripe fruit matured in breathless air'. In China and Burma the stupa was given a different form, and name—the pagoda. In Ceylon it is a dagoba, and in Siam it soared skywards till its spire looked like an arrow.

The main themes for the Buddhist artists were the *Jataka* tales—stories of Buddha's previous lives as Bodhisattva and incidents of his life. Side by side with these are scenes of everyday life. Animals figure largely in these tales, showing how before the final human incarnation, in which he attained enlightenment, the Bodhisattva himself had been reborn innumerable times as an animal. (The Jataka tales themselves are spiced with a sly humour and are known to have inspired La Fontaine.) While the attitude of Buddha towards nature is made clear enough in ancient writings, it is brought out even more strongly in the visual arts. Even the earliest sculptures known to us (dating back to the third and second centuries BC) are impressive for the loving care and skill with which the forms and attitudes of animals are shown. The striking thing about this early art is its profound kinship with nature. Processions led by gaily caparisoned horses and elephants, men, women and children, animals, luxuriant vegetation, flowers, fishes, birds, deer, tree spirits, snakes, are modelled with a natural quality which carries with it the pulse of life, of tenderness, of movement and vitality.

The lotus flower, or 'Padma' is widely used in the art, and in the religious symbolism of Buddhism. Long regarded as a sacred plant, the lotus and its flower aptly symbolizes life's fulfilment. With its roots in the earth, its stem in water, its blossom in the air, and blooming in the rays of the sun, the lotus symbolizes the four elements. It is also the symbol of rebirth; its seeds pass from the air to the water and then into the earth where they germinate. It symbolizes purity.

This chapter seeks to give both a panorama of the great masterpieces of sculpture, architecture and painting of Buddhist art in Asia, and a glimpse of some of the ethical ideals, and the message of peace, gentleness and mercy which Buddhism 'one of the greatest edifices of thought ever created by the human spirit' has inspired.

The life and teaching of Buddha

Sarvepalli Radhakrishnan

Gautama, the Buddha, the teacher of infinite compassion, the master mind from the East, had a deep influence on the thought and life of the human race and was the founder of a religious tradition whose hold is hardly less wide and deep than any other. He was born in 563 BC at Kapilavastu on the Nepalese border, 150 miles north of Benares. The spot was afterwards marked by the Indian Emperor Asoka with a column which is still standing.

Gautama was of a religious temperament and found the pleasures and ambitions of the world unsatisfying. The efforts of his father to turn his mind to secular interests failed, and at the age of twenty-nine he left his home, wife and family, put on the ascetic garb and became a wandering seeker of truth. This was the great renunciation. Determined to attain illumination by the practice of asceticism he withdrew with five disciples to the beautiful forest of Uruvala. Despite his severe fasts and austerities, he got no glimpse of the riddle of life. He therefore decided that asceticism was not the way to enlightenment. He remembered how once in his youth he had an experience of mystic contemplation and now tried to pursue that line. It was thus that he found the answer, in the last watch of the night. 'Ignorance was destroyed, knowledge had arisen . . . as I sat there earnest, strenuous, resolute.' Gautama had attained *bodhi* or illumination and became the Buddha, the Enlightened One.

He adopted a mendicant missionary's life with all its dangers of poverty, unpopularity and opposition. In the deer park near modern Sarnath in India, he preached his first sermon. Disciples began to flock to him, and he sent them far and wide to preach. He himself travelled widely for forty-five years and gathered many followers.

There is nothing esoteric about Buddha's teaching, and little of what we call dogma. With a breadth of view rare in that age, and not common in ours, he refused to stifle criticism. Intolerance seemed to him the greatest enemy of religion. There was never an occasion when the Buddha flamed forth in anger, never an incident when an unkind word escaped his lips. He had vast tolerance for his kind. He thought of the world as ignorant rather than wicked, as unsatisfactory rather than rebellious. He met opposition with calm and confidence.

The message of the Buddha was not only for his age, but for all time. The impermanence of the world, its sorrow and suffering provoked his religious quest: Buddha felt the threat of nothingness, of non-being which one experiences when one looks upon the passing world of birth and death, of disease and old age. The question is whether we can acquire strength and courage, whether we can discover the centre of freedom in ourselves which will save us from the insecurity of time, from the body of this death. Buddha gives us the answer: 'By deepening our awareness and by changing ourselves.' The way to change the world is to change the nature of man. Buddha asks us to find the teacher within ourselves and attain enlightenment. His morality was not one of outward conformity, but of inward cleansing.

After observing that those who wish to lead a religious life and avoid the two extremes of self-indulgence and self-mortification, and follow the middle way, he enunciates the four truths about sorrow, the cause of sorrow, the removal of sorrow and the way leading to it.

The eightfold path represents a ladder to perfection. Right views, right aspirations, right speech, right action, right living, right effort, right mindfulness, right contemplation. The eightfold path is more than a code of morality. It is a way of life.

Respect for animal life is an integral part of morality. A good Buddhist does not speak of sin, but only of ignorance and foolishness which can be cured by enlightenment and sympathy. When the individual overcomes ignorance, breaks the power of his own deeds to drag him back into expiation, ceases to desire and to regret, and attains enlightenment, he passes into the world of being as distinct from that of existence, being which is free from form and formlessness, from pain and delight, though that state is not humanly conceivable. It is deliverance, freedom from rebirth – Nirvana.

The exact number of Buddhists in the world is not known. In Asia some 500 million people are followers of the religion of the Middle Way. Buddhist thought and teaching fall into two main schools – the *Hinayana School* and the *Mahayana School*.

The *Hinayana School* (Lesser Vehicle) exists in Ceylon, Burma, Thailand and Cambodia. It seeks to retain the earlier teachings of Buddha down to the letter, views the Buddha as a human being, a teacher whose Enlightenment raised him above others. His Nirvana was the same as that of any other person who attains it. He dispensed no divine power. Man's destiny is moulded by his own acts; salvation comes by following monastic self-discipline.

The *Mahayana School* (The Greater Vehicle) spread from India to Nepal, Tibet, China, Korea and Japan. It is less rigorous and does not limit salvation to the monastic order. Every person, however humble, may become a candidate for Buddhahood if he but wills it and holds to his purpose. The historical Gautama falls into the background making way for a Pantheon of Buddhas viewed as redeemers or gods. The path to salvation lies in love for the holy Buddha and Bodhisattvas of the past, love for one's fellow creatures by self-sacrifice for their needs, active compassion and charity. There is also the *Zen* system of Buddhism (which flourishes in Japan) which eschews all intellectual processes in the progress towards individual enlightenment. Enlightenment comes to a man in a sudden flash. Buddhahood pervades every single aspect of nature; it is as evident in a grain of sand as in a saint. Zen Buddhism makes an appeal to both intellectual and non-intellectual.

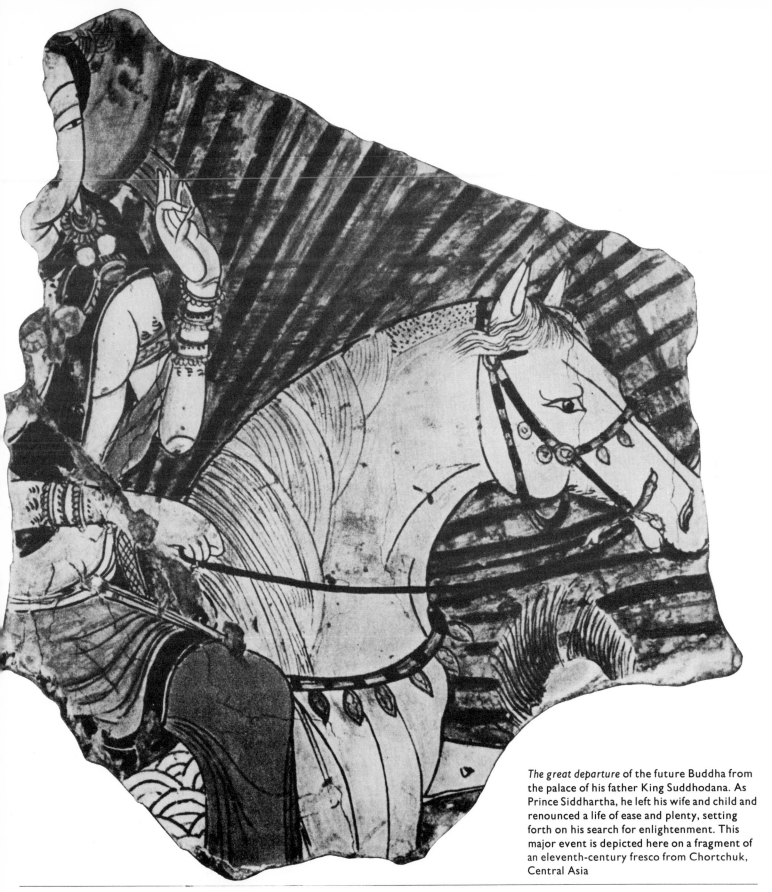

The great departure of the future Buddha from the palace of his father King Suddhodana. As Prince Siddhartha, he left his wife and child and renounced a life of ease and plenty, setting forth on his search for enlightenment. This major event is depicted here on a fragment of an eleventh-century fresco from Chortchuk, Central Asia

The spread of Buddhist art

One of the first notable monuments to perpetuate the memory of Buddha was built at Sanchi in central India some 2,200 years ago—about two centuries after his death. And although Buddhism disappeared from its native soil, it spread to other countries of Asia to become the living faith of millions who, in their turn, built monuments to honour Buddha throughout the vast Continent.

Some of these lay hidden for over 1,000 years, buried under sand, or lost in the solitudes of impenetrable tropical jungles. It is only in the past seventy years or so that explorers and archaeologists have made systematic studies of these monuments, hacking their way through entangled undergrowth, or digging in the desert wastes to reveal art that has amazed the world—great Buddhas in eternal sleep or standing in watchful meditation.

Indian influence on the art of Asia of the time is reflected all over the continent—in the flying figures of the Yun Kang caves in Shansi in China; in the calm nobility of the reliefs of Borobudur in Java, in the strength of the early Siamese Buddhas, in the wall paintings of Pagan in Burma, in the sensuousness of the women of Sigiri in Ceylon and in the movement of the dancers in the grottoes of Kizil in central Asia.

49

The spread of Buddhism through Asia came in several waves, emanating from India from the first century AD. Bronze statues of a later period have been unearthed from the jungles of Annam, Borneo and Celebes. Buddhist culture apparently superimposed itself on the whole of South-east Asia. Nevertheless, each region retained much of its own personality and character. In the eighth century AD Buddhist art began to mature and flower in these countries, gaining in movement and vigour, when local tradition dominated. We see this clearly at Borobudur in Java, where the Javanese pattern of composition, harmony and repose are blended with the Indian style of art. Later, Javanese art threw off this influence and asserted its own national characteristics. Chinese Buddhist sculpture includes some of the most beautiful religious sculpture in the world. The essential contribution of China towards Asian Buddhist art is the expression of the Buddha's face. The mystic smile is purely a Chinese creation, and is the expression of a profound religious sentiment. Wherever we find the suggestion of this smile, in Cambodia, in Japan, in Java, Siam or Burma, we see the affinity with China.

In Japan, the technique and even the aesthetics that guided the artists after the sixth century AD came from China and Korea. The spirit is entirely Japanese, the most characteristic sculpture being powerful, virile, frequently leaving a disturbing impact.

As South-east Asian cultures were coming into maturity in the eighth century AD those of Afghanistan and the central Asian kingdoms, ravaged by repeated invasions, started to decline. The Muslim invasions of the Middle Ages destroyed the last stronghold of Buddhism in India. Artists and monks living in the University City of Nalanda fled for refuge to Tibet and Nepal. Nepalese art continued the medieval tradition of Indian Buddhist art. Tibetan painting and sculpture shows a strange mixture of central Asian, Chinese, Indian and local tradition.

BUDDHIST ART IN INDIA

It is a great paradox that Buddhism, as a religion, has gradually ceased to exist in its own birthplace, India, since the twelfth century AD. But the art which was created and developed in India under the direct influence of Buddhism has bequeathed to this country works of art whose beauty

The south gate at Sanchi, which continues the story begun on the north gate, of Prince Visvantara (the last of Buddha's incarnations before he was born as Gautama) who practised the virtue of the perfection of giving. Banished by the people for giving away to a drought-ridden country a white elephant endowed with the magical power of bringing rain, he suffered a series of trials during which his steadfastness and charity were put to the test. The story of the south gate frieze shown here begins on the right, when the exiled prince and his wife Madri have reached the foot of the Himalayas after a thousand hardships. They are shown clad as forest dwellers, tending the fire in front of their leaf-domed hut. In the peaceable jungle, the children, the animals and the trees are friends. Then, while Madri has gone into the jungle to seek fruit and roots, a wicked Brahmin arrives and asks Visvantara to give him his children as servants. Despite their tears and his own anguish, Visvantara acquiesces. Even when he sees his children being tied and beaten (left of centre) he does not interfere or protest. Finally another Brahmin appears and asks the hermit-prince to relinquish his beloved wife (centre left). But as the Prince accepts, the trials end, for the Brahmin is none other than the god Indra who has come down to earth in disguise to subject the prince to this supreme test. Directly above, Indra crowned and carrying his thunderbolts is shown reuniting the prince and his wife. The rest of the relief reads from the left It shows (bottom row) the prince's father who has purchased the children's freedom from the Brahmin setting off to meet his son and daughter-in-law. Top row, the parents and children (mounted on an elephant) are seen regaining their kingdom

These two images of serenity are Bodhisattvas or potential Buddhas, modelled in clay and painted from the caves at Maichisan. They have been depicted in a most unusual cheek to cheek pose which suggests two people in intimate conversation. The tenderness and gentle expression they reflect is typical of Wei period sculpture

and magnitude place them among the foremost of mankind's cultural treasures.

Little remains of the earliest Indian Buddhist art that was done on perishable buildings of wood. What do remain are the rock temples and dwellings of the early Buddhist monks, like those at Karla, Ajanta, Ellora and many other sites whose semi-obscurity gave an added touch of mystery to the paintings and sculpture decorating their walls and pillars.

Sanchi, in the Indian state of Madhya Pradesh, contains some of the oldest (first century BC) and best-preserved of Buddhist carvings. Sanchi art, one of the earliest of Buddhist art forms, depicts scenes from the *Jataka* and from the life of Buddha in continuous narrative reliefs. The carved gateways of the Sanchi Stupa mark the transition from ivory to stone carving and at least one of the gateways was donated by the ivory carvers' guild of the Andhra Kingdom. In effect, these carvings give the impression of a delicate work of ivory, with their figures crowded closely together and the great attention given to detail.

The Ajanta caves, north-east of Bombay, are justly renowned as one of the remarkable collections of the world's religious art, and among the noblest memorials of Buddhism in that country.

It is interesting to note that the rock-cut temples of Ajanta emerged from their millennial oblivion by pure accident when one day in 1819 some British soldiers on manoeuvres came upon these magnificent cave temples hewn out of the rocks.

The enchanting wall paintings of Bodhisattvas, female figures, various flower and animal motifs are now fairly well known in most countries. These forms and figures are so vibrant with life that the earliest Europeans who saw them could not believe that they were religious. But the main themes of the Ajanta paintings centre round the *Jataka* stories. Human life with its drama of love, compassion, happiness, death, suffering and sacrifice is illuminated by a glow of religious feeling and profound piety. When the caves were first discovered the paintings were fairly well preserved, but today only a few caves still retain them.

The paintings of Ajanta hold a supreme position in Asian art history. They have for Asia and the history of Asian art the same outstanding significance that Italian frescoes have for Europe and the history of European art. One Italian authority on fresco painting has said that they 'will bear comparison with the best that Europe could produce down to the time of Michelangelo'. As the late Prime Minister of India, Pandit Jawaharlal Nehru said, 'the appeal of Ajanta is not merely to the artist or the expert, but to every sensitive human being. Anyone who would understand the past of India must look at these frescoes which have exercised such a powerful influence not only in India, but in distant countries also.'

Speaking of the Ajanta painting of the Compassionate Bodhisattva, the French Orientalist Réné Grousset has said, 'this is a figure that must be placed in world art history alongside the highest incarnation of the Sistine Chapel, alongside those drawings most inspired with a soul, such as the drawings of Christ in the Last Supper by Leonardo da Vinci'.

Ajanta's sculpture, architecture and decorative pillars deserve to be better known too. It is difficult for anyone who has not actually seen these temples hewn from the mountain, to imagine their grandeur. These monastery temples are among the earliest rock-cut remains in India; in their monumental galleries the whole of India's ancient life can be seen anew. The caves are of two main types— the *Chaityas*, shrines or meeting places in the form of an apse (semi-circular in shape at the rear) and the *Viharas*—four sided monasteries or living caves. Some *Chaityas* have a monumental portico and the vaulting is supported on both sides by massive colonnades, flanked by secondary side-aisles—the style of these shrines seems to be inspired from wooden structures of the secular communities mentioned in early Buddhist literature.

A walk round these many-levelled temples is like a journey by magic carpet to the ancient world of early Buddhist times.

The earlier of the thirty cave-monasteries and chapels, all hewn from the rock in the second century BC, reflect the simple, ascetic character of Hinayana Buddhism. In the later examples the primitive austerity and purely spiritual appeal have completely vanished, and the art has become rich, mellow and gracious under the influence of the Gupta style (the fifth century AD), the Golden Age of Indian art. In this era, religious ideas developed and changed without persecution.

Most art historians regard the fifth century AD as the richest period of India's Buddhist art. From the new ideas brought by contacts with other lands and from the greater skills and improved techniques of the Indian painters and sculptors came a great flowering of art. This period can well be described as 'classic' in the sense of describing a degree of perfection never achieved before or since and in the perfect balance and harmony of all elements stylistic and iconographic. The magnificent paintings at Ajanta are a reflection of this supremacy of aesthetic achievement.

Despite the great evolution it underwent, and the many styles it developed during its history of fourteen centuries, Indian Buddhist art maintained a striking unity, due to the fact that the various styles followed each other in the same religious sites; the temples and sanctuaries which art and faith enriched down the centuries.

BUDDHIST ART IN CHINA

Buddhism appeared in China for the first time about AD 65, when Indian monks were travelling northwards across the mountain passes as missionaries. When Buddhism came to China, over trade routes like the famous Silk Route through central Asia, it had already developed a ritual with definite needs, temples, monasteries, statues and paintings. It therefore brought with it a new idea about the function of art; namely that art had to serve the divinity.

Between the fourth and sixth centuries, Buddhist art experienced a great deal of expansion, especially in northern China

Detail of a painting on silk dating from the ninth century AD, and found in one of the caves of the Thousand Buddhas at Tun Huang

under the Wei dynasty. This development continued under the Sui dynasty (581–618). The richest period of Chinese Buddhist art came in the years of the T'ang dynasty (AD 618–906). In the T'ang capital, a great Buddhist monument, the Grey Goose Pagoda was raised, and in all parts of the newly-expanded Empire temples were built and richly decorated with carvings, sculptures and frescoes. In the eleventh and twelfth centuries, the quality of Buddhist painting was still high, but sculpture was already in a state of decline. The same is true, though at a much later date, of Buddhist painting, which never again reached the heights it had achieved under the great artists of the T'ang dynasty.

Some of the finest treasures of Chinese Buddhist painting and sculpture are preserved in the three great 'art galleries' hewn out of the cliff sides of northern China—the Buddhist cave temples and shrines at Lung Men in Shansi Province and at Tun Huang and Maichisan in Kansu Province. Though many paintings have been damaged by time and weather, thousands of others, still in remarkably good condition offer a panorama of Chinese Buddhist art from the third to the thirteenth century AD.

The great temples like the Cave of the Thousand Buddhas at Tun Huang (where caravans travelling on the great Silk Road from China to Persia and Iran halted before crossing the Gobi or Lop Nur desert), were visited by travellers who came to pray for safety and success and to give donations. During the thousand years that this practice continued, hundreds of temples were dug out of the rock and richly decorated with paintings, and images of the Buddha. These caves reveal the skill and imagination of ancient Chinese artists in executing delicately painted figures.

The richest store of Chinese Buddhist sculpture and paintings which has become available to the world recently lies in the cave-chapels of Maichisan—or the corn rick mountain, since this gigantic rock, rising abruptly to a great height, perfectly circular in appearance, resembles the shape of a peasant's corn rick. On the precipitous walls of its upper half were carved many Buddha figures, and a thousand chambers in the rock to serve for niches for other figures. The Maichisan caves were excavated at various periods—the earliest in the fifth century, but there were continual additions in caves and statues right up to the Ming period in the fifteenth to the seventeenth century AD.

Today there are 194 cave-chapels ranging from those as large as Churches and Abbeys to those as small as shrines. All the walls are covered with paintings and numerous statues of the Buddha, Bodhisattvas, attendant figures, disciples, lay donors—both men and women, celestial nymphs (*apsaras*) carrying offerings of flowers and incense, heavenly musicians playing the harp, flute or cymbals. At Maichisan there are excellent examples of the art of all the various styles and periods, particularly the Wei period which produces some of the most spiritual and beautiful religious art in the world. One of the figures recalls the 'smiling angel' of the Cathedral of Reims, while another is reminiscent of French Gothic sculpture.

The three great Buddhist cave-temples in China are undoubtedly among the marvels of the Asian world.

BUDDHIST ART IN BURMA

Buddhism reached Burma in force from India about AD 1057, though Buddhist colonies had appeared in Burma much earlier. Today it is virtually a one-religion country. Thus in every Burmese village are found golden-spired monasteries and pagodas. It is amazing how many pagodas jut out of every part of the Burmese countryside. No hill is too steep or rocky to prevent one from being erected.

Greatest of Burma's pagodas, and Holy of Holies to the Buddhist world, is the superbly beautiful Shwe Dagon in Rangoon. It is the most universally visited of Asia's Buddhist shrines, its peculiar sanctity being due to the fact that it contains several original relics of Gautama including four hairs from the head of the Buddha. Built on the highest point of land in Rangoon, the Shwe Dagon is visible for a distance of twenty miles or more, brilliantly lit by floodlights at night, dazzling in the sun by day. Its spire is covered with pure gold which is renewed each generation by public subscription.

Of all the great centres of Buddhism in Asia, few can boast a more impressive concentration of monuments than the ancient holy city of Pagan (accent last syllable). Pagan was a teeming capital of Burma a thousand years ago. It was built by King Anawrahta in the eleventh century and once had no fewer than 4,000 pagodas. It remained one of the great royal and religious cities of Asia until it was reduced by the armies of Kublai Khan

Garbed in white and capped in gold, glittering in the afternoon sky, Ananda pagoda is the most famous and best preserved of the temples of Pagan

in 1287. For eight miles along the Irrawaddy River, in central Burma, and for two miles inland, a forest of pagodas and stupas of every size and shape extends into the horizon. Some stand out glistening white against their red-brown weather-beaten neighbours like medieval cathedrals in a fantastic landscape. About them rise round towers, bulbous mushrooms, slender pinnacles, bell-shaped pyramids, knoblike domes and pumpkin pagodas.

Ananda pagoda is the most famous and best preserved of the temples of Pagan. It is considered one of the wonders of Burma's former holy capital. Completed in the eleventh century, its form may have been inspired by the great cave temples of India, accounts of which were brought to Burma by a group of Indian Buddhist monks from Orissa. Outside the temple are 1,500 plaques depicting Buddha's previous lives.

Most of the temples of Pagan were covered with elaborate frescoes, the earliest of which recall the masterpieces of Ajanta in India. Many of the temples were also decorated with delicate wooden sculptures.

BUDDHIST ART IN CEYLON
The great Indian Emperor Asoka despatched missionaries who preached the doctrines of Buddhism in Ceylon in the middle of the third century BC. The adoption of Buddhism by the Sinhalese marked the beginning of a period of great building activity, designed to serve the needs of their new faith, which gave an impetus to the growth of the arts, including sculpture and painting.

Some of the earliest remains of pictorial art in Ceylon are found in a rock pocket at Sigiri. The colossal figure of a seated lion projecting out of the cliff face has given the name 'Sigiri' (the Lion's Rock) to the enormous mass of stone rising 600 feet from a plain in the Matale district of Ceylon. Here in the fifth century a parricide king, Kasappa, took refuge from his enemies and built a handsome palace. A pathway giving access to the summit was protected at its outer edge by a brick wall averaging eight feet in height and coated with lime plaster so highly polished that even today, after the lapse of fifteen centuries, one can see one's reflection in it. Hence the wall is known as *Kadapat-pavura*, 'Mirror Wall'. The tempera paintings of women similar to those which exist in an almost inaccessible rock pocket at

Sigiri may also once have covered a large area of the western face of the Sigiri rock. These figures of women depicted as rising from clouds date from one of the greatest periods of Sinhalese art (fourth and fifth centuries) about which early Chinese historians spoke in raptures. By their originality and their capacity for depicting the human form, the Sigiri paintings stand isolated from later works, but resemble the famous contemporary Ajanta paintings in India. These figures, somewhat less than life-size, are depicted in three quarter profile as rising from clouds, being cut off below the waste. Some are in pairs, a golden coloured lady being attended by a dark-hued one, while others are single figures. The faces are oval in shape with sensuous lips while the hands are delicate and expressive.

There are also fragmentary remains of frescoes in a cave at Hindagala, six miles to the south-east of Kandy, which are coeval with or somewhat later than those at Sigiri. The paintings depict the Buddha surrounded by figures, presumably divine, in attitudes of adoration.

The paintings on the walls of the shrine at the medieval capital Polannaruva, dating from the reign of Parakramabahu I (AD 1153–1186) or the decade immediately

following, are, next to those of Sigiri, the most important monuments of pictorial art which Ceylon possesses. They prove that the classical tradition of Indian painting, represented at Ajanta, was kept alive in Ceylon after it had lost its vitality in India itself. Almost every shrine at Polannaruva of the twelfth century contained paintings on the walls; even the exterior was brilliantly painted with floral designs. These paintings have suffered badly from neglect since they were first brought to light over half a century ago, but what remains today is impressive enough.

After the thirteenth century, Buddhism, which provided the inspiration for most of the artistic achievements of the Sinhalese, started to sink to a very low level. There was a revival in the eighteenth century, when a number of religious edifices were built anew and many ancient shrines were restored. The ancient works of art in Ceylon have had, and still have, a profound influence on the artists of present day Ceylon who are striving to bring about a cultural renaissance in the island.

BUDDHIST ART IN INDONESIA
Today Indonesia is a largely Muslim country, but when Indian influence spread to the country in the first century and

A detail from one of Borobudor's hundreds of bas reliefs, relating one of the apadanas, the Buddhist legends of saintly deeds. According to this particular legend there existed in the time of Buddha a realm called Roruka ruled by a Buddhist king named Rudrayana. One day a tremendous sandstorm buried the kingdom, but the King's minister, Hirus, managed to save its treasures and escaped by sea (the boat is shown here). After a long and perilous voyage, he finally reached a friendly land and founded a great city

took root, it stimulated some of the greatest masterpieces of art. One of the most noble monuments of Buddhist art is the gigantic sanctuary raised from AD 750 onwards at Borobudur on the island of Java. Borobudur consists of five walled-in rectangular terraces, and above them, three round platforms on which are seventy-two bell-shaped stupas. By walking round the monument, pilgrims can read on its 504 statues and 1,400 bas reliefs, the story of man's journey through birth and death to ultimate enlightenment, with the culmination of the career of the Bodhisattva in the realms of the mystic Buddhas. The three miles of carvings are arranged in such a way that by following the rite of 'pradakshina' (walking round them and always turning with the right shoulder to the wall) pilgrims follow the footsteps of the Buddha. Crowning Borobudur, a 'terraced mountain' clothed in stone, is a sealed terminal stupa.

BUDDHIST ART IN CAMBODIA

Almost a century ago, Henri Mouhot, a French botanist who had been intrigued by reports of ancient cities hidden deep in the jungle, was making his way through the great forests of the Mekong River in Cambodia. One morning he saw an amazing spectacle—a series of stately towers rising like peaks above a sea of jungle. Mouhot had come across the city of Angkor, ancient capital of the Khmer Empire (ninth to fifteenth century) and the masterpiece of an art and an architecture that had hitherto been hidden from the world.

When the Khmer Empire collapsed about AD 1440 after a hundred years' war with Siam, the capital was withdrawn from Angkor to Phnom Penh, the present capital of Cambodia.

It was only at the end of the nineteenth century that archaeologists were able to make proper studies of the Angkor temples freed at last from the invading jungle. They found on the site more than twenty major monuments covering some 10,000 acres. Gradually they reconstructed the story of an empire whose dominion extended over what is today South Vietnam, Laos and part of Cambodia, and retraced the development of the singularly harmonious Khmer art.

The first city of Angkor and its Great Temple were the creation of Suryavarman II (1112–1152), who was not a Bud-

dhist. In 1181 one of his successors, Jayavarman VII, a Buddhist king, founded a new capital, Angkor Thom, close by. It was Jayavarman VII who adorned the Great Temple of the former capital (previously dedicated to the Hindu god Vishnu) with Buddhist decorations and gave it the title which this great temple fortress still bears—Angkor Wat (the palace monastery).

In the centre of Angkor Thom, stands the Bayon Temple, built at the end of the twelfth century as a Buddhist shrine of the Mahayana school dedicated to Lokesvara, the compassionate Bodhisattva. The Bayon

itself is not so much a work of architecture as one of sculpture with towers like so many statues in the round. The entire site of Angkor Thom is a vast brilliantly planned and ordered arrangement of buildings. Not only are the temples magnificent in themselves, but the great roads along which the faithful passed to the holy place were conceived and executed with genius.

BUDDHIST ART IN THAILAND

Thailand has been called the land of Buddhist images. Early Thai Buddhist art drew its inspiration from ancient India, Cam-

This meditating Buddha was cast in bronze at Ayudhya, for four centuries (1350 to 1767) the capital of Thailand, where a remarkable school of Buddhist sculpture developed. Characteristic of the Ayudhya style was the crowning of the Buddha's head with a high conical mass formed by two, three or more rungs surmounted by the traditional lotus-bud

bodia and China, while developing its own original style. For more than 1,300 years, Thai artists have been making images of the Buddha, ranging in size from tiny miniatures to huge giants. Carved from many materials—stone, plaster, terracotta, wood, crystal or jade, silver or gold and, most characteristic of all, bronze—images of Buddha today far outnumber the inhabitants of Thailand. The countryside of northern and central Thailand is studded with large numbers of temples and monuments such as those at the ancient cities of Ayudhya, Chiengmai, Sukhothai and Lopburi.

Thailand's wealth of monuments has come chiefly from the devotion of its kings who built magnificent resting places for their own ashes. The great 'wats', as they are known, also serve as monasteries, schools and hospitals as well as places of Buddhist worship.

Bangkok, the capital, is perhaps one of the most impressive Buddhist cities of the world. It offers a glittering spectacle of Buddhist sculpture and architecture, yet the capital is no more than two centuries old. The elaborate roofs and spires of Bangkok's temples and palaces (all built since 1782) reveal the richness of detail which marks Thai Buddhist architecture. The sanctuaries are built largely of wood with elaborately carved gables. A distinctive feature of these modern buildings are the projecting 'Ox-horns' on the gables.

BUDDHIST ART IN KOREA

Buddhism was introduced into Korea from China in AD 327 and reached its apogee between the tenth and fourteenth centuries, after which Confucianism replaced it as the state religion. 24 May, the Buddhist Festival, is still commemorated in Korea in the picturesque Feast of the Lanterns, when people hang lanterns of many shapes and colours on high poles. Still standing are some of the magnificent temples built in Korea when Buddhism was at its height. It was from Korea that Buddhism reached Japan along the sea routes, and Korean carpenters laboured ten years to raise the great temple of Horyuji near Nara in Japan.

BUDDHIST ART IN JAPAN

According to legend, a Buddhist image made of camphor wood floated ashore at Nara, Japan's first great captial, from the Bay of Chinu (present Osaka Bay) and henceforth Buddhism flourished.

Buddhist art in Japan starts from this

The Buddhist sanctuaries which form part of the Horyuji monastery at Nara are renowned as being among the world's greatest treasure houses of art. In one of these, the famous five-storeyed Pagoda, there is still preserved a series of clay statuettes remarkable for their poignant realism, their expressions of emotion, tenderness and grief. This photograph shows some of the figures from a cave which depicts a scene of the Nirvana or passing away of Buddha Sakyamuni with various saints, disciples and ascetics lamenting his departure

period. Like Athens in ancient Greece, Nara was the gateway through which religion and art, education and culture entered and spread through the land of Yamato (the ancient name of Japan). Within eighty-four years, temples and monasteries were built under the patronage of the court.

The period of eighty-four years, when the capital of Japan was established in Nara in AD 710 until its transfer to Kyoto in 794, is known as the Golden Age of Japanese sculpture. It was in this period that the famous Great Buddha, the biggest bronze statue in the world, was made. It is said that the casting of the statue required 437 tons of bronze, 288 pounds of gold and seven tons of charcoal. It is enshrined in the Todaiji Temple, the Buddhist cathe-

dral meaning 'The Great Temples of the East' which is the largest wooden structure in the world.

In the famous Five-Storeyed Pagoda, at Horyuji of Nara, there is still preserved a series of statuettes remarkable for their expressions of emotion, tenderness and grief.

The story of Japanese architecture and sculpture is one of successive waves of influence from China, but like Greece, which absorbed and reforged the aesthetic elements it received from Egypt, Assyria and Phoenicia, and like China itself in regard to India and Afghanistan, Japan moulded to its own mode of thought and expression the artistic traditions it received from China and distant India. It gathered them up, gave them new life,

This seventh-century camphor-wood statue of the young Buddha (Miroku Bosatsu) has been called 'one of the noblest images of meditation ever created by the hand of man'

added a new conception of Buddhist tenderness and dignity and a new spirit of grandeur and exaltation that we discern in the masterpieces of the Asuka, Nara, Heian and Kamakura periods (seventh to fourteenth century).

In 1180 civil war and fire ravaged the great sanctuaries of Nara. The repairs and restorations which followed (demanding meticulous knowledge of the older styles) ushered in the great school of the Kamakura period in the thirteenth century which attained its supremacy with the sculptures of such geniuses as Unkei, his fellow pupil Kaikei and his son Tankei. The Kamakura spirit of renascence affected not only sculpture. Old Buddhist sects of the Nara period were revived and new sects, such as Zen Buddhism, appeared after the renewal of contact with China in the eleventh century (suspended in the ninth). An outstanding example of Kamakura portrait sculpture is the statue of the hermit Basuen which is now at Kyoto. This statue has been described as 'one of the most powerful monastic figures of all time'.

The wooden temple of Koryuji is one of the richest yet least known storehouses of Japanese art. Some of the temple's masterpieces surpass anything to be found even in Nara. Of all the works of art in the temple, the seventh-century statue of Miroku-Bosatsu (a Bodhisattva, or future Buddha) is probably the most graceful and subtle. It is carved from a single block of plain Japanese red pine. This pose, known as the 'Hanka shi-i' attitude, was the one Prince Gautama assumed when he was plunged in meditation just prior to his enlightenment. The figure which is in the same half cross-legged pose, has been compared to Rodin's 'The Thinker' but the smiling lips and the non-oriental shape of eyes and face strangely recall Leonardo da Vinci's 'Mona Lisa'. It has been called 'one of the noblest images of meditation ever created by the hand of man'.

BUDDHIST ART IN AFGHANISTAN

In 1922 French archaeologists brought to light some remarkable sculpture in the ruins of Hadda, near Jelalabad, Afghanistan. The figures, made of lime plaster or stucco and originally brilliantly coloured, had decorated the walls of innumerable stupas and monasteries. But the real significance of this sculpture is its obvious Greco-Roman inspiration. In this region, a 'No man's land' of ancient conquerors, there had flourished a Greco-Roman Buddhist art of singular beauty. The fragment of the figure holding a lapful of flowers, for example, is believed to be a model of the Roman portrait of Antoninus, favourite of the Emperor Hadrian. And the title 'Warrior of ancient Gaul' could easily be applied to the head. Most of the sculpture at Hadda dates from the third to the fifth century AD. Further artistic development was prevented by the invasion of the Huns in the sixth century.

To the north-west of Kabul, capital of Afghanistan, in a green and fertile valley surrounded by pink and rose red mountains, lies Bamiyan. In ancient times it was a stopping place on the caravan route which linked central Asia to India, and through it passed Buddhist pilgrims and missionaries. Between the fourth and fifth centuries AD Buddhist monks at Bamiyan carved innumerable shrines and monastic cells out of the sandstone rocks. The invasion by the Mongol hordes of Ghengis Khan in the thirteenth century brought ruin to the countryside around Bamiyan and devastation to the Buddhist shrines and sculptures. The two most imposing relics which still exist are colossal statues of Buddha, one 173 feet high, the other 120, carved out of the cliffside. A man can easily walk upright in the opening between the toes.

BUDDHIST ART IN NEPAL

In Nepal, the birthplace of the Buddha, religious architecture has a character of its own, as is shown by the famous ninth century stupa at Bodnath near Katmandu. It was from Nepal and the neighbouring state of Sikkim that Buddhism spread to Tibet where it led to the founding of the Lama order of Buddhist monks.

BUDDHIST ART IN TIBET

With the caravans which toiled their way through the Himalayas from Sikkim and Nepal in the seventh century AD, Buddhism came to Tibet. Its influence soon spread with the help of the great king Song-tseen Gam-po who had married a Chinese princess of Buddhist faith. About

AD 750 an Indian Buddhist monk named Padmasambhava crossed the mountains into Tibet and preached a doctrine known as Tantrism. This was a mixture of Mahayana Buddhism, and certain local traditions. In its popular aspects, it involved prayers, ritual dances and the exorcism of devils. Padmasambhava founded the branch of monks, or lamas, known as the 'red caps' and transformed a nation of warriors into a vast community of monks.

In Tibet, Buddhism brought forth a strange art in which influences from India, China and central Asia were intermingled. A whole world of symbols came to life in sculpture and painting. Artist monks made spiritual preparations including fasting before painting the *than-kas* or temple banners which are a special feature of Tibetan Buddhist art. Painted on silk or other fabrics, these banners usually contain a spiritual portrait of one or other of the saints and deities, and also many other figures and scenes, which tell the story of the central personality.

A great historian of Asian art, the late Heinrich Zimmer, wrote of those works:

'One sees here an impressive, really frightening genius for the rendition of the terrible aspect of the spiritual powers. Even the Buddhas and Bodhisattvas, who elsewhere in the extensive Buddhist domain are represented almost exclusively in benevolent guise, here appear as veritable demons.'

The Buddhist paintings of Tibet and Nepal have much in common with the art of medieval India of which they were originally the faithful copies. This tradition of Tibetan painting has been maintained down the centuries.

Buddhist art has an amazing unity and an amazing diversity. It can be compared only to the unity and diversity of Christian art in Europe. All art seeks to bring us nearer to the values which guide all men. The Buddha brings a message of peace: Christ brings us a message of peace; the artist tries to interpret this message in his own way. In the knowledge of the similarity of all men lies also the fact of the unity of all men, and with an understanding of other arts we deepen our understanding of our own.

6 Nubian monuments of Egypt and the Sudan

Introduction

Four miles south of the present Aswan Dam in central Egypt, a new High Dam (Sadd el Aali) has been built across the Nile by the United Arab Republic with Soviet help, to usher in an era of great regeneration. Food production will be increased by nearly half; hydroelectric power increased nearly tenfold; some 2,500,000 acres of desert has been brought under cultivation, and an additional 750,000 acres once flooded has been reclaimed. The new dam is an economic necessity for Egypt but it created a vast lake which threatened to engulf in Nubia some of the most glorious of monuments built by man.

Egypt is the cradle of Mediterranean civilization and the archaeologists' living book of history. Nubia (the junction point at which the cultures of Inner Africa met with the cultures of the Mediterranean) will vanish under the waters of the Aswan Dam; yet it bears the imprint of 5,000 years of history on a narrow, semi-desert land bordering the Nile. It is difficult for those who have never set eyes on the shore of the Nubian Nile to imagine the majesty of the sites, the fascination of the sanctuaries and the charm of the villages. It is like an extraordinary open-air museum nearly 300 miles long containing monuments often surpassing Gothic cathedrals in size, temples, tombs and fortresses.

An agonizing dilemma therefore faced the authorities charged with developing the Nile Valley: how to choose between the needs and welfare of their people and the treasures which belong not only to their country, but to humanity as a whole. As André Malraux has said: 'Nubia, like Chaldea, belongs to the dawn of our history.' In the region to be flooded, scientists feel, may well lie some of the important clues to the riddle of man's unknown past.

Accordingly in 1959 the United Arab Republic and the Government of the Sudan appealed to Unesco to obtain the international aid which was required to save such gems of ancient art as Abu Simbel and Philae from disappearing under the raised waters of the dam and to save the treasures which lay buried in the sand on sites which had not till then been systematically excavated. On 8 March 1960 Unesco's Director General, Mr Vittorino Veronese launched the now famous international campaign to save the treasures of Nubia.

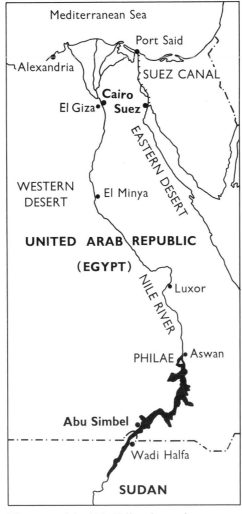

This map of the Nile Valley shows the vast artificial lake (shaded) which was formed when the new Aswan High Dam was completed in 1968. Its waters would have submerged numerous historical treasures and monuments in Nubia in both Egypt and the Sudan

Eight years after it was launched this campaign has attained its objectives. Sixty countries took part in this unprecedented enterprise. The United Arab Republic and the Republic of the Sudan under Unesco's auspices and with the collaboration of these sixty countries worked to save all that could be saved as the waters of the Nile rose behind the Aswan High Dam. Twenty-two temples were moved; all monuments, inscriptions and rock carving were inventoried and photographed; all frescoes from the Christian period were removed from ancient walls and taken to safety; teams of archaeologists from every continent explored 500 kilometres (300 miles) of the Nile Valley; all archaeological sites were reconnoitred and prospected, with the exception of a strip 80 kilometres (50 miles) long between the second and third Cataracts of the Nile (the last area

to be flooded) which is still being explored.

The science and technology that can put men on the moon is more than equipped to preserve even so fragile a monument as Abu Simbel. The two temples of Abu Simbel have now been preserved by what has been described as 'the most daring project of modern times'. This bold, imaginative and grandiose scheme has transferred into twentieth-century idiom something of the ancient massive thinking which could contemplate the Great Pyramid with its 2,300,000 separate blocks each weighing $2\frac{1}{2}$ tons.

After the escarpments above and around the rock-hewn temples had been excavated, the temples were sliced from the mountain side into which they were built 3,000 years ago in 1,041 sections each weighing 20 to 30 tons, and put together, and now stand 64 metres (200 feet) above their original site, today under water. Concrete domes are now being erected above the temples to take the weight of the hill top to be reconstituted around the site so that it may closely resemble the original one in every detail. When the Aswan Dam is filled, the Nile will be approximately in the same relationship to the temples as it used to be and since the orientation of the temples is precisely as it was, the morning sun will contrive to bring out of the darkness the faces of the ancient gods. Begun in April 1964, the monumental task at Abu Simbel was completed by the spring of 1969 – more than a year ahead of schedule. International contributions from public and private sources totalled nearly $21 million. This figure includes contributions already made or pledged by 50 nations ($17,600,000), the yield from a United Arab Republic tourist tax introduced in 1964 ($860,000), proceeds from exhibitions, particularly those organized in Japan by Asahi Shimbun Press ($1 million), and sums collected by the American Committee for the Preservation of Abu Simbel ($1,300,000).

As a token of gratitude, the government of the United Arab Republic is handing over certain Nubian temples and a large collection of antiquities from other regions of Egypt to museums in other countries. The temple of Dendur has already been attributed to the USA and that of Ellesyia to Italy.

It now remains to provide protection for the monuments on the island of Philae in the Nile. These temples are downstream from the High Dam, and unlike the sites upstream are not in danger of complete inundation. They are, however, submerged to about half their height. A plan for the work at Philae is under study by Unesco and the United Arab Republic Government.

The extensive work undertaken by the Documentation Centre of Ancient Egypt (set up in May 1955 by the Antiquities Service of Egypt with the direct co-operation of Unesco) will give the world's Egyptologists the possibility of adding to our knowledge of the areas of the ancient world which has by no means finished yielding up its secrets. We should indeed be grateful for the building of the High Dam for it has drawn the attention of scholars the world over to this forgotten reach of the Nile.

This chapter attempts to give some idea of the ancient culture of Nubia—its magnificent monuments which, but for international action might have been lost for ever, as well as showing the riches that the Aswan High Dam will bring today to the peoples of the Nile Valley.

Journey to the land of Kush

Rex Keating

What we today call Sudanese Nubia was known to the ancient Egyptians as Kush. What makes Sudanese Nubia so important to archaeologists ? It is the ancient towns, the cemeteries and the old fortresses of Nubia, which cannot be considered beautiful but which are absolute treasure houses of information about the life, conditions, hopes and aspirations of our forbears.

But Sudanese Nubia holds more than monuments and relics, it contains the people of the Second Cataract and they are a living example of life in Nubia's remote past. They must now leave their ancient land before the waters of the Aswan Dam close over it. Their folklore is fascinating and before they are moved and the threads of tradition broken a social anthropological survey must be made. This should note carefully the architecture and decorative designs of modern Nubian houses; some of the emblems used date right back through the Fung Kingdom of the fifteenth century to the early Christian era and earlier still to Pharaonic times. Even today these people cross the Nile on long flat-bottomed craft that would have been familiar to a soldier of the Pharaohs.

The Christian kingdoms of Nubia, lasting roughly from the sixth century till at least the fourteenth century, are hardly known. They begin with the coming of missionaries from Byzantium, sent by the Emperor Justinian in the middle of the sixth century, who came up through Egypt to the then pagan peoples of Nubia.

Still in existence are the writings of the Syrian, John of Ephesus, which give a vivid account of the coming of one of these missionaries, of how he suffered from the heat and hid himself in a cave with his feet in a basin of cold water to keep cool during the hot weather, an action with which many of us who know the Sudan during the summer months will be in great sympathy.

On many of the little ruined churches of the area are frescoes of gods, of the Virgin, of saints, all showing very strong Byzantine characteristics. The pottery of the people is also of extremely good quality, a fine painted ware with many motives derived from the Mediterranean.

The Nubians live in the Valley of the Nile, which has been the main overland route between north and south—between the Mediterranean coast and the vast ethnic group of the Negro people of equatorial Africa. Man must always have used the Nile Valley as a convenient highway. Anthropologists have even suggested that central Africa may have seen man's first triumph over his material surroundings. This is a measure of the importance of the prehistoric sites which have yet to be discovered on the banks of the Nile.

Traces of prehistoric man are plain to see on all sides of the Second Cataract. For example on the Island of Vronati was found what might be described as a 'Stone Age workshop'. There lying on the surface were typical Mesolithic implements.

The earliest of the people of ancient Egypt regarded the area south of Wadi Halfa with awe. Its inhabitants were the fierce cattle owners against whom they built the immense fortresses which still stand along the length of the Cataract, spectacular even in their ruin. Yet a thousand years before the fortresses frowned over the river, travellers and expeditions from Egypt came this way.

Standing back from the river Nile is an isolated hill which contains on its inner face by far the earliest inscription in Sudanese and Egyptian Nubia. It records in archaic hieroglyphs that an expedition sent by King Djer of Egypt passed this

rock on its way to the south. King Djer was the third king of Egypt's first dynasty, an incredibly remote figure who ruled at the very dawn of Egypt's history some 5,000 years ago. Yet here, in effect, is his signature, a clear indication that he did once exist.

All over west and central Africa strange similarities of form have appeared in widely separated areas. The ancient name of Kush is still preserved in the names of Nubian-speaking peoples living today in south-west Sudan.

The Kushites were great iron-workers. Their capital Meroe has been called the 'Birmingham of the ancient world' and from their factories weapons and objects of iron spread across Africa, influencing profoundly the neighbouring African cultures of that day. They have left many indecipherable inscriptions; it is possible that in Nubia lies buried the key to the Meroitic Tongue.

Nubia has been described as the cockpit of the ancient African world. From the north the Egyptians representing the highest civilization of that time were pushing south to exploit the gold mines and to trade in ivory, precious woods and other products. The people of the south were pushing north to the more fertile parts of the Valley of the Nile, and the results of the continuous battle between the two have greatly influenced the course of European civilization and through European civilization, that of the world at the present time.

Every effort must be made by the nations of the world to save history from the floods so to speak and to preserve the cultural heritage of this part of Africa for future generations.

Nubia's Christian age

L P Kirwan

When we think of the historic monuments of Nubia we think mainly of the great temples of Abu Simbel and Philae, built by the Pharaohs several thousand years ago. In style and origin, these memorials of the Pharaohs are not Nubian at all, they are Egyptian. By contrast with these Pharaonic monuments there are many other relics of ancient and medieval times more truly Nubian in character. Some belong to the Sudanese Kingdom of Meroe which ruled during the Greco-Roman Age over most of the Sudan and most of Lower Nubia from its capital, Meroe, a hundred miles or so north of Khartum.

Others belong to Christian Nubia, to the era of the Christian Nubian kingdoms which flourished from AD 542 to 1323 and thus endured for 700 years after the Muslim conquest of neighbouring Egypt.

This age of Christianity in Nubia was one of great prosperity and power. Thriving cities and townships, churches and monasteries, were thickly clustered along both banks of the Nile. The administration of Church and State alike was elaborately organized, largely on Byzantine lines. A Nubian school of painters flourished and adorned the walls of the domed and vaulted white-washed Nubian churches with religious scenes in brilliant colours.

The first of the Nubian kingdoms to be converted to Christianity between AD 542 and 545 was the northernmost, and the most powerful, kingdom of Nobadia. When the first Christian missionary, Julian, arrived in Nubia from Turkey a few years after AD 535 he was received not with hostility, but with considerable ceremony by the Nubians and their king. The first visible result of the preachings of Julian and the missionary, Longinus, and other missionaries was the conversion into churches of the pagan temples of Lower Nubia; the small temple of Rameses II at Wadi es Sebua, and the temple at Dendur, built by the Roman Emperor Augustus, which was rededicated as a church in AD 559. Then, or soon after, came the building of the first churches in Nubia, at Farus, near the present Sudanese-Egyptian border, and at Kasr Ibrim, both influential centres in earlier times. By the early years of the seventh century Nubia, outwardly at least, was a Christian land.

Greek was probably the language of conversion and this, like the distinct traces of Byzantine influence in religious painting and architecture, reflects the predominantly Byzantine rather than Coptic (or Egyptian) character of Nubian Christianity in its earliest phase. Probably after the middle of the seventh century, as the result of a great influx of Christian refugees from Egypt, Nubia swung over to Coptic Church doctrines.

The ruined churches of Nubia must also be saved from the waters of the Nile. The delicate remains of frescoes like those which adorn so brilliantly the walls of the little church of Abd el Kadir near the Second Cataract must be removed and

preserved. Tombs, some of them pillared, and cupola tombs such as those at Kasr Ibrim must be explored and their skeletal remains studied so that we may learn something of the racial origins and characteristics of the Christian Nubians.

When this is done a new chapter will be added to the history of Christianity in Africa and a new page to the history of the medieval Christian world.

Philae, the sacred isle

Etienne Drioton
The riches of the island of Philae with its exquisite temples and colonnades and the graceful 'kiosk' of Trajan have consecrated its renown. The temples are not the work of a single pharaoh. Each new king embellished and extended what his predecessor had done. But practically all the buildings which still stand are due to Pharaohs of the Hellenistic period or to the Roman Emperors who governed after them.

But it was not for its beauty alone that Philae was famous in ancient times. In the last period of its history, it had, with the adjacent islands, become one of the great religious centres of Ancient Egypt, replacing Abydos in the cult of Osiris. The island of Bigeh was sacred to Osiris and had become according to the Greek term, an *Abaton*, that is, an area within which it was forbidden to penetrate. The sleep of the dead god beneath his sacred wood must not be disturbed.

Close by this island dedicated to the dead god, Isis in her temple of Philae belonged to the world of the living. For this very reason, so as to provide a link with the world of the departed, she devoted herself to maintaining the cult of her brother-husband. On all holy occasions, the idol of Isis was taken from its tabernacle, embarked on the river and disembarked at Bigeh, where it presided over the solemn libations at the tomb of Osiris.

The history of Philae mirrors the religious trends which inspired Egypt in the days of the Ptolemies and the Roman emperors. During the Assyrian, Babylonian and Persian invasions, the people gradually turned away from the gods of the State religion, the sun gods who had been unable to protect Egypt. The faith of the people was transferred to Osiris, whose legend explained all ills and authorized all hopes.

Another feature of religion at this time, unknown in the Pharaonic period, was the tendency to give more importance to Isis than to Osiris. This tendency is apparent in the religious establishments of the Philae group.

How Philae will be saved

Michel Conil Lacoste
It was Herodotus who first referred to Philae as the 'Pearl of Egypt', but the phrase has now become a cliché, and it is perhaps time we dispensed with it. But there can be no doubt that the spectacle offered by the sacred island of Isis with its pylons, its porticos and temples all reflected in the iridescent waters of the Nile is a sight which never fails to move the beholder.

Poised on the edge of the Aswan desert, Philae, the first stop in Egyptian Nubia, is unequalled in beauty except for Abu Simbel, the last stop before entering Sudanese Nubia.

Philae is young not only in beauty but also in time, for none of its temples date beyond the fourth century BC. This is a short period indeed when compared to the 470 million years of the natural granite amphitheatre which forms the setting for the 'pearl' which is Philae.

But the island is not merely a prodigious site; it is also a sanctuary, because it was from here that the cult of Isis, the universal goddess and mother of Horus, spread during Roman times far beyond the realms of Egypt.

Philae is a museum, or more exactly a city of five temples, the largest of which is dedicated to Isis. It is fronted by two gigantic pylons and the famous *Mammisi* or 'birth house' devoted to the annual mystery of the birth of Horus, the Sun-God.

To the east lies Trajan's celebrated Kiosk, to the south the Kiosk of Nectancho from which an avenue of sphinxes (or *dromus*) leads to the first pylon of the Temple of Isis. These buildings are completed by the famous gate of Hadrian with its chapel and three colonnades.

All these monuments with their delicately moulded pillars and their exquisitely intercolonnaded walls, recall the influence of Greek architecture and form a unique ensemble in art.

Two plans exist for the salvage of Philae. The first was originally suggested

The sacred boat of the goddess Isis, depicted here on a bas-relief in the Isis temple of Philae

The interior courtyard of the temple of Isis at Philae with the famous colonnaded mammisi or birth house of Horus. The monuments of Philae have been saved by a system of three protective dykes, a plan proposed by Netherlands experts

The tops of pillars are all that show of the birth house on Philae when the gates of the Aswan Dam are opened in the month of October and the Nile slowly submerges the island's monuments

by an Egyptian engineer and an advance project has been prepared by the Netherlands Engineering Consultants (Nedeco) on the instruction of the Netherlands Government. This is designed to safeguard the island in its original setting by the construction of three dykes that will isolate Philae within a low-lying artificial lake between the Aswan Dam and the High Dam. The second plan has been prepared by the Egyptian Government and envisages dismantling the monuments on Philae island and reconstructing them on the nearby island of Agilkia in their original form and well above the water-level. The first plan was finally adopted and these beautiful temples have been preserved.

Abu Simbel

The two rock temples of Abu Simbel (the Great Temple of Rameses and the Small Temple of Nefertari) rise on either side of a river of golden sand running down from a natural amphitheatre of pink sandstone. The most important sanctuaries built by Rameses in Lower Nubia, they are also the most remote, the most harmonious and the most colossal. Rameses built temples all over Nubia, each dedicated to one of the gods of the Empire. At Abu Simbel he brought the three gods together and added his own image, raised to divine rank.

Here, therefore he reigns, a god among gods, surrounded by his entire family. Rameses imposed the cult of the Sun-King, born of the sun, the spouse of a goddess, transformed into a woman, the ravishing Nefertari. The queen is depicted in the flower of her beauty in the temple dedicated to her by Rameses to the north of his own sanctuary, identifying her with Hathor, the presiding goddess.

The magnificent monument lay buried in the sand of the desert for many centuries and it was not until 1817 that it was freed from the sand by Giovanni Batista Balzoni, but it was only in 1909–10 that all the sand was at last cleared from the four colossi, from the terrain, the forecourt and the approaches. It is heartening to know that international solidarity has saved the great temple of Abu Simbel from the watery grave that might have swallowed it up.

At any hour of the day the Great Temple

of Abu Simbel built more than 3,000 years ago is an impressive sight, but at dawn it offers its most breathtaking spectacle. There was nothing haphazard about the choice of its site or the construction of the multiple galleries and chambers deep in the mountainside. The sudden illumination of the statues, the sun shining in the sanctuary deep in the heart of the rock at Abu Simbel is a breath-taking spectacle. Its religious implication seems clear—divine light seeks out from the very bowel of the earth the man who holds divinity within him.

Engineers of 3,000 years ago

Ritchie Calder

The greatness of Egypt is popularly identified with the petrified geometry of the pyramids, those remarkable examples of civil engineering, veritable mountains of masonry. Experts, however, would agree that the sublimation of funerary art, combined with shrewd scientific insight, were the rock temples.

There are great free-standing Egyptian temples, superb in their proportions, in their pillars and their sculptures, but the architects of these were able to choose the best quarried blocks for their building and ornamentation. A sculptor, carving a statue, would pick the most suitable, most enduring and most flawless stone for his purpose.

The architects and the masons of the rock temples had no such latitude; instead of choosing blocks of stone they had to discover an escarpment or a mountain which would conform to their exacting requirements. Once committed, their artistic ingenuity was hostage to the site.

Among the greatest of these temples hewn from the living rock were the Great Temple and the Small Temple of Abu Simbel in which the immortality of the Gods and of Rameses II was embodied in the indestructible rock. They were executed by Rameses II in his prodigious reign of sixty-seven years from 1300 to 1233 BC.

Thirty miles north of the Second Cataract, on the left bank of the Nile, where the river turns east, were two rocky prominences divided by a gully. Here was a site which met a first elementary requirement: that the temple, dominating the river, face the rising sun.

To quote one of the technical reports

Above left: through the temple portals the sun bathes the huge Osirian pillars with its golden light and at certain times of the year reaches 200 feet into the heart of the mountain. Here it picks out from the Stygian darkness the seated figures of divinities like Amon. *Above right*: the God of Thebes. *Below*: The four immortals seated at the end of the sanctuary: Ptah, whose statue remains eternally in darkness for he is king of the underworld; Amon, Rameses II and Ra-Horakhti, morning sun god

drawn up by engineering experts 'The temples of Abu Simbel are a wonderful achievement. Apart from the importance of the monuments themselves, we are struck with admiration at the deep knowledge of geology which the ancient Egyptians possessed. The presence of hard sandstone banks alternating with softer ones was used to advantage in creating the temples and the statues. The more compact layers were chosen for the ceilings of the temples and inner rooms, or to support the greater weight of the sitting statues. They also made the most of the fissures in the rock: the facades of the two temples run parallel to the more fissured lines.'

On what we would nowadays call the 'feasibility report' the ancients went ahead with the construction of the two temples—some 300 feet apart—overhanging the banks of the Nile. But they did something more; they contrived the design of the temples to fit into the natural landscape so that art and science conspired with nature to make Abu Simbel one of the wonders of the world.

The larger of the two rock temples, facing to the east and to the rising sun, has a façade 33 metres (over 107 feet) in height and 38 metres (over 123 feet) in width. It was dedicated by Rameses to Ra-Horakhti, Amon-Ra and Ptah, the most important gods of Egypt. In its proportions and structure it equalled a temple that might have been built on the surface instead of underground.

A narrow passage leads to the inner sanctuary where are seated the statues of the three gods to whom the temple is dedicated, and of Rameses himself. And here is seen the purposeful ingenuity of the architects and engineers. Like skilful stage-lighters, they contrived that the rising sun would penetrate 200 feet into the heart of the mountain and illumine the faces of only three of the immortals. The fourth, the god of the Underworld, Ptah, on the extreme left remained eternally in darkness. This essential feature of Abu Simbel was one of the things taken into account in deciding how the temple should be finally preserved from the rising waters of the High Dam.

To Nefertari, his wife, Rameses dedicated the Small Temple, several hundred feet away across a sandy gully. Its façade measures 88 feet in width and 39 feet in height. It is ornamented by six colossal statues each 33 feet high.

To quote the engineering experts once again: 'The inspiration of the Abu Simbel monuments rises above and beyond the traditional conception of the ancient Egyptians, for whom the pyramid was the maximum of architectural perfection, as the only conclusion of a long process tending to geometrical abstraction. What prevails here is the plastic sense of the mass; the monument merges into its environment, the architecture marries with sculpture, and sculpture actually acquires a dominant character in the ensemble.'

The modern pyramid of Aswan: Sadd el Aali

Albert Raccah

'Egypt is a gift of the Nile.' Thus wrote Herodotus, the Greek historian and traveller of the fifth century BC. Indeed, all of this land of nearly 400,000 square miles would be nothing but a vast desert from the Libyan frontier to the Red Sea and from the Mediterranean to the Sudanese frontier if the Nile did not cross it from south to north before fanning out in a vast delta 100 miles from the coast.

This is a rain-starved country. On an average there are six rainy days in Cairo per year and only one at Aswan. It is easy to understand why the ancient Egyptians considered the Nile of divine essence: it was the very source of all life in Egypt.

One also understands why all agricultural development is at the mercy of the amount of water taken from the Nile. During the flood season, an immense volume of water is lost to the sea. The present Aswan dam was built to harness a part of it for irrigation in spring and summer.

Called in Arabic 'El Khazzan' (the reservoir), it was built at Aswan between 1899 and 1902 on the granite rock of the river bed in the middle of the First Cataract. The dam, 100 feet high, was to make it possible to store 930 million cubic metres of water in an artificial lake extending upstream for 140 miles, thus inundating the island of Philae and its sanctuaries, as well as part of the cultivated land.

By 1934, the dam had been raised by 46 feet bringing the reservoir's total capacity to five thousand million cubic metres. The artificial lake reached back as far as Wadi Halfa, 225 miles up the Nile from Aswan.

The present dam contains one and a half

million cubic metres of masonry (the Great Pyramid of Cheops had two and a half million originally). The dam wall is over a mile long and has 180 sluice gates operating on two levels. The iron control gates are all opened in July, during the high water season, so that the Nile's muddy waters may flood and fertilize the country. Early in October the sluices are closed and the river is kept back. In early spring when Egypt begins to lack water, the Aswan dam acts as the reservoir which irrigates the country.

But the Aswan reservoir is inadequate for Egypt's presentday needs. For the past half-century, agriculture and industry have been unable to keep pace with the problem of food for its rapidly rising population. Egypt urgently needs more land for cultivation, better and higher crop yields, hydroelectric energy for its expanding industry.

This 'living space' can be won thanks to the Nile, the real wealth of Egypt, and by the construction of a new dam, the Sadd el Aali. The purpose of the High Dam, the preliminary engineering work on which has already been done, is the total utilization of the Nile's waters. Not a drop of the river will be lost in the sea.

The dam wall, to be erected on a site four miles upstream from the present Aswan dam, will rise 225 feet and have a crest three miles in length. It will create an artificial lake 300 miles long with a capacity of nearly 130,000 million cubic metres and a surface area of 1,150 square miles. Since the rapids of the Second Cataract will disappear under 30 feet of water, regular navigation between Egypt and the Sudan will become possible for the first time.

With the great reservoir which the Sadd el Aali will create, Egypt will be able to increase its arable land surface by nearly half. In reality it is expected that as much as two and a half million acres of desert land will be brought under cultivation and that 750,000 acres now flooded will be reclaimed.

Although the greatest advantage of the Sadd el Aali lies in the possibility of opening up new areas for farming and ensuring their regular water supply, the energy output foreseen for the dam would in itself be enough to justify its construction. Four tunnels for water evacuation during flood periods and four chute tunnels will service sixteen turbine units buried more than 300 feet under the granite rock. They

Stages in the removal of the colossi at Abu Simbel. *Far left*: clearing the accumulation of sand, and *left*: one of the last blocks of stone being lifted by a giant crane towards its place on the new site of the temple. This block is the face of Rameses II cut away with an L-shaped section of stone to anchor it in place. Hooks for lifting are cemented into the block with a synthetic resin compound. Cut up with infinite precaution and lifted two hundred feet up a hillside, the temples of Abu Simbel have risen again in all their ancient majesty

will operate all year round with a 'head' (height from which the water drops) averaging 200 feet. The turbines will have an estimated total capacity of 2 million hp and an annual production of 10–12,000 million kilowatt-hours a year, nearly ten times present total consumption in Egypt. The Boulder Dam in the United States produces only half as much power. The combination of the hydro-electric potentials of both the Sadd el Aali and Aswan dam will raise Egypt's capacity to more than 15,000 million kilowatt-hours a year.

When the High Dam of Aswan is completed, four years will be needed to fill its basin capacity. In that period, the population of Egypt will probably continue to increase at the same rate as in previous years and this increase (8 million persons within the next ten years) makes the building of the Sadd el Aali a vital necessity.

7 New year festivals

Introduction

Festivals provide a useful introduction to the culture of a country. The festivals in the East are many and varied with a rich heritage of religion and folklore. To appreciate them to the full, it is necessary to have some knowledge of the religion, literature and ethics of the country concerned. Lack of curiosity and indifference can prevent the foreigner from sharing in a unique cultural experience.

In India, for example, spring has been given a more exalted place than perhaps in any other part of the world. It has been embodied in divine legends that for three thousand years have been the never-failing inspiration of poets, sculptors, painters and philosophers. Spring festivals are celebrated with colourful *melas* or fairs and open-air performances of the *Ramayana* epic and the Krishna Leela ballet. To add to the enjoyment and pleasure of watching these one must have a working knowledge of Hindu mythology and the Hindu Trinity – Brahma, the creator; Vishnu, the preserver, and Siva, the destroyer. Vishnu is the hope of all mortal things, that is why, every few hundred or thousand years when the world seems threatened with collapse, he comes down in bodily form to give it new strength and life; the two most splendid and famous reincarnations are Rama and Krishna.

The Indian epic of *Ramayana* is comparable only with the *Iliad* in the lasting influence it has exerted on the thinking of a whole people. The story of Rama not only extols the finest feelings – especially loyalty and faithfulness to one's word, but is also an inexhaustible source of inspiration for essayists and story-tellers. It is roughly comparable with the part played by Don Quixote in Spain. Many a scholar in India and beyond its borders regards it as the origin of the tale of Prince Charming in Western legend, where the hero overcomes countless natural and supernatural obstacles before being reunited with his beloved.

These children have put on traditional costumes and masks with grotesque features for their parts in a performance of the Ramayana. This great Indian epic, dating back over 2,000 years, tells the story of Rama, a 'Prince Charming' who overcame a thousand and one obstacles to win his beloved Sita. Today, as in the past, the legendary adventures of this hero captivate audiences in India and other Asian countries

By the process of mental association, animals too can acquire the significance of cultural values. In India, the monkey king Hanuman, assisted Rama to triumph over the evil spirits of ancient Ceylon. Almost inevitably monkeys should conjure up in the minds of Indians the army of Hanuman, just as a reader of the *Little Flowers of St Francis* is reminded by birds of the great saint, or a lover of poetry cannot help reciting Baudelaire when he sees cats.

The Krishna Leela ballet performance is one of the most fascinating aspects of a heritage which belongs not merely to the past, but keeps on growing. It is celebrated in the spring, and re-enacts the story of Krishna (the reincarnation of the Hindu god Vishnu) from his childhood in the fields and woods among cowherds and milkmaids, describing the pranks played by this child whose charm no one could resist. He has a number of girls among his playmates, and they are ready to put everything aside—work, family, the past and present—to follow him, or just to go on looking for him in the forests. As an adult, he plays a central part in the feudal cosmic war in which a host of princes of the same blood destroy one another. All who come in contact with him, either as a child or a young man, have momentary visions of his divinity, seeing him in a flash as Vishnu. While to the outside observer it may seem no more than a pantomime— an unending succession of good and evil spirits and tableaux with no apparent connection, the Indian public's reaction to the Krishna Leela is, in many ways, similar to the feelings invoked in Europe by the Oberammergau Passion and Mystery plays –charged with emotion and with no trace of surprise because they are familiar with the story brought to light in the acting and dancing.

Whole volumes would be required to describe the rich variety of the many national festivals in the East. To compare and contrast how only one festival—New Year—is celebrated throughout Asia is both interesting and instructive. Not only is the festival celebrated in different ways, it is also celebrated at different times of the year, depending on the type of calendar in use. This is shown in the descriptions which follow of the New Year in China, Sikkim, Bali, Japan and India. Yet, despite all these differences, there is a certain unity in the fact that the New Year represents a triumph of the forces of good over the forces of evil.

The Koreans call New Year's Day the day of discretion because of the belief that what will happen in the coming year is conceived on this first day of the first month: *Chong-wol* or *Il-wol*, the first month is thus always considered as the most important of the year. Korean families are supposed to stay awake throughout the night of New Year's Eve, and to offer sacrifices to their ancestors at midnight.

In Vietnam the New Year is known as the festival of Tet. The festivities have a ritual and mystic character: offerings are made before the temple altars: purification baths are taken, and the people cleanse themselves for the New Year. The Tonkingese fix branches of flexible bamboo to the roofs of their houses in order to drive away evil spirits.

A nostalgic recollection by a Chinese philosopher of his childhood celebrations of New Year gives a picture of the Old Chinese New Year. Nowadays, New Year is celebrated in China on 1 January.

Amid the noise and smoke of exploding fire crackers, the traditional lion dance is performed in the streets of San Francisco's Chinatown where more than 30,000 Chinese live today. Thousands of fire crackers are set off to drive away evil spirits. The lion, despite its ferocious mask, is the symbol of good luck in the coming year. This exuberant dance is a leading feature of the Chinese New Year celebrations

Old China

LANTERNS, GONGS AND FIREWORKS
Lin Yutang

My memory goes back to those exciting, indelible childhood years. I lived in an inland village near the south-east coast of China. It was about the turn of the century, the Manchu Empress Dowager was still on her throne, and customs had not yet changed.

As far back as I can remember, when I was four or five, I felt New Year coming weeks ahead, the way a western child would feel the portentous arrival of the Christmas season. Not shopping and packages, but my mother would grind rice flour on a home mill, to make nienkao, or New Year pudding, made of rice flour, turnip and dried shrimps. It was no small excitement since this was done only once a year.

My sisters would assist my mother at the small mill, consisting of two horizontal mill-stones about a foot and a half across, the upper stone turned by a wooden crank suspended from the ceiling. It was a very tricky job, and full of fun. There was a small hole in the upper stone, and while one person turned the stone around, another had to drop rice and water with a porcelain spoon expertly, at the exact moment when the hole came round. Naturally I demanded to aim the rice at the hole too. I may or may not have broken a few spoons.

The next thing I remember was falling asleep trying to sit the Old Year out. For it was the custom that the whole family should sit up after a sumptuous dinner, in which, besides fried clams, a special roll made by mother, also only once a year, invariably figured. It consisted of finely chopped ingredients made into a paste and wrapped around with a layer of peritoneal fat from a pig. Red candles burned brightly on the centre table against the wall. We would sing hymns and we would pray, for we were Christians.

Then my eyes would feel drowsy and the next thing I knew when I woke up was the expectation of something akin to the Christmas stocking. It was not a stocking, but a cheap black satin gown with a deep rose vest on top, which the younger children were allowed to wear only once a year on the occasion of the New Year.

The Old Chinese New Year, of the lunar calendar, was the greatest festival of the year for the Chinese people, compared with which every other festival seemed to have something less of the holiday spirit. For five days, the entire nation dressed in its best clothes, shut up shop, loafed, gambled, beat gongs, let off firecrackers, paid calls and went to the theatre.

The humblest maid had the right not to be scolded on New Year's Day and, strangest of all, the hard-working women of China loafed and cracked melon seeds and refused to wash or cook a regular meal

or even handle a kitchen knife. The justification for this idleness was that to sweep the floor on New Year's Day was to sweep away good luck, and to wash was to wash away good luck. Red scrolls were pasted on every door containing words like Luck, Happiness, Peace, Prosperity, Spring. For red was the colour of happiness.

And all around in the home courtyards and in the streets, there was the sound of firecrackers, and the air was filled with the smell of sulphur and narcissus – sulphur outdoors and the incredible subtle fragrance of narcissus indoors.

Then the Republic came. The Republican Government of China, officially abolished the lunar New Year, but the lunar New Year was still with us, very much so and refused to be abolished. It lodged too deeply in the people's consciousness.

It was then about 1930, and I was in Shanghai.

I am ultra-modern. No one can accuse me of being conservative.

I didn't want Old New Year. But the Old New Year came. It came on February the fourth.

My big Scientific Mind told me not to keep the Old New Year, and I promised him. 'I'm not going to let you down,' I said, with more good will than self-confidence.

My downfall started when I went to the City Gods' Temple to see what I could get for the children. I should not have gone to the City Gods' Temple in the first place. Once there at this time of the year, you know what would happen. I found on my way home that I had not only rotating lanterns and rabbit lanterns and several packages of Chinese toys with me, but some twigs of plum blossom, besides.

After coming home, I found that someone from my native place had presented me with a pot of narcissus, the narcissus which made my native place nationally famous and which reminded me of New Year's Day in my childhood. I could not shut my eyes without the entire picture of my childhood coming back to me.

At lunch, the smell of the narcissus made me think of the New Year rice-pudding, made with turnips.

By three o'clock in the afternoon I was already in a bus on my way home from North Szechuen Road with a big basket of nienkao weighing two and a half pounds.

At five, we ate the fried nienkao, and with the room filled with the subtle frag-

rance of narcissus, I felt terribly like a sinner.

By six o'clock, I found red candles burning brightly on the mantelpiece, their lapping flames casting a satirical glow of triumph at my Scientific Consciousness.

'Who bought the candles?' I demanded.

'Why, you bought them yourself this morning.'

'Oh, did I?' It cannot have been my Scientific Consciousness that did it. It must have been the Other Consciousness.

I thought I must have looked a little ridiculous, the ridiculousness coming less from the recollection of what I did in the morning than from the conflict of my head and my heart at the moment. I was soon startled out of this mental conflict by the 'bomb-bah' of fire crackers, in my neighbourhood. One by one, those sounds sank into my deep consciousness. They have a way of shaking the Chinese heart that no European knows. The challenge of my neighbour on the east was soon taken up by my neighbour in the west, until it grew into a regular fusillade.

I was not going to be beaten by them. Pulling out some money, I said to my boy:

'Ah-ching, take this and buy me some heaven-and-earth firecrackers and some rattle firecrackers, as loud as possible and as big as possible. Remember, the bigger and the louder the better.'

So amidst the 'bomb-bah' of firecrackers, I sat down to the New Year's Eve dinner. And I felt very happy in spite of myself.

Celebrations in Sikkim

DANCE TO WELCOME NEW YEAR

Tucked away in the towering Himalayas, the little state of Sikkim with its 170,000 souls and 2,800 square miles of territory lies to the east of Nepal between India and Tibet. Throughout its length and breadth embracing tropical to alpine vegetation and boasting a wide variety of rare flora and fauna (of orchids alone there are over 400 species) prayer flags flutter in the Himalayan breeze to ward off evil spirits. They flutter on the fringes of lush green rice, barley and millet fields, on hill tops and in the courtyards of modern buildings and of ancient monasteries.

On the 28th and 29th day of the tenth Tibetan month (which falls sometime in December or January) dances are held in front of Tsuglakhang monastery of the

The two-day Tibetan New Year ceremony is designed to drive away the demons of the old year and welcome the good spirits on the road of the months to come. *Above left:* The deep tones of the ancient trumpets of the lamas mingle with the voices raised in prayer and thus add rhythm to the sacred New Year dance, the Thiam. *Above right:* The High Priest, the Lentshi-Lama brandishes a ritual bell and 'thunderbolt' to evoke the forces which animate the Thiam

On the evening of the second day there is peace and silence. Assured that the good spirits are satisfied the lamas withdraw to the temple. In the shadow of a richly decorated statue of their deity, Guru Rimpoche, they stand in fervent prayer

Palace at Gangtok, Sikkim's capital. The dancers are lamas and Sikkimese youth and its purpose is to drive away evil spirits and to welcome Losoong, Sikkimese New Year's Day, with a clean slate. The Losoong falls on the first day of the eleventh Tibetan month, corresponding to sometime in December or January, that is, two months ahead of the Tibetan New Year's Day.

In the dances, the deep tone of Ragdhungs (long medieval brass trumpets), the sadly sweet melody of Gyalings (Sikkimese clarionets) and roll of Ngas (ancient drums) mingle with the voice of praying lamas and add solemnity and rhythm. The 'Dhutor' or 'Kagya' dances, as these dances are collectively known, start with the Black Hat Dance, in which the High Priest dances with a bow and arrows, and enrapturing with his dancing skill the evil being of bygone days shoots an arrow through the latter's heart. Later, two cemetery ghouls dance over a human-shaped effigy of dough, which represents evil spirits, cut it into pieces and throw them in four directions. To help these defenders of the Dharma, a host of guardian deities in a variety of costumes and displaying an exquisite array of masks (ranging from a stag's to a tiger's) leap, spin, double-march and make mystic gestures to the rhythm of the Ragdhungs, Gyalings and Ngas, while the Acharyas, who play the Jesters, provide spells of comedy and, by their pranks and jests, send the spectators into peals of laughter.

Finally, Tormas (cone-shaped dough images) are thrown away amidst more music and chanting of prayers.

NEW YEAR'S DAY

New Year's Day is an occasion for feasting and merry-making, when the Sikkimese feast on delicacies like Honton (dumplings stuffed with lavishly seasoned cheese), Sheto (Sikkimese pastry), roast pork and Chang (Sikkimese millet beer served in bamboo containers and sucked through bamboo pipes) and hold archery contests.

Bali

THE GIFTS TO THE GODS ARE EATEN BY MORTALS

Each year in Bali lasts only 210 days. The date of the *Galungan*, or Balinese New Year, thus changes annually. The festivities are spread out over a ten-day period during which it is believed that the de-

New Year in Bali: the Barong

parted ancestors return to earth to receive offerings and bring happiness. Before the festivities, houses and temples are freshly decorated and the offerings carefully prepared. Many of these 'constructions' are more than six feet tall and are made of straw, interlaced with yellow, red or white rice and ornamented with frangipani flowers and palm fronds. During the *Galgungan* festivities, the *Barong*, a beneficent animal dear to the hearts of all Balinese, makes its appearance. This dragon-like animal is manoeuvred by two dancers who weave their way along the island paths. The leaps and capers of the *Barong* delight old and young alike, the more so as they symbolize the fight between the forces of good and evil.

Work in preparing the ancestral offerings lasts more than two weeks. Once ready, they are taken to the temple where they remain on view for some days. After this period, the Balinese, a realistic people full of common sense, come to collect them, for they realise that although the offerings are made for the gods, they can only be eaten by human beings.

Japan

LOBSTERS FOR A LONG LIFE; SEAWEED FOR A HAPPY ONE

Shigeo Kimura

The celebration of *O-Sho-Gatsu*—the Japanese New Year Festival—has both a moral and religious significance. Morally, it is an expression of determination for a new life in the coming year. Mythologically, it is a complicated form of offering to *Toshi-Gami*, or the God of the Year, who supposedly grants blessings and protection from misfortunes throughout the year.

The New Year season lasts for one month beginning on 1 January, as the special name of the first month—*O-Sho-Gatsu*—means. However, the festivities take place only on the first seven days, of which the first two or three are regarded as the most important.

The Imperial Household, symbol of the Japanese people, offers prayers for further benevolence of its ancestral deities, the Government suspends its administrative activities, and factories, shops and offices are all closed. In short, the whole country is in a state of festive relaxation during the holidays.

Although the hustle and bustle of modern life tend to destroy some of the traditional distinctive features of Japanese New Year celebrations, nevertheless many still follow their age-old pattern.

The last day of the year is called *Omisoka*. It is New Year's Eve. It is, in a sense, a day of purification. We Japanese, eager to welcome the New Year in a happy and reverent mood, clean our houses and purify ourselves.

Late at night we eat a few bowlfuls of *Soba*, or Japanese noodles, which are long and slender and are believed to possess magical qualities which will ensure longevity. We then sit by the fireside or around the hearth resting and talking until just before midnight. A few minutes before twelve the temple bells throughout the country start ringing. The bells are rung 108 times to drive away 108 evils. Resounding on the wintry air, the bells toll the knell for the parting year.

We decorate our houses with special devices. Outside decorations include the *Kadomatsu* and *Shimekazari*. *Kadomatsu*, meaning the gate pine, is usually set up on both sides of the front entrance to invite *Toshi-Gami* there. It consists of pine-branches, plum-twigs and bamboo-poles bundled into the shape of a stock. Often two tall bamboo-fronds are used as substitutes. We believe these plants to be symbols of good omen, and because of their hardiness, to denote longevity. *Shimekazari* is a straw rope decorated with a kind of orange, called *Daidai*, and fern leaves. It is usually hung above the front door. The word *Daidai* has the same pronunciation as the words meaning 'from generation to generation', while the fern leaves with their multiplicity of fronds suggest expanding prosperity.

For interior decoration we have *Osonae* which is placed on a little stand of plain wood in the alcove. On it are a pair of *Mochi* or rice-cakes and several other things of good omen. Among these is sometimes included a lobster. Since the lobster's back is bent, this symbol expresses the wish that one may enjoy a very long life until one's back is bent until it resembles that of a lobster.

At break of day we get up and go to a nearby stream or well for *Wakamizu*, or the first water of the year. With this we wash ourselves. This water is believed to have the power of preserving health throughout the year. We then exchange New Year greetings with our family and offer prayers at the family altar. At breakfast we sit down together in a circle, clad in our best clothes with the grown-ups in formal dress and young ones in colourful kimonos. It is also customary for adults to go out into the garden and pay respect to the morning sun by clapping their hands.

The first feast of the New Year is very special. We first of all take, in the order of family seniority, a thimbleful of *Toso*, sweet *sake* spiced with fragrant herbs, which is believed to promote health. Then follow various sumptuous dishes. *Zoni* comes first. It is a kind of soup which is as indispensable for the New Year celebrations as rice is on any other day of the year. The chief ingredient is *Mochi* or rice-cakes, cut in round or rectangular pieces and boiled with different vegetables.

Mochi signifies fullness, abundance and plenty. Other foods which accompany the *Zoni* include carp, famous for its energy and determination to surmount obstacles; black beans, symbolic of robust health; chestnuts for success, and dried seaweed, *Kombu*. The yellow petals of a variety of chrysanthemum (eaten as a salad) are frequently used to enrich the colour scheme of the table, the preparation of this meal, in fact of all Japanese meals, being made with a special concern for colour.

Before or after the first meal we visit, usually with our family, the nearest shrines and temples to seek divine bliss for the year. This visit is called *Hatsu-mode* which means literally first pilgrimage.

In the morning or afternoon we make a round of visits to our friends, carrying a large stock of visiting cards. Merchants and shopkeepers usually bring with them a bundle of new *Tenugui*, literally hand towel, with their names inscribed on them. These are courtesy visits; an expression of gratitude for patronage during the past year, *Tenugui* serving as tokens of thanks.

On New Year's Day we are visited by a troupe of *Shishimai* dancers, a feature of this festive season. The dancers wear a big mask, the *Shishi*, or a conventionalized lion with a grotesque red face. They perform a gay dance to the accompaniment of a drum and a flute.

Oibane or battledore and shuttlecock is an outdoor game particularly favoured by young girls. When they miss a stroke they sometimes have to undergo the penalty of having their faces smeared with ink. The battledores which they use are artistically decorated with all kinds of woven silk figures and flowers.

Boys enjoy kite-flying—*Tako-age*—in the streets and fields. The kites designed in gay colours make an amazing pattern as they rise into the sky.

In the evening we have a *Karuta-tori* party—a poem card game. The game is played with a set of two hundred cards, named in Japanese *Hyakunin Isshu*, literally a hundred poems from a hundred people. It is an anthology of a hundred *Waka* or thirty-one-syllable odes composed by historically celebrated poets and poetesses. Half the cards, each containing the whole poem and usually the author's portrait are used for reading. The other half, each containing only the last two lines of the poem, are used for playing.

All the participants hunch forward over the playing cards arranged on the *Tatami* or straw mat, exchanging quick glances so as to pick up the card corresponding to the poem which is being read aloud.

Matsunouchi, or the days of the gate pine, which comprise the first week of the New Year, ends on 7 January. On the preceding night we gather up all the decorations and burn them for exorcising purposes. The New Year festivities gradually die away and everything goes back to normal.

India

LAND OF MANY CALENDARS

India is not only a land of many races, religions, languages and cultures, but also one of many calendars. Practically every linguistic and religious group has one of its own, and some have different ones for different purposes. So the matter of sending a New Year greetings card to Indian friends is not as simple an affair as it is in Europe or the USA. Outside Hindu society, there are other religions which have their own calendar and their own New Year's Day.

The Muslims use the lunar system, starting with *Hegira*, the flight of the Prophet Mohammed from Mecca to Medina. Since the lunar month is shorter than the solar, the Muslim New Year's Day falls at different times of the year.

The Christians use the Roman calendar. They celebrate it in much the same way as Christians elsewhere—exchanging greetings cards and wishing each other happiness. The smallest of all India's religious

Above: candlelit diwali eve: for those Hindus who follow the Vikrama calendar diwali night is both a festival of light and a New Year celebration. Here, several Hindu women in exquisite saris light the candles in front of their house. *Below*: a building in New Delhi brilliantly illuminated for diwali night

minorities, the Parsees, start their calendar with the accession year of *Yezdajrid* to the Persian throne in AD 632. Their New Year's Day is the first day of *Farvirdin* which corresponds to 5 September.

Along with this conglomeration of calendars and communities goes a vast variety of celebrations differing with each sect in every part of the country. The only thing all these festivities have in common is that New Year's Day itself does not have as much significance as the mythical or historical events associated with it.

For six million Sikhs, New Year's Day is really holy. On the morning of the first of *Baisakh* (also New Year's Day for other peoples in certain parts of India) the last of their ten *Gurus* (spiritual guides), Gobind Singh (1666–1708), inaugurated the *Khalsa*, the martial wing of the Sikh religious movement, with five dedicated disciples.

On every first *Baisakh*, Sikh temples and homes have a special religious ceremony. In the afternoon, their sacred book, the *Granth*, is taken out on a gaily decorated carriage guarded by five men with drawn swords—in memory of the first converts.

New Year celebrations take place in Bengal and Assam in the month of *Baisakh*, or April, and picturesque spectacles are seen during the New Year *melas* or fairs.

The people of Kerala have their political New Year on the first of the month of *Simha*, Leo (August–September), but observe their religious New Year, the *Vishu* (the *Bihu* of the people of Assam) on the first of the month of *mesha*, Pisces, almost corresponding to the first of Baisakh. It is a unique festival of which the most important part, apart from feasting, is the *kani* or 'holy vision'. Every member of the household wakes up in the morning with eyes tight shut, proceeds to the family shrine and opens the eyes to a symbol of God artistically decorated and lit up. This is followed by presentation of silver coins by seniors to juniors.

What 1 April is to the business world in some Western European countries—namely, the start of the new financial year, so *Diwali* is to the Indian merchant community. Although it is only a matter of closing one set of account books and starting new ones, it is done with great ceremony. Houses are whitewashed, and Lakshmi, the goddess of prosperity, worshipped, with the new account books lying at her feet. Presents are sent to relations and friends. At night the houses of all Hindus are lit with oil lamps and candles—hence the name *Diwali*, the cluster of lights. All over North India specially, and almost all over India generally, it is an inspiring sight to see the dark night of the *Diwali* (it always falls on a new moon day) lit up by innumerable tiny oil lamps and candles.

Diwali has many origins ascribed to it. The most popular explanation is that on this day, the god Rama, an incarnation of Vishnu, returned home after his victory over the demon King of Ceylon who had abducted his wife, Sita. Amongst the Marathas of central India, *Diwali* is the occasion for the worship of the god King *Mahabali* who was banished to the nether world by Vishnu in his incarnation as Vamana. In Bengal lamps are lit and carried on long poles to light the way of departed spirits to their ultimate destination.

The common factor in all the celebrations is the use of illuminations and fireworks. Anyone travelling by air on *Diwali* night could see as many lights beneath him as in the heavens above, and many more meteors shooting upwards. The philosophers believe that *Diwali* symbolizes the triumph of light of knowledge over the darkness of ignorance, of truth over falsehood. What better wish could one make on a New Year's Day than affirm one's faith in the ultimate triumph of good over evil?

8 Tradition in transition: Japan

Introduction

Although Japan, unlike many other Asian nations has long been powerful on the international scene, most westerners know little about her life, customs and tradition. However, it must be admitted that it is not a simple matter to 'understand' a nation whose whole social structure, way of thinking and philosophy of life are so different from one's own. Any attempt to understand Japanese thinking and behaviour must take into account the fact that until a relatively short time ago Japan was an island universe all of its own that had deliberately cut itself off from all contact with the Western world. The modern era was ushered in with the Meiji Restoration in 1868. Japan then flung open its ports to the commerce, science, institutions and customs of the West.

And then the Japanese who had embarked on only one foreign war of aggression in 1,500 years of their history (the ill-fated Korean expedition of 1592–98) plunged headlong into military adventure—war with China, Russia, Germany and finally Pearl Harbour in 1941 which ended with Japan's total defeat and unconditional surrender in 1945.

The Japanese look at the West as materially powerful and thereby enviable but not truly cultivated and a little lacking in soul.

There is an old Japanese riddle which asks, 'Why is a son who wants to offer advice to his parents like a Buddhist priest who wants to have hair on the top of his head?' (Buddhist priests shave their heads.) The answer is, 'No matter how much he wants to do it, he can't.' Although the attitude of young people towards their family is undergoing important changes today, the riddle does help to illustrate two fundamental aspects of Japanese life—the idea of hierarchy and filial piety.

Hierarchy was basic to Japan's whole notion of social relations until the end of World War II. It was to be found in the many infinitely complex rules, customs and conventions that regulate everyday life; every greeting, every contact indicated the kind and degree of social distance between people. The Japanese have built up a 'respect language' which they accompany with bows and kneeling. It is not enough to know to whom one should bow but also to exactly what degree, for this may range from a slight bow to kneeling with the forehead touching the hands on the floor.

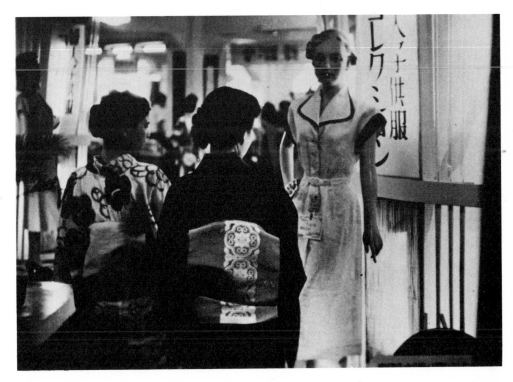

Above: Yofuku versus Kimono. Many Japanese, especially in the cities, live a dual life wearing Yofuku (Western clothes) out of doors and kimono (Japanese dress) at home, though the reverse can also be seen. Western dress is preferred in the street because it is easier to get about in.
Below: Two Tokyo girls stride the street in the busy Marunouchi district with confidence and a sense of total equality. They no longer walk the small, mincing steps of their mothers and grandmothers in their kimonos

Hierarchy was observed above all in family life. The Japanese family was a tightly knit social—and economic—unit. The sense of family—of belonging to a family, of acting in the family name, of defending family honour, of doing things on behalf of the family, of being worthy of the family ancestors—was extremely powerful, particularly in the rural regions.

The status of Japanese women was fixed according to the Confucian maxim: 'A woman owes obedience three times in her life, to her parents when she is young, to her husband when she is married, and to her children when she is old.'

Perhaps no country in Asia has changed more rapidly than Japan; revolutionary transformations have taken place in postwar Japan. New types of behaviour and new modes of thought have grown up in competition with traditional forms. The Emperor remains, but only as a symbol of national unity; his absolute powers have gone and sovereignty belongs to the people, but attachment to imperial and national tradition remains strong. In Japan, as in most countries, traditions are maintained more strongly in the countryside than in the cities. Laws concerning the family and inheritance as well as the legal status of women have changed entirely. Before 1945 women had no vote and were only allowed to own property conjointly with their husbands. Today they have equal rights with men. Women now crowd the polling booths at election time, but their political life usually stops there. Schoolgirls have been growing up under the influence of a new feminist slogan: 'Let's develop the power to think and act for ourselves.' The entire educational system has been recast. Young men are free to marry as they wish and no longer need the consent of their families. The established religion has been abolished root and branch and freedom of worship has been granted to all faiths.

The youth of Japan today are caught by the conflicting pull between traditional ways and the new social evolution in Japan; torn between the age-old tradition of respect and obedience to their parents and the desire to display more independence and initiative. The articles which follow on 'Wedding day in modern Japan', 'Teenager's day' and 'Student's profile' show how this process of change is affecting Japan.

The Japanese are a great reading nation. Illiteracy, contrary to popular opinion in the West, is practically non-existent despite Japan's complex system of writing. The public's reading taste is highly developed. Daily newspapers are numerous and the most important have circulations among the highest in the world. Many weekly and monthly magazines exist and the output of books is considerable. Interest in Japanese translations of foreign publications is high. Three articles in this chapter deal with Japanese literature.

Wedding day in modern Japan

In the West love usually precedes marriage, but in traditional Japan it came after marriage. It was considered dishonourable for a young person of either sex to select a life-mate. According to a feudal idea a girl was married more into the family of the bridegroom than to the young man, and in the past if a boy and a girl got married through mutual love their union was considered a 'free marriage' and condemned. In modern Japan, however, with the increased independence of women, love marriages are now more common and accepted occurrences.

Although the feudal custom of arranging marriages without consulting the wishes of the future couple has not completely vanished, it has been replaced in recent times by two other ways of arranging a marriage: (1) the type of marriage in which the wishes of the couple concerned are exclusively the deciding factor; (2) a type of arranged marriage in which both the interests and preferences of the two families and the wishes of the prospective husband and wife are taken into account.

Negotiated marriages are arranged in Japan by a matchmaker, known as a *Nakodo* (literally, go-between), who may be a close friend, a senior or a relative. Go-betweens do not seek payment for their services but simply the happiness of the married couple and the maintenance of the two families' lineage. The main function of the go-between is to find suitable candidates, act as liaison between the families by providing photographs and *curricula vitae* of the young persons, and especially to arrange an interview (*miai*) between the prospective bride and groom and to carry out an exchange of gifts between their families.

Western and Oriental elements found in many aspects of Japanese life are found in modern wedding ceremonies for which the brides are garbed in the traditional kimonos and the bridegrooms are dressed in western style. The elaborate hair-do's worn exclusively by brides, *taka-shimada*, are wigs.

A Japanese bride of old wore a raw cotton hood to hide her face at a wedding. Modern brides have a piece of white cloth called *Tsuno kakushi* (horn hider) over their dressed hair. It is proverbially said that a jealous woman has horns and her imaginary horns are thus symbolically hidden by the headband. According to *Onna Daigaku* (Women's Great Learning), a seventeenth-century book which a Japanese bride in feudal days put in her trousseau, jealousy was included among seven causes for which a wife could be divorced. (Among other causes formerly accepted as justifying divorce: dis-

obedience to her parents-in-law, talkativeness and indiscreet speech for which 'she shall leave lest she should cause discord among the relatives of her husband or discord in her home'.)

Today Japanese wives are recognized by the law as human beings with the same rights as their husbands. 'Marriage shall be based only on the mutual consent of both sexes and it shall be maintained through mutual cooperation with the equal rights of husband and wife as a basis,' says the Japanese Constitution. If a wife owns property in her own right her husband cannot take it from her. And if the worst comes to the worst she can apply for a divorce.

Although a Japanese usually reaches his maturity when he is twenty, the traditional line of demarcation between adolescence and adulthood is generally considered to be marriage.

In Japan most weddings are celebrated according to the Shinto ritual. The ceremony usually takes place in a special marriage room or at home. According to custom the marriage room is decorated with emblems—cranes and tortoises for longevity and bamboo for endurance. Once all the guests have been seated by the ushers, robed musicians sitting crosslegged begin to play wind instruments. This is the signal for the Shinto priests in full regalia to enter with their attendants. Then begins the solemn service during which many prayers are offered at the altar.

The wedding ceremony is called *San-san-kudo* (literally 3–3–9 times), for the bride and bridegroom exchange rice-wine cups 3 by 3 = 9 times, i.e. they drink nine symbolic cupfuls from a set of three lucky wine-cups beautifully lacquered with lucky designs painted on them.

A toast is drunk to the future happiness and longevity of the newly-weds. The couple then proceed to the altar, renew their pledges to the gods and offer branches of the sacred *sakaki* tree. Western style weddings are also popular in Japan, where the bride wears a white robe and veil and her husband-to-be wears a frock-coat and striped trousers.

Teenager's day — Tokyo

Michiko Jinuma, nineteen-year-old daughter of a Tokyo judge, lives with her parents and three sisters in a typical Japanese wooden house with nine rooms.

Below: Confidences in the lunch-hour. A classical head is eavesdropping
Above: Tea in the family circle, 'the most delightful time of day' says Michiko

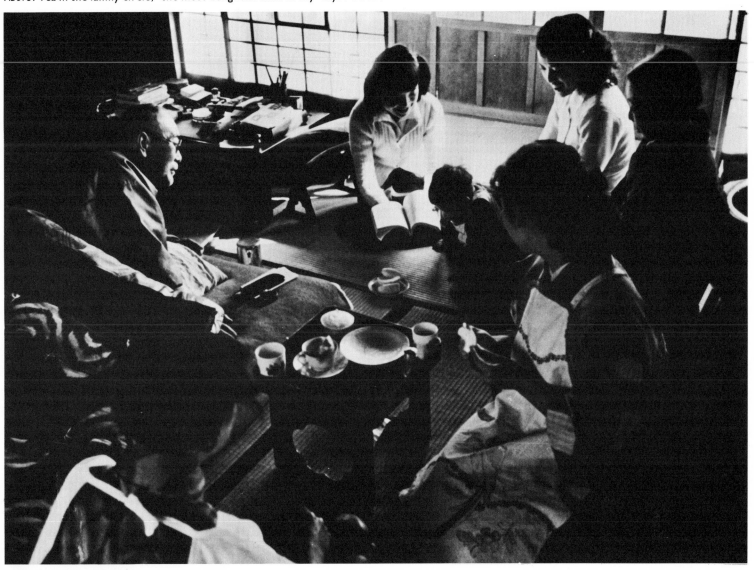

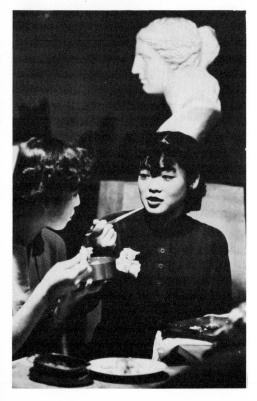

Every other day she travels into Tokyo by the electric train—rarely getting a seat, for young men do not make room for girls —to attend classes at a fashion school where students learn dressmaking and designing. Out of classes Michiko loves to stroll through Tokyo's streets, 'window shopping' and admiring the dresses with a growing professional eye. Returning home in the evening, she prepares her work for the next day or sets about altering one of her dresses. She has quite an extensive wardrobe: four two-piece dresses, five one-piece dresses, two kimonos and six pairs of shoes. With the kimono she always wears the Japanese *geteas* (wooden clogs). Michiko, in fact, lives the easy and carefree life of a middle-class girl. She is on good terms with her parents who allow her plenty of freedom. 'If you think it is right, then do it; if you think it is wrong, then don't,' her father tells her. She uses powder and lipstick, nail polish, face lotion and oil for the hair.

In the home she helps her mother with the housework—but without much enthusiasm. When she is not in school she likes to read the paper and listen to the radio (plays and Western classical music are her favourites). In the evening she helps her mother to prepare dinner, and then comes the most delightful time of the day for the family. They are all together and tell each other the happenings of the day. Michiko has plenty of friends, but no boyfriend in the Western sense. She would like one older than herself with whom she could talk about everything. She hopes to marry and have three or four children, but no more. 'Overpopulation in our country is a menace,' she says, 'and we women have an obligation there.'

Student's profile—Kyoto

Goro Suma is a law student at Kyoto University. As his family lives far away in the north of Honshu, the main Japanese

A rare relaxation—a chat and sake in a Kyoto bar

A light burns on till the early hours

An old tradition—sport, but nowadays just for sport's sake

island, Goro rents a tiny room where he studies and sleeps. He takes his meals in a restaurant nearby—rice, *miso* soup, *natto* (steamed and fermented beans) and *tsuku-dani* (preserved small fish, shellfish or seaweed in soy) figure largely on the menu —or preferably at the student canteen where food is cheaper. Apart from his books, he owns three suits, two uniforms (student clothes), a pullover, two pairs of shoes and a pair of gumshoes. To pay for his studies he works as secretary of the university professors' and employees' union. As much of his time is taken up with his work for the University Union, Goro 'burns the candle' until about two each morning to catch up with his studies. But he still finds time for games of baseball and ping-pong and occasionally for skiing. Like most Japanese youth he is interested in films, especially 'realistic' ones, and is fond of Western classical music. He disagrees with his father on many matters, but when he is in trouble he seeks his father's advice. He does not belong to any religious sect. Goro wants to become a teacher and he hopes to marry soon. He intends to have two children.

The wonders of Japan's literary world

Eight hundred years before the Brontës, six centuries before Mme de La Fayette, a lady of the Japanese imperial court sat down with brush and writing case and composed what is still considered the greatest novel in her language. Lady Murasaki's *Tale of Genji* is not only a classic for her countrymen; until recently it was one of the rare pieces of Japanese literature to have been translated into Occidental tongues.

Unlike the Brontë sisters, Lady Murasaki felt no qualms lest her work be treated condescendingly because of her sex. Her own contemporaries included a number of women authors, and the earliest known anthology of Japanese writing—the *Manyoshu* or *Collection of Ten Thousand Leaves*—is studded with poems by ladies of noble birth.

Compiled long before most of the languages now spoken in Europe had developed (about AD 750), the *Manyoshu* initiated a series of anthologies in which the Japanese systematically tried to preserve what was finest in their poetry. In the three hundred years between the

The Gate of Hell, one of the most striking Japanese films of recent years, was based on a story by the famous writer Kikuchi Kan. Another story by this author was brought to the screen in the Japanese film *Rashomon*

ninth and the twelfth centuries, eight such anthologies were drawn up by imperial command.

But for many centuries to come the work of Japanese writers was to remain virtually unknown outside Japan. Two anthologies have been compiled by Donald Keene for the Unesco collection. The first covers the ancient and classical periods; the second, the writing produced since the Meiji Restoration in 1868.

In the first of Mr Keene's two anthologies poetry holds a major place. Whether cast in the tight, demanding verse forms of the *haiku* and *waka*—containing seventeen and thirty-one syllables respectively —or in a larger, looser mould, all these poems reflect the Japanese love of nature (a constant in the national character) and most have a melancholy tinge. Human life, their authors never forgot, is just as frail and uncertain as the cherry blossoms that

flower and fade or the foam that glistens and melts away. A fatalistic and stoical religion added to their resignation, as did disasters like the periodic earthquakes that shake their islands, and the spectacle of man's own perversity in making war upon his fellows, forgetting his loved ones, or throwing his long trusted counsellors into disgrace.

But Japanese authors of the classical period also found expression in many other ways than poetry. Storytellers and chroniclers, essayists and diarists, reflected the history and manners of their times while two distinctive forms of the drama—the No play and the puppet theatre—were developed to a high degree.

In a society where the same exacting code of behaviour had been followed for centuries, where convention dictated the slightest gesture, where etiquette forbade the direct expression of feeling, art had to

The Cannery Boat. A dramatic film was made from the story of the voyage of a floating cannery in the waters of Kamchatka, written in 1929 by Kobayashi Takij

suggest by symbol, metaphor and understatement. But when the floodgates from the outside world were opened, restraints were washed away.

Lady Murasaki had made an emperor's son the hero of her masterpiece. Higuchi Ichiyo, Japan's principal woman novelist of modern times, wrote about children growing up in Tokyo's licensed quarter. Her rowdy adolescents might be taken as symbols of a whole population that was elbowing its way to the forefront of the writer's attention.

In the pages of the modern anthology we meet some characters who are lost survivors of an earlier day—like the *haiku* poet and his sister the elocution teacher in Nagai Kafu's *The River Sumida*—but many more who are an integral part of the world they live in.

There are soldiers, actors, thieves, geishas and government officials, misunderstood women and a husband who has killed his wife and cannot honestly tell the judge whether it was by accident or design. There are sons struggling to get free of their families and young men setting out to study in the West. There is a country schoolteacher—a most influential personage—and a war prisoner's wife supporting herself and her little boy by peddling black-market tea in Tokyo.

Three of the writers represented in the anthology have been introduced to audiences outside Japan through the medium of the cinema in *Rashomon* and *The Gate of Hell* where authors have recast old material in a modern and personal mould, and *The Cannery Boat* which describes the grim life of fishermen and sailors in a floating cannery off Kamchatka.

This simultaneous interest in the past and present seems to point toward a more complete fusion of influences into something newer still.

Modern Japanese fiction

A BREAK WITH TRADITION

The present literary scene in Japan is one of immense activity. Publishers and literary magazines abound, and the number of novels and stories published every year is overwhelming. With books extremely cheap and the reading public large and alert, sales are vastly in excess of those before the war, the material rewards for literary success are considerable. Some of the largest incomes in Japan are at present earned by popular writers.

The *shi-shosetsu* tradition of semi-autobiographical fiction has survived into the postwar period but it is no longer as widely followed as some decades ago. Nevertheless, the confessional diary type of writing, in which everything is seen through the eyes of one lone, sensitive individual, continues to be far more popular in Japan than in the West.

To what extent, then, is current Japanese literature influenced by that of the West? On the whole the influence is not nearly as direct as is often assumed by Western readers.

Although in many ways the Pacific War and its aftermath constituted a break with the past as great or even greater than that provided by the Meiji Revolution (1867–1910) there was no rupture with native literary tradition such as occurred in the nineteenth century. Whereas the new Meiji writers tended to look entirely to the West for their models, the writers of the present day receive their influence both from the West and from their own writers of the past sixty years.

Japanese novelists have usually assimilated only those elements of foreign literature that are in some way close to the recipient. This is more than ever true today when the Japanese writer has such an immense selection of world literature at his disposal.

Although the most conspicuous influences have certainly come from Europe, it would be a mistake to discount the effect of Chinese and Japanese classical literature on certain modern writers. This classical influence is reflected in the imagery, the descriptions, the general mood and sometimes the structural techniques of many outstanding post-Meiji writers and their successors. One of the most interesting aspects of these writers is precisely the way in which they succeeded in moulding classical traditions with modern Western thoughts and technique.

However, the fact remains that the modern Japanese novel and story are essentially Western forms; in so far as literary influence has played a part, most Japanese prose writers are indebted to modern Western literature far more than to their own country's classical tradition. It is writers like Hugo, Poe, Whitman, Baudelaire, Dostoevsky, Tolstoy, Hardy, Zola, Huysmans, Maupassant, Wilde and D H Lawrence that have exercised influence rather than Murasaki Shikibu, Saikaku Bakin and the other famous prose writers of earlier centuries.

Japan is, of course, not the only country in which imported literature has exerted an influence, but the historical conditions of the Meiji Period made this influence of primary importance. As Mr Mishima (who among the younger writers is particularly conscious of his own country's classical heritage) has said:

'In most other countries there exists a strong literary tradition into which writers can assimilate whatever is imported. In Japan our literature does not rest on any such tradition. Although our talented writers have managed to utilize their abilities individually, there are very few of them who have managed to ground their works on secure tradition.'

The history of the modern story in Japan can be considered to date from the introduction of Maupassant's work in the 1890s. One of the earliest writers to attempt to produce in Japanese the type of story that was current in Europe was Mori Ogai, who after his return from Germany in 1888 did so much to familiarize Japanese readers with Western literary forms.

Of the two masters of the late nineteenth century short story in Europe, Maupassant exerted considerably greater influence in Japan than Chekhov. The reason is not far to seek: the introduction of Maupassant's short stories coincided with the rise of naturalism in Japanese literature and, indeed, was one of the important influences in this movement. It was Maupassant's direct, realistic and often harsh approach to his material that affected Japanese writers, rather than his mastery of the short story form itself.

On the whole Japanese writers do not make the clear differentiation between the novel and the short story that is accepted in the West. The line of demarcation in Japan between the two genres has always tended to be vague. This is reflected in the terminology. Both forms are known as *shosetsu*, the word for short story being differentiated only by the prefix *tampen* (short piece). *Shosetsu* is also used with the prefix *chuhen* (middle piece) to describe an intermediate length of work having about 40,000 to 60,000 words; this roughly corresponds to what is sometimes known as a novelette, but the form is very much more popular in Japan than in the West.

By general standards a considerable proportion of *tampen shosetsu* are not short stories at all; frequently they appear to be sketches, essays or truncated novels. A large number of Japanese story writers are primarily novelists for whom stories tend to be what Miss Elizabeth Bowen has called 'side-issues from the crowded imagination'.

In a country that has produced the most compressed forms of poetry in world literature, it is remarkable that stories should so frequently be marked by a turgid verbosity which cries out for the ministration of a red pencil.

Fortunately a number of good modern writers in Japan have treated the short story as an equal and separate genre of literature, not merely as an abbreviated novel or as a sketch. Of the authors represented in *Modern Japanese Stories*, the three who stand out in Japanese letters as short-story writers are Shiga Naoya, Akutagawa Ryunosuke and Nakajima Atsushi.

Published by Unesco, this collection consists of one representative story of twenty-five important writers and provides a thorough introduction to Japanese fiction in this century and, in a sense, a picture of the contemporary Japanese mind.

'The Makioka Sisters'

A GREAT CONTEMPORARY NOVEL
Irving Jaffe
How does a Japanese woman find a husband? What are the important factors governing her choice: romantic love, money, physical attraction, the man's health, family, social position? The answer, as revealed in a recently published translation of a famous Japanese novel—*The Makioka Sisters*—is *all* of them but least important of all, perhaps, at least for girls of the upper middle classes, is romantic love.

The Makioka Sisters represents the culmination of a lifelong intellectual and artistic evolution by the author, Junichiro Tanizaki, who is generally regarded as Japan's leading contemporary novelist. In his earlier days, under the influence of such Western writers as Poe, Baudelaire and Oscar Wilde, Tanizaki wrote bizarre,

sometimes grotesque stories, often dealing with aberrations in human behaviour.

In his more mature years, Tanizaki acquired a growing interest both in the traditional Japanese aesthetic as evidenced by his modern-language translation of the early eleventh-century Japanese classic novel *The Tale of Genji*, and in the unfolding of ordinary Japanese lives.

As a high point in this development, *The Makioka Sisters* is ideally suited to take us 'inside' the Japan of the recent past and of a certain milieu; the immediate postwar Japan of the upper middle classes in the Osaka–Kyoto region where something of the traditional Japanese ways and *douceur de vivre* still exist.

Begun toward the end of the war, *The Makioka Sisters* (published in Japan as *Sasame-yuki*), was completed in the early postwar years. Structurally, the novel, with its lack of any strong plot or dramatic climaxes, its up-in-the-air ending, may disconcert the Western reader. But this very absence of a 'story' structure, this meandering through all the details of daily living, produces a fidelity to life which is highly informative to the foreign reader.

With infinite patience, Tanizaki threads his way through some five years immediately preceding Japan's entry into World War II in the lives of the four Makioka sisters, members of a respected merchant family which is gradually declining both in wealth and in social standing. Tanizaki has said he tried to confine himself to 'what was attractive' in the graceful prewar life, 'but I was not able to withdraw completely from the enveloping storm. This was the necessary fate of a novel born of war and peace.'

The main theme of the novel is the series of repeated failures in the family's attempt to find a socially acceptable husband for the third sister; silent, mild-mannered, retiring Yukiko, the most 'traditional' Japanese of them all. The impact of the modern world on traditional Japanese ways, and the disturbances this causes, are reflected in the hectic life of the bright, modern, independent and somewhat rebellious youngest sister, Taeko, who finally is excluded from the family circle.

Yet no ultimate, irretrievable tragedy befalls any of the main characters: life just goes on. Yukiko finally finds a husband, and Taeko ends up as the wife of a bartender—but, even here, it is clear that the bonds of affection and loyalty between

Taeko and her sisters will endure despite official ostracism.

The main interest of the novel for Western readers lies in the wealth of intimate detail about Japanese life—glimpses both of thoroughly modern daily life and of ancient customs which, even though some of them are undoubtedly on the decline in present day Japan, show us a side of life which still persists.

9 History and culture

Introduction

The story of man can be told in the language of travel—both of people and of goods. An important European contribution to the knowledge of the globe and to cultures in Eastern lands was represented by the journeys into Asia made by missionaries and merchants in the thirteenth century. A number of European travellers have left more or less detailed records of their journeys which provide not only fascinating accounts of the history and culture of these eastern countries, but also interesting insights into the attitude of the Westerner towards the East. Two European travellers are represented here—the Venetian traveller Marco Polo and the sixteenth-century Portuguese trader Ferdinand Mendes Pinto. Marco Polo's book gives a vivid account of the geography, ethnography, politics and science of thirteenth-century Asia; the flourishing trade in China, the splendour of the Mogul Empire are all reflected in this work. An interesting feature of Ferdinand Mendes Pinto's writing is that it gives a most sympathetic picture of non-European civilizations. Mendes was one of the early writers who did not believe that the European viewpoint was the only right one and did not treat men with beliefs differing from his own as mere objects whose sole interest lies in the profits and advantages that can be gained from them.

We are often inclined to forget the important place that the Arab world holds in the history of thought. The Arab renaissance flourished in the eighth century AD anticipating the Western renaissance by seven hundred years. The humanistic values flowered among the Arabs when Europe was still sunk in the darkness of the Middle Ages. The most important element of the legacy from the Arab to the Western world is the intellectual element consisting of the sum of knowledge inherited from Greece and transmitted to medieval Europe through the Arab scientists and philosophers of Spain. Thanks to them Euclid, Archimedes, Ptolemy, Hippocrates, Galen, Aristotle and Plato were known to Western thought, however imperfectly, long before Europe could renew direct contact with them.

After the founding of Islam by the Prophet Mohammed around 630, the new civilization rapidly spread outwards from Arabia, its centre, until by the middle of the tenth century, when it was at its zenith, it included by far the greater part of the in-

habited world. To the west it took in Egypt and the entire North African coast, the islands of Sicily and Crete and nearly all of Spain. To the north, Syria, Armenia and the south-east regions of the Caucasus were under Islamic rule; further east, Mesopotamia, Iraq, Persia and Afghanistan, Transoxania and parts of India's northern plains.

Both the cultural and geographical horizons of Europe were bounded in nearly all directions by Islam, which enjoyed the summit of its prosperity at the time when the civilization of the West slumbered in its deepest darkness. Navigation, commerce, architecture, together with nearly all the arts and crafts were cultivated, and their fruits and techniques handed on to the West. The Arabs pro-

duced eminent scholars and practitioners in medicine, astronomy, physics and the natural sciences. They were the inventors of algebra and trigonometry, and they contributed much to the development of arithmetical calculation.

By the twelfth century the works of Arab scholars had begun to be translated and accepted as authorities in the West—in Europe; and in the thirteenth century the Arab world and the West were intellectually much more closely aligned than they have ever been since.

In the sixteenth century the revolution brought about by Copernicus in astronomy, the reform of alchemy and medicine by Paracelsus and the new anatomy of Vesalius struck great blows at traditional Arab erudition. Then when the Moors

A great adventure begins for the young Marco Polo as he sets off from Venice on his journey among the 'kingdoms and marvels of the East'. These old engravings showing the departure of Nicolo and Matteo Polo, Marco's father and uncle, and Marco himself, are taken from the de Mandeville *Livre des Merveilles* now in the Bibliotheque Nationale, Paris

were defeated and the Muslim empire in Europe came to an end, all the eastern learning that had not already been assimilated was lost.

Glimpses of the role of Islam in world history and the Arab cultural heritage are contained in this chapter which also includes brief insights into the cultures of Pakistan, Korea, Thailand and Lebanon.

Marco Polo

A THIRTEENTH-CENTURY GLOBE TROTTING BUSINESSMAN

Jose de Benito

In September 1298 a Venetian nobleman, Marco Polo, was taken prisoner by the Genoese navy. He related the tales of his travels to a fellow prisoner—a learned man from Pisa and this was the genesis of *The Book of Ser Marco Polo, the Venetian, concerning the kingdoms and marvels of the East.*

It was thanks to the trustworthy and detailed accounts of Marco Polo's travels that the cartographers of Charles V of France were able to trace the map of Asia into their famous *Catalan Atlas* embodying in it a great deal of new information. But in addition—and this is of supreme importance in the history of civilization—the news about the wealth of Asia and its trade in spices was certainly a powerful factor in inciting the Portuguese to launch their great voyages of discovery, and in encouraging Christopher Colombus to plan and carry out the great adventure which was to lead to the opening up of a new continent.

Thus as Marco Polo's words flowed on between the four bare walls of that Genoese prison, a new historical era was born. The centre of world interest began to shift from the Mediterranean, sailed by Greek and Phoenician vessels centuries before Christ, to the ocean, that 'dark sea' of the ancients, which has now become a bridge between the old peoples of Europe and the new nations of the Americas.

But who was Marco Polo? Born in Venice in 1254, he was the son of Nicolò Polo, who, with his elder brother Marco and his other brother Matteo, ran an important business at Constantinople with a branch at Soldaja (Crimea), from which they traded with the East. Marco Polo was barely seven when his father and his uncle Matteo decided to make a business trip into the heart of Asia. They set out from Soldaja in 1261, and their journey lasted eight years. In 1269 they returned, bearing gifts from the great Kublai Khan to the Sovereign Pontiff of Christianity, and a request that the latter should send to China several masters of the liberal arts who could also bring the religion of Christ to Kublai's subjects. The Holy See was vacant at the time, owing to the death of Clement IV, and was not to be filled for three years.

Marco, who was by now nearly fifteen, was thrilled by the stories told by his father and his uncle Matteo and begged to be allowed to accompany them on their second journey to the East. The brothers agreed, but as they were unwilling to set off again for China without meeting the Great Khan's requests, they spent two years in Venice, waiting for the election of a Pope and making careful preparations for the new expedition.

In 1271 the Polo brothers obtained from the new Pope, Gregory X, letters and presents for Kublai Khan, a descendant of Ghengiz Khan.

Everything was now in order; and in 1271 Marco, Nicolò and Matteo Polo set out from the port of Lajazzo on the eastern Mediterranean. They were not to return until twenty-five years later, in 1296.

Marco Polo's was by far the most extensive trip ever made up to that time. Many would hesitate, even today, before undertaking such a journey. Harsh climates, the risk of illness and the dangers of the road across huge and lonely steppes (including the possibility of encounters with bands of desert robbers) would make it, even now, an adventurous trip.

The tremendous effect, which the story of these travels must have produced on the minds of contemporary readers, and indeed on people living in the fourteenth and fifteenth centuries, can be imagined.

Yet Marco Polo, with a modesty rare in adventurers, hardly puts himself into the picture at all; his is a strictly objective and realistic account of the countries he visited, or of those about which, without having been there himself, he had reliable sources of information. The absence of the fictitious element—lack of fantasy—invests his story with unique power and authenticity, and makes it a monument of geographical and commercial information.

In a time like his, when there was much commercial movement and competition to open new routes for Venetian, Genoese, Pisan, Catalan and Florentine trade his story was to pave the way for every sort of project and ambition, to foster every dream of adventure in medieval man.

The Belgian historian, J. Pirenne, summing up Marco Polo's description of the Chinese economy, says: 'In northern China, coal deposits (as yet, unknown to the rest of the world) had been discovered; Hang-Chow, the largest city of the universe and China's most flourishing port, was the anchorage for powerful fleets, equipped by the Empire, which sailed as far as the Indian Archipelago. In the commercial cities, business men rich as kings were grouped into corporations. Peking was the centre of the silk trade in the North; Chung-Tu was the concentration point for all the export trade to Central Asia; Nanking and Su-Chow manufactured cloth of gold; Yang Chow was the rice market; Hang-Chow was the sugar market and simultaneously the most important centre of international commerce; Fu-Chow and Chin-Chow controlled the traffic in spices and pearls, as well as the imports from India. Navigation was so intense that for every one ship loaded with pepper which sailed from India to Alexandria, at least one hundred anchored at Chin-Chow.'

This was the Mongol emperor's time of greatest splendour. The shades of Ghengiz Khan, the conqueror of Asia who had been so great a threat to Europe, still hung over the eastern world, with memories of the terrible massacres that his hordes had perpetrated among the Chinese peoples accustomed to the enlightened authority of the Sing dynasty. And Kublai Khan had made good use of that terror so as to impose order in all his vast dominions. How else could the Polos have wandered for twenty-five years over the remotest of areas without mishap?

Successive chapters of the book of Marco Polo describe Turkestan, Lesser and Greater Armenia (from Anatolia to the Caucasus); the kingdoms of Mosul, Baghdad, Tauris and the Khanate of Persia up to Ormuz; Mongolia, China, India and Siberia; the seven thousand islands of Japan; South east Asia, including Cochin-china and Annam; the islands of Java and Sumatra (or Little Java), the Malay Peninsula and Ceylon; Arabia, Abyssinia, the East African coast and Madagascar; and finally, Trebizond and Constantinople.

Europe's pioneers of oceanic navigation to the Far East were the Portuguese. In 1497 Vasco da Gama sailed to India and opened a maritime trade route to the Orient. By 1519 a Portuguese cartographer was able to depict with commendable realism in this picturesquely illustrated map, countries from the Red Sea to south east Asia

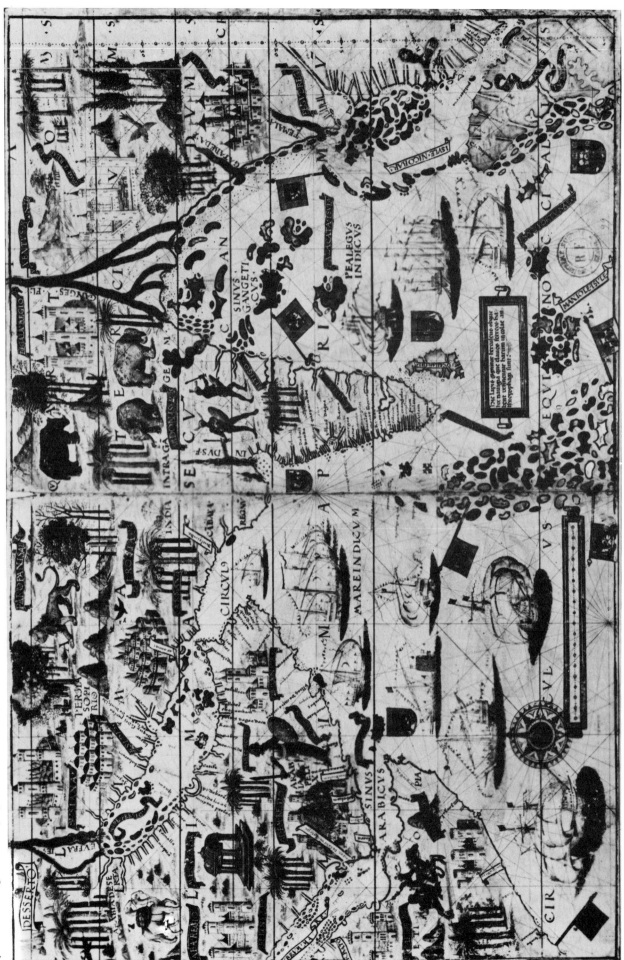

A Portuguese Sancho Panza in the Far East

Antonio José Saraiva

One of the oldest examples of the acceptance of a voyager of the world's diversity and a sympathetic understanding of non-European civilizations is contained in the sixteenth-century *Peregrinação,* by Ferdinand Mendes Pinto, a Portuguese trader in the Far East who died in 1582. Though almost forgotten today, *Peregrinação* was at one time known throughout Europe. First published in 1614, it was translated into a number of languages, including French, English, German and Dutch during the seventeenth and eighteenth centuries.

The Portuguese navigator Vasco da Gama arrived at Calicut, the present seaport of Kozhikode, on the Malabar coast of India, in 1498. In 1511 the Portuguese annexed Malacca which gave them a firm control over the trade in the Far East for some time. In 1517 they sent an Embassy to the Emperor of China, but at that time the Ming Dynasty had turned its back on the sea and closed its frontiers to foreigners; and so the ambassador of the King of Portugal failed in his mission.

Nevertheless a few venturesome Portuguese merchants and adventurers managed to trade between China, the Malay Archipelago and the Pacific Islands, by accepting the risks which this involved. Private individuals, unconnected in any way with the Portuguese state, they operated in a more or less clandestine way, building small stores and depots on the Chinese coast which eventually grew into self-governing mercantile communities and trading stations. If the opportunity came their way, they were not above acts of piracy. On occasion their voyages took them to places hitherto unknown to Europeans.

Thus, about 1542 a ship with Portuguese merchants aboard, including Ferdinand Mendes Pinto, who by then belonged to this strange world of adventurers, arrived at the island of Tanegashima in Japan. Mendes Pinto has left us an account of this first meeting between Europeans and Japanese.

He was charmed by the chivalrous spirit and noble nature of the islanders and impressed by attention paid to questions of honour which was the cause of endless feuds between the nobles. He also tells us how one of his companions, Diego Zeimoto, introduced firearms to Japan. The first time they saw Diego killing game with his gun, the local people took him for a magician, but they quickly learned to

A Chinese view of the earth in the mid-seventeenth century offered by this page from the Ko Chih Tahao, a rare treatise on astronomy and geography, by Hsiung-Ming-Yu, which includes a diagram explaining the sphericity of our planet. Some 16 centuries earlier a great Chinese astronomer of the Han era, Chang Heng, described the heavens as 'like a hen's egg and as round as a crossbow bullet'; the earth is like the yolk of the egg, and lies alone in the centre. Hsiung-Ming-Yu also used the phrase 'as round as a crossbow bullet' to describe the earth, but graduated the sphere into 360° instead of 365¹·4° used by the Han astronomers. The sphere shows ships of Chinese rig, pagodas and at the antipodes, a large European building like a cathedral

make guns themselves since, as Mendes Pinto tells us, their craftsmen were extremely skilful. Pinto also remarks on the graciousness of the women and the exquisite politeness of the courtiers.

This delightful picture of the Japanese is only part of the book. Its author boasts of having covered the whole Asian coast from the Persian Gulf to Siberia, with detours through the Indonesian Islands and the Island of Taiwan, and of having travelled in China by river and canal between Peking and Nanking, where he was astounded at the huge 'towns' of boat-dwellers.

He claims to have worked as a convict on repairing the Great Wall of China and to have been able to measure its height and thickness with his own hands. He asserts that he was enlisted into the Mongol army which invaded China about 1544, that he was taken before the famous

king who burnt the suburbs of Pekin (probably Dayan, King of the Ordos), and that he visited the Holy City in Tibet.

These travels, some of them undoubtedly true, and the others imaginary, serve him as a framework for a vividly romanticized autobiography. It is packed with incident, with shipwrecks, land and sea fights, wanderings, dreadful crimes, glorious exploits and popular risings, with anecdotes, with descriptions of customs, rites, beliefs, ceremonies, towns, palaces and temples of the most wonderful kinds. From its pages speak a multitude of characters into whose mouths the author puts eloquent discourses studded with Eastern imagery. The whole is a blend of narrative and description almost Homeric in its variety and power.

The main character, the author himself, is successively agent of the Governor of Malacca, merchant, pirate, slave, vagabond, beggar, soldier, and finally, simultaneously ambassador of the Viceroy of Goa to a Japanese baron and Jesuit missionary.

He never depicts himself as a hero but rather as a poor booby muddling his way as best he can out of innumerable misfortunes. Most of the time he is at grips with hunger and fear. In a word, he is the complete *picaro,* the anti-hero of the Spanish picaresque novels. If we prefer, we can look on him as a Portuguese Sancho Panza of the East. He has no notion whatever of knightly honour and he is the absolute reverse of a hidalgo or conquistador.

At most, he is a trader and that is why, even when he is acting as an ambassador, he always appears to be of a lower order than his Eastern interlocutors, be they Malay Sultans, Chinese mandarins, Japanese Samurai, priests anywhere and everywhere, or even the poor fishermen whose slave he was for a while. From all these people he receives lessons of every kind to which he is obliged to hearken submissively.

The women too, for whom Mendes Pinto has the utmost affection, have something to teach the plunderers. A storm hurls them on the shores of the island of Lequia (Taiwan). They are borne off to prison on suspicion of being sea-rovers disguised as merchants, but the wretched state in which they arrive, naked and covered with cuts and bruises, stirs the women to pity.

When the travellers are on the point of

being executed the women flock to the main square of the city with a moving petition to the King, signed by hundreds, begging him to spare the prisoners. The King is moved and releases the condemned men, but says that he will not receive them 'because it ill becomes a king to look on men who, though knowing God, do not obey His laws and are wont to steal their neighbour's goods'.

To Mendes Pinto's Orientals, the Europeans are little better than savages, they eat with their fingers, quarrel loudly and sometimes come to blows for futile reasons. To the East, they are objects of amazement or derision.

Above all, however, *Peregrinação* gives us a wholeheartedly admiring picture of the civilizations of the Far East. As for China, Mendes Pinto depicts it as an absolute Utopia: justice is swift, humane and completely fair to the accused; the structure of the state prevents the corruption of its magistrates and the oppression of its subjects; there is no unemployment or famine; manufacturing and trade supply all the needs of man; there is a complete system of communications; manners are perfect; and 'Rome, Constantinople, Venice, Paris, London, Seville, Lisbon or any other famed city of Europe' do not begin to compare with the capital, Peking. Mendes Pinto even goes so far as to wish that the laws of China could be copied in Portugal.

This description of China is of course rather idealized and the indications are that our author did not know China as well as he knew Japan. What counts, however, is his admiration and lack of prejudice, and his admiration is not purely intellectual, but comes also from the heart.

At every turn we find him moved to wonder by the works of art, the towns, the crowds, the colour and music, the manner of speech, the ceremonies, the beauty of the women and the delightful ways of the children. He even gives us descriptions of Chinese and Japanese plays, translates forms of greeting and courtesy, and provides transcriptions (though how faithful, it is hard to say) of occasional words of the tongues of the East.

Naturally the picture he paints is not without its blemishes. It includes accounts of unbelievable atrocities. Yet the fact remains that Mendes Pinto was, I am sure, the first person to attempt a synoptic sketch of the civilizations of the Far East and that he produced one that is lively and artistic, and that seeks to penetrate to the heart and essence of those civilizations and to understand them from within.

That is why, in any history of European feelings and attitudes towards non-European civilizations, Mendes Pinto has earned an honoured place.

Islam in world history

Marshall G S Hodgson

When Mohammed first preached Islam, in a rather obscure part of the Arabian peninsula in the seventh century AD, the other major religions had already penetrated, among them, most of the civilized lands of the eastern hemisphere. Christianity prevailed in the Mediterranean basin, Zoroastrianism in Iran, Hinduism in India and the southeast, Buddhism and Taoism in the Far East. There seemed little room for a new religion; and indeed Mohammed did not claim that Islam was new. He believed he was bringing the same message from God that Moses and Jesus had brought to the Jews and the Christians of old; that God alone was to be worshipped, that His will was to be obeyed as made known through His prophets and that at the Last Judgment the disobedient would be punished and the believers rewarded in Paradise.

The Jews and Christians, Mohammed believed, had corrupted this simple message, and in Islam the purity of God's truth was restored. In contrast to the nations around them, the Arabians, pagans till then, were now offered the uncorrupted truth in their own language in the Koran. Within Mohammed's lifetime the greater part of Arabia offered him its obedience as God's prophet, and the formerly feuding Arabians were forged into a strong new society on the basis of Islam.

At its beginning Islam had the appearance of a reformed version of the Jewish-Christian faith, adapted to the local needs of the Arabian tribes. It would have been hard to guess, then, that it was to play so great a role in the world; first in the creation of a great Middle Eastern empire, the Caliphate; then, when the Caliphate broke up, as a basis for the most powerful international civilization of the medieval world; and finally in our time as a world religion which is by some standards the most widely distributed of all faiths. In the Middle Ages Muslims believed themselves to be on the way to taking over the whole world and turning it into a single divinely guided society. They came nearer to uniting the world than we usually realize; and the brotherhood of Islam still provides one of the most active ideals at work among mankind.

When the Arabian tribes were brought together by Islam into a single state, they quickly burst the bounds of Arabia, and within decades found themselves masters of the Middle East, heirs to half the Roman Empire and the whole of the Persian. At first Islam was the badge of the ruling Arabs; but the subject peoples—Christians, Jews, Zoroastrians, Buddhists—were not slow in adopting the new and dynamic creed, sometimes despite the objections of the Arabs, many of whom preferred to keep their privileged faith for themselves.

Within two centuries Islam had become the predominant religion in most of the lands ruled by the Arab Caliphate, while the Arabic language had become the common vehicle of its burgeoning cultural and commercial life. In this way a great civilization, with its own literary, artistic and intellectual traditions, was built around the Muslim faith. When the Caliphate broke up in the tenth century the civilization remained, to be carried round the world and enriched by the various Islamic peoples.

This civilization was now given its social unity no longer by a single state and a single language—Persian soon became an international cultural language rivalling Arabic, and in time many other languages became important locally—but by a single system of sacred law. This law covered in principle every aspect of personal life, etiquette and ritual and belief as well as points of contract or of inheritance. Though not all parts of the sacred law were equally applied among all Muslim peoples, it produced enough uniformity in essentials to make it possible for a Muslim from any country to have citizenship rights throughout the Dar al-Islam, the territory under Muslim rule.

A learned man from Morocco, travelling to see the world, might be made a judge when he lived for a time in India as easily as if he were in his own country thousands of miles away. At the yearly pilgrimage to Mecca, Muslims from the most distant lands met and might share their concerns. With such relatively free interchange, Islamic culture, though it was diverse from country to country, maintained a common heritage in all its forms. Thus in its exquisite grace the Taj Mahal reflects Indian traditions differing widely from those of the Balkans or of North Africa; but it was as obviously built for Muslims as any mosque in Istanbul or Tunis.

The culture which such effectively flexible institutions fostered was worthy of them. Straddling the crossroads of the world, the Islamic society was in a position to gather its inspiration from most of the civilizations that had arisen before it. It did not fail to do so; but whatever it learned from the past it made its own, and generally improved.

Apart from the grand simplicity of the religion itself, its glory was in its literature, especially its poetry. This grew out of the classical genius of pre-Islamic Arabia, which Muslims never ceased to respect, but which in Islamic times achieved far greater amplitude and variety. The untranslatable subtlety of Arabic verse and the versatile sweetness of the Persian poets have inspired local literatures wherever Islam has gone.

Muslims proved industrious scholars, and notably indefatigable historians. Above all must be mentioned their natural science. The Muslims inherited a formidable body of learning from the classical Greeks—philosophy and logic from Plato and Aristotle, mathematics, astronomy, and medicine from Euclid and Ptolemy, Hippocrates and Galen, and the rest. To this inheritance they joined much of the results of Sanskrit learning—including the use of the zero. They then accumulated a wealth of further data: astronomical observations which helped prepare the way for the acceptance of the Copernican theory, alchemical experiments which much enlarged the realm of chemistry, algebraic solutions, geographical data, philosophical problems, botanical discoveries, medical techniques. The age of creative Islamic science did not last so long as that of creative art; after five or six centuries the Muslim peoples ceased to produce much that was new. Yet the scientific heritage did not cease to discipline the minds of cultivated Muslims everywhere.

In the course of the centuries the Muslim faith, and with it the Islamic culture, was spread far beyond the old limits of the Caliphate by the preaching of mer-

chants and mystics, or by the prestige or force of conquering monarchs. In some areas, as in China, though many were converted to Islam the Muslims never gained power. In most parts Muslim rule spread at least as fast as the Muslim faith. Islam had been first established in the Middle East, and Muslim rulers there long made it a point to carry Islam into the two great populous regions on each side, Europe and India. India proved the more vulnerable and by 1300 Muslim rule had been momentarily extended almost to its southern tip; on the other hand, by 1529—and again in 1683—the Ottoman Turks were besieging Vienna in the heart of Europe. In other directions Islamization was perhaps less romantic, but more lasting. By 1500 Islam dominated much of northern Africa and of central Eurasia, and the coastlines around the Indian Ocean.

Even where they did not convert or conquer, the Muslims had an important cultural influence. Thus in Africa, peoples which had not yet accepted Islam often adapted elements of Muslim practice to their own cultures. In most parts of India even Hindu courts recognized the excellence of Indo-Muslim culture: Islamic handicrafts and art objects were eagerly received everywhere; and in lands as far apart as western Europe and China, till the end of the Middle Ages astronomy and the other sciences were studied in large part from Muslim masters. It might easily have been supposed that Islam from its central position was destined to unite the Old World under its own leadership.

In the midst of this expansion the West Europeans, emerging from relative obscurity, upset all expectations. In the generation of about 1500 the Europeans proved themselves masters of the oceans.

By the nineteenth century, Western domination, in one form or another, spread over the whole world, and ended by altering radically the circumstances in which henceforth all peoples must live. The Muslim peoples, either under direct European rule or under constant interference by European powers, had to adapt themselves perforce to the European world order, adopting Western rules of commerce and of citizenship, the new Western means of transportation and communication, Western military methods and scientific discoveries.

Gradually they began to undergo like transformations to those which had already affected the West; and in the

twentieth century, as Western power receded, they have taken up (in common with the rest of the world) the task of forging new destinies for themselves in the new age, on an equal basis with the Western peoples.

The Arab cultural heritage

A Scotsman who spent many years of his life on the far away islands reaching northward to Norway recently recalled his youthful excitement when he learned that the designs which were used on the jerseys of his native district in Scotland were of Arabic source. They had come all the way from Spain. He recalled the thrill that had come to him on learning, in school, that the word algebra was of Arabic origin, that chemistry was derived from the Arabic word alchemy and that Sinbad the Sailor and the Thousand and One Nights were only a part of a vast poetic literature. It was the Arabic people who kept alive the intellectual tradition of the Greeks and not least, the teaching of Aristotle between the fall of Rome and the European Renaissance.

HISTORICAL CONTINUITY

The arts and skills of algebra and trigonometry and mathematics and geography and medicine and botany owe their historical continuity throughout the Dark Ages to the Arabic peoples. In fact one can truthfully say that European civilization was saved by the wisdom and enlightenment of the Arab Courts that followed 700 AD. Indeed, it is not astonishing that King Richard I found Saladin the cultured character which Sir Walter Scott described in *The Talisman*. The twelfth century in England was meeting its own sixteenth century without knowing it.

The ancient ways of communication were slow. When Arabs travelled to China, or gave as they did the first written account of Czechoslovakia and the city of Prague, their stories of observation took a long time to come and were dispersed even more slowly.

The designs of Persia took hundreds of years to travel by way of Arabic architecture, illuminated manuscripts and designs from Persia to Spain.

'IN QUEST OF LEARNING'

The problem of explaining the influence that the Arabs have had on Western civilization can be approached in two ways. It is possible either to make broad statements, which while impressive and true may fail to touch the reader because of their remoteness from everyday life, or we may touch here and there on the most ordinary objects which the West owes to the Arab world and which the West takes for granted until some twitch of the thread of history jerks back into our minds the realization of what has, in fact, happened.

Handfuls of Arabic coins of the tenth century found on a remote island in the Baltic Sea; a 'journey in quest of learning' made by the historian Al-Mas-udi to Zanzibar; a regular trade route linking Spain with Central Asia. These are only a few of the indications of how the Arabs ranged round the seas eager for knowledge leaving their mark on the world about them.

The interest of the Arabic people in geography brought them rich dividends, but this interest came originally not from a desire for trade. It sprang from a very different source—the need for pilgrims to find their way across the trackless sands to Mecca, the need to site mosques, so that they pointed to the Holy City and the desire of faithful Muslims to be sure that, at their prayers, they faced toward the Kaba.

The discoveries of the voyagers, the findings of the thinkers and investigators of the day were recorded on paper for the first time in history. At the same time, centuries before Gutenberg, mechanical duplicating systems were introduced to make possible the diffusion of these writings. Even the problem of copyright was strictly legislated by the Arabs centuries ago.

Julep, soda, syrup and sherbet (the ancestor of ice cream) are not only words derived from the Arabic, but their nature is indicative of a civilization in which there was the ability to enjoy some of the small, pleasant things of life.

SILKS AND SATINS

In making life more agreeable for themselves the Arabs developed to a high degree the art of producing textiles, the silks and satins and tapestries mentioned above. Damascus made damask, muslin came from Mosul, Baghdad produced baldaquins, and so on, in a rich flood of colour and design. Arab culture thus was slowly absorbed by the West. From the Arabs in Spain, Arabic skills and customs made their way to Provence (garnished by the charming songs of the troubadours), from Provence into Lorraine, and thence all over Europe.

The tragedy of this contact, however, is that there is so much that the Westerners never did learn. The great literature of the Arab world is still almost literally contained in sealed books unknown to most of us.

The Arab world had its first great flowering a thousand to twelve hundred years ago, but even now, in some branches of thought, the West is only beginning to catch up with it. Thus, for example, the Arabs long ago insisted that a medical doctor be not only a physician but a metaphysician, a philosopher and a sage, and thus understand fully the value of psychology in healing.

Indeed, such was the work done in the field of medicine that Avicenna (Ibn Sina, AD 980 to 1037), who was not only a doctor and a philosopher but a philologist and poet as well, served as the chief medical authority to the West until the seventeenth century.

Another Arab philosopher, Ibn-Roschid, known to Western Europe as Averroes, and whose numerous writings (he is said to have used over 10,000 sheets of paper) summed up the work of Muslim thinkers up to the end of the twelfth century, was described by Renan as the 'Boethius of Arab philosophy'.

The introduction of Averroes meant the end of the Dark Ages. To Dante, he was the Commentator *par excellence*—'Averroes, che il gran commento feo'. Discussed, prohibited, but always widely read, he was for many centuries one of the main forces which lead to the Renaissance. By the beginning of the sixteenth century he had become, to quote Renan again, 'almost the official philosophy of Italy in general'.

As one sees the new Arab world of today, one recalls that the phoenix, which rises splendidly from its ashes to a new life, is a bird whose dwelling place is Arabia and that his miraculous powers of reincarnation are not yet exhausted.

Avicenna, scientist and philosopher

Camille Aboussouan

In the Middle Ages, about 1150, some fifty years before Aristotle's *Metaphysics* was rediscovered, works by a Persian named Avicenna brought to Western Europe the essentials of an extensive and well-constructed system. This Persian scholar gave the world a body of 335 works, scientific even more than philosophic, which was to play an important part in the development of knowledge. Up to the eighteenth century, his works on medicine were still standard textbooks in all the universities of Europe. His studies of mathematics, physics, chemistry, astronomy and botany, his treatises on the administration of the army and on the state land taxes, his epistle on love, his correspondence with other scientists of the time, his philosophical, legal, linguistic and poetic works, and even his commentaries on magic, entitle him to be considered as one of the most striking figures in world civilization.

A thousand lunar years ago, in AD 980, Abu Ali al Husain ibn Abdallah ibn Sina, called Avicenna, was born at Afsana, near Bokhara, in Persia. Thanks to the care lavished upon him in childhood, he very early acquired a wide learning unusual among his contemporaries. Although a Persian, he wrote all his works in Arabic, and only a few poems, a treatise on pulsation and another on the principles of science were written in his native language.

Like all good Muslims, he first learnt the Koran; he then made the acquaintance of Arabic literature, Greek philosophy, law, theology, medicine, geometry, physics and mathematics. Porphyrius, Euclid and Ptolemy occupied most of his time until he reached the age of sixteen, when, being more learned than any of his teachers, he established his own school, with many doctors working under his guidance. He was particularly interested in philosophy.

When he was eighteen and had acquired all the learning of the time, he was summoned, because of his reputation as a doctor, to attend the Sultan, who had been stricken with a serious illness. He cured him and, as a reward, the ruler gave him permission to work in his magnificent library; he also consulted him on state affairs and, generally, on other matters, and enabled him to spend much time in study.

At twenty-one Avicenna wrote his first book, *Al Majmuh*, a collection of philosophic writings. He was then beginning to take an interest in political life and, leaving Bokhara, wandered from one court to another among the Emirs of northern

Persia and the lands around the Caspian Sea. He finally arrived at Hamadan where he cured the Emir, who appointed him Vizier. There Avicenna spent his days on the business of the state and his nights on his own works. The *Al-Shifa* and the *Qanun fit-tibb* his masterly work on medicine, which was the bible of all doctors in the East and West for centuries, were written then. In the latter treatise, there are many lucid explanations of the functions and diseases of the human body.

On the death of the Emir of Hamadan, his enemies imprisoned Avicenna in the fortress of Ferdajan. There he almost completed the sections on logic, mathematics, physics and metaphysics in the *Al-Shifa* and went on to write several works on philosophy and medicine.

This enforced retirement gave him leisure for work, but it did not last very long. He fled to Ispahan where he completed the *Al-Shifa*. In the last years of his life in Ispahan there was a very definite development in his work, particularly in the *Kitab el-Jcharat wa' tanbihat*, or 'Book of Theorems', the last of his works which has come down to us complete. Unfortunately, this work has never yet been translated in full. We are informed that Mlle Goichon, who is one of the foremost specialists on Avicenna, has just finished a translation into French. This will help Westerners to understand more clearly Avicenna's remarkable contribution to medieval philosophy at a time when, one thousand years after his birth, he still stands an acknowledged master.

Pakistan, spiritual home and national reality

Claude Levi-Strauss

Of all the countries which make up our inhabited globe, Pakistan is perhaps the one which presents the most unusual characteristics. The laws defining its existence declare that it was founded as a state where all Muslims could live according to the principles of Islam. As such it provides a spiritual home for all members of a single religious community regardless of their national origin. Nevertheless, Pakistan remains in the deepest sense of the word a nation. It groups under one unified authority lands that for thousands of years have been inhabited by the same people, most of whom have shared for centuries the same moral, political and religious principles forming the basis of the new State.

This dual aspect—the spiritual home and the national reality—characterizes the Pakistan of today. It explains too, certain paradoxes. For although Pakistan's hope is to bring together Muslims from all over prepartition India, in reality 50 million Muslims are still scattered in other parts of the subcontinent.

As a nation, Pakistan has defined frontiers and distinctive geographic and sociological features. As a spiritual home, it somewhat anticipates its national individuality. For it must mould itself—with undiminished creative zeal—in the image of the great promise it wishes to be, not only for its own people but also for all those who some day may come seeking a means of life in keeping with their faith.

One has only to glance at a map to understand the complexity of the problems confronting this nation which has set itself such lofty requirements. Not only do a thousand miles of Indian territory split East and West Pakistan but differences in climate, physiography and even language separate the two regions. Eastern Pakistan, though by far the smaller area, has the larger population; yet it is West Pakistan, which is less fertile, that compensates for the food shortages of the eastern zone. This zone (East Bengal) is almost entirely devoted to the cultivation of jute, the crop which enables the government to balance its national budget.

Pakistan happens to hold practically a world monopoly of raw jute but when Pakistan was set up the country was unable to convert the fibre for lack of any jute goods industry and inadequate port facilities impeded its exportation.

To remedy this situation, the Government embarked on a series of vast industrialization projects for the construction of the first jute mills at Narayanganj, a hydroelectric dam and a paper mill on the Karnafully River, additional port facilities at Chittagong, a new port at the Ganges Delta, power stations at Malakand and sugar refineries at Mardan. Additional projects have been added in successive Five Year Plans.

Pakistan's third Five Year Plan involves an expenditure of £3,900 million. But the immense problems of financing these projects and of transforming a large portion of illiterate peasants into technically and socially educated workmen present formidable obstacles. Here United Nations and Unesco Technical Assistance and Pakistan Aid Consortium programmes may help in meeting some of the difficulties.

Partition and with it the independence of Pakistan brought in its wake immense misery and suffering. Millions of refugees trekked into West Pakistan (Sind and Punjab) from all parts of India, leaving behind them everything they cherished—their personal belongings, their fortunes, their land and the tombs of their ancestors—in order to join the spiritual community of their own choosing.

Similar problems—and others even more specialized—also face East Bengal. To solve them will require no small degree of imagination and international collaboration. For even the most intensive jute cultivation cannot be expected to absorb the manpower or assure the livelihood of a population which exceeds in density 2,500 inhabitants per square mile. In fact, for centuries the people have sought a secondary means of income in cottage industries such as the manufacture of muslin cloth which has made Dacca famous. But even these rural crafts are conditioned by unique circumstances. They depend on international markets not only as a source for raw materials but as a sales outlet for the finished products.

To take a specific case, in East Bengal I visited in 1951 a number of villages of incredible poverty in the region of Langalbund not far from Dacca. There, over 50,000 people lived only by the manufacture of mother-of-pearl buttons. These buttons, of the kind used for cheap shirts and underwear, were produced in huge quantities by hand tools which might well have belonged to the early Middle Ages.

The raw materials needed for their production such as chemicals, cardboard and foil spangles used to mount the buttons on the cardboard, have ceased coming in from abroad since Pakistan became independent. Following a world slump in demand, pearl button production in the villages had declined from 60,000 gross per week to less than 50,000 per month, while the price paid to the village craftsman had fallen 75 per cent.

This is only one example of the distressing problems facing Pakistan today. It would be a mistake, however, to view them merely as economic problems. No doubt the key to the dilemma lies first with the technicians.

For example, the material conditions of

the Bengali peasant could be almost unbelievably improved by the introduction of small, specially manufactured, hand operated machines. These would simplify the different stages of work in the button industry. Surely the purposes of science are not only to solve scientific problems but to find answers to social problems as well. The efforts of science should not only enable mankind to surpass itself; they must also help those who lag behind to catch up.

A young nation founded on an ancient civilization, Pakistan like other nations of Asia or America, synthesizes in its problems the whole of human development. At one and the same time, it suffers and lives in our Middle Ages which its villages perpetuate; in our eighteenth and nineteenth centuries which its first attempts at industrialization reproduce; in our twentieth century whose advantages it is determined to secure. Perhaps the more developed nations, by providing Pakistan with some of the means to bridge these gaps and overcome such contradictions, may learn in return how man can succeed in attaining his full individual stature without denying any part of his heritage and of his past.

The cultural heritage of Korea

'LAND OF THE MORNING CALM'

At the end of the fourteenth century, there was the Third unified dynasty of Korea, the kingdom of Cho-sun – Land of the Morning Calm, with its capital at Seoul. The land had maintained a close relationship with the Chinese Ming Dynasty. The rare travellers who tried to tell the rest of the world about the treasures of this kingdom attributed a Mongolian origin to this homogeneous people. They remarked on the individuality of the language and the simplicity of its alphabet of twenty-four letters. They recounted a formidable list of discoveries and inventions:

The south gate of Seoul: the first king of the Yi dynasty conscripted 200,000 workmen to construct a great wall around Seoul, his new capital. It was 7 miles long, up to 20 feet wide, from 10–20 feet high, and contained 4 great gates and 4 smaller ones. Today, the remains are well inside the city which has grown to over one million inhabitants

Long known as the 'Hermit Kingdom', Korea is said to have evolved, quite alone, many things which other nations produced only by united effort: the celestial observatory, the spinning wheel, the art of pottery, movable metal type, paper money, the rain-gauge, even the armour-plated warships used by Admiral Yi Soon-sin to defeat Japanese invaders in 1592.

TRAVELLERS' TALES

Ancient travellers told how education flourished. They actually meant Chinese education, for the Koreans, it seems, did not consider themselves learned unless they could, with the light strokes of a brush, show themselves conversant with the language of Confucius and work their way up in the administrative hierarchy, relying only on the Chinese classics. They judged their own fine alphabet too simple, and good enough only for children.

What high ramparts enclosed this people. Only the most poetically inclined historians were interested in them. Records provide a description of thatched cottages where the Korean peasant lived, the marriage ceremonies and a few ritual dances and traditions of native cooking. Most travellers gave only a superficial picture of their own adventures in Korea. Only a few of them recounted Korean proverbs.

Yet Korea has a rich collection of folklore and songs, fables and fairytales: Cinderella is called Kongji; little Red Riding Hood will be eaten up by the tiger. Both the tiger and the tortoise figure as prominently in Korea as in China; the genii or jinns are as powerful as those in Norway.

Well, in what niche at last can be pigeon-holed this 'culture' of the old ancient lords, of peasants always in white, always in mourning, of beribboned dancers and of the silent silkworm breeders crouched on the mud floor unwinding the silk that they will never wear?

OLD BELIEFS DIE HARD

Religion may give an answer. Buddhism made inroads into Korea in AD 372 but it was not until early in the sixth century that this religion started to bloom. Buddhism spread its influence through the princely courts in marvellous works of architecture, piety and philosophy; the temples, still rising noble and serene above the fir trees are favourite subjects of the modern photographer.

Then, Confucianism replaced Buddhism: and the official doctrines of family and national loyalties were built on the ruins of monasteries where the monks eked out a miserable existence, though still receiving the humble devotion of the womenfolk. The ancestor cult was confined to the educated class: and shamanism, which had once been the nucleus in popular faith, still has a hold, though to a far lesser degree, on simple minds. Holy places are still revered, mountains shelter genii and under the sacred trees the passer-by still places pebbles . . .

It was late in the sixteenth century that literature on Catholicism was first introduced to Korea. This Western religion started to gain popularity in the middle of the seventeenth century. The first European Catholic priest, Father Maubant, entered Korea in 1835 and Protestantism came to Korea in 1884.

In the fifteenth century, Korean learned men compiled an *Annals of Koryo Dynasty*, an encyclopaedia at the time (1454) in 139 volumes, but it is doubtful whether they even wrote about the daily practices of the common people. In any case, the average Korean would not have access to these works, for, like the Official Public Records, they were not written in his language.

What first strikes any traveller to Korea are the elegant and stately palace buildings in and around Seoul and the Buddhist temples located deep in picturesque mountains. Ordinary residences, whether thatched or tiled, have the unique heating system called *ondol*. The system comprises a hot floor and an oven in the kitchen where fuel is burned to warm the floor.

The traditional Korean dress consists of loose robes and wide trousers for men and short, close-fitting jackets and flowing skirts for women. Women still prefer their traditional costumes whereas men, especially urbanites, prefer Western dress. Men wearing traditional loose white robes and horse hair hats and holding long bamboo pipes are rarely seen nowadays.

Best known among Korean foods are *kimchi*, a highly spiced pickled combination of radishes, cabbages and other vegetables, and *pulgogi*, delicious beef barbecued over a charcoal fire.

THE ARTS

The historical literature of both Korea and China records the great attachment of ancient Korean society to music and dance.

The *Komun'go*, a six-stringed zither, was invented by a prime minister of Koguryo in the fifth century while the *kayagum*, a twelve-stringed zither, was invented and played in the kingdom of Kara in the middle of the sixth century. At present the Court Music Department of the Royal Household preserves sixty-four oriental musical instruments and 242 compositions dating back to ancient times. The sixty-four instruments comprise eleven metallic, two stone, thirteen string, thirteen bamboo, one gourd, three earthen, eighteen leather and three wooden instruments.

For more than a thousand years, many aspects of Korean art have been truly great. Experts have spoken of the pottery of the country as the finest in the world, especially the refined Koryo fine arts represented in its celadon ware. This jade-coloured celadon won great admiration for its elegant colour and lovely shape. At the same time, the white celadon of the Yi dynasty, noted for its simple colour and shape, shows another unique aspect of Korean fine arts.

The masterpiece of ancient Korean sculpture is the figure of Buddha in the Sokkulam, a stone cave shrine, built in 752 near Kyongju, the capital of Silla. The artificial cave was built with granite blocks. The five-metre-high entrance is so placed as to allow the first rays of the rising sun to illuminate the enormous white granite Buddha in the centre of the cave. Disciples are carved in exquisite bas-relief on the circular interior walls of the dome-shaped cave. It is known that Japanese sculpture developed in the sixth century from Korean art and that, generally speaking, Korea was an indispensable channel through which civilization was introduced into Japan; for many centuries the Japanese called Korea the Treasure Land of the West.

The enchantment of Thailand

Leonard Cottrell

Thailand—what does the name conjure up? Pagodas with steep, many-tiered roofs of red and green tiles, with gilded, pointed eaves? Buddhist priests in yellow robes gliding among the tricycle taxis and swarming traffic of Bangkok? A group of dancers in scarlet and green robes spangled with gold, and high, golden head-dresses, moving gracefully through the movements of the classical dance to the

Two centuries ago, King Rama I chose the small village of Bangkok as the site for his new capital. Today it is a city of 800,000 people, whose skyline is scattered with the elaborate roofs and spires of 400 temples

clashing music of xylophones and high, thin, flutes ? Those who have visited Thailand, the modern name for old Siam, will certainly recollect those impressions, as I do whenever the name is mentioned.

But there is another side to Thailand. In Bangkok, the capital, one can buy practically everything the West can provide; the latest motorcars, refrigerators, washing machines, cameras, radiograms. There are luxurious hotels, restaurants with a European cuisine and, in the suburbs, beautiful modern villas set in landscape gardens, and as well-appointed as any in London or Paris.

Yet, side by side with huge modern ferroconcrete cinemas showing Hollywood films, cheek by jowl with the modern banks and office blocks, are the ancient *klongs* or canals on which lives an enormous, literally floating population of Thai families in covered-in boats. And as one drives beyond the broad, smoothly asphalted Raj-Damnern Avenue one comes upon dusty lanes between rows of wooden houses raised on stilts above the flood-water, and sees mothers washing their babies in the same muddy water which most of them have to boil for drinking as against the well-to-do people who order distilled water in bottles called 'Polaris'.

It is partly this clash between East and West that has brought about the need for new educational methods in Thailand. Not only is there an urgent need for Thai technicians to operate western machinery; engineers for the power-houses,

builders, garage mechanics, machinists and so on, but, in the words of a Thai teacher: 'It is necessary to make the children understand the relationship between nations, to make them know their own country better and to understand their responsibility to improve it.'

In 1949 Thailand invited Unesco and other UN specialized agencies such as the Food and Agricultural Organization and the International Labour Office, to take part in an experimental pilot project in the area round Cha-choeng-sao, a small town some seventy miles from Bangkok.

I travelled by train from Bangkok to Cha-choeng-sao, through mile after mile of completely flat country. Immediately outside Bangkok there are a few trees, chiefly bamboos, and here and there small cultivated plots—long straight rows of vegetables with irrigation canals between them, and men with bare feet and huge straw hats moving among the plots. Then come the ricefields, mile after mile of pale green—the green of an English meadow in spring—stretching to the horizon. Thailand is one of the greatest rice-producing countries in the Far East and the country's prosperity largely depends on the quality of the rice crop.

Cha-choeng-sao itself is a small town, built mainly of wood, like most Thai country towns, and standing on a broad, brown river, the Bangpakong. Scattered around it, on the riverside and beside the innumerable canals, are smaller villages, each with its wooden school-building, usually with a balcony overlooking the

river. It is in these schools that UN agencies personnel and their Thai counterparts (for each adviser works alongside a Thai teacher or 'counterpart') are conducting their experiment. The project's headquarters is in a big wooden building adjoining one of the schools at Cha-choeng-sao, which is now being extended to accommodate members of the mission.

The Europeans and Thais live and work together, there are offices, a conference room, a dining-room and dormitories, but life at Cha-choeng-sao is by no means luxurious. Water has to be carried by the common people from the river in big earthenware jars, from which one pours water over oneself when taking a shower, which, during nine months of the year is pretty often, or alternatively they must keep a lot of big earthenware jars to capture rainwater during the rains for use during the dry season. At night the staff sleep under mosquito nets, and DDT sprays are used in the constant war against the mosquitoes which swarm in after dark.

In spite of these discomforts the atmosphere is happy and comradely at Cha-choeng-sao. One could hardly help feeling happy in Thailand for the Thais are a friendly people, generous almost to a fault. The UN advisers and their Thai counterparts discuss together, and the discussions which take place over the dining-room table, or in the little riverside cafe are both friendly and outspoken.

'They work together alongside us,' the head of the mission told me, 'they watch our methods and discuss them with us. Sometimes they agree with us; sometimes they have better ideas of their own. But it is a joint effort all along the line.'

At one school I watched a fascinating experiment in history teaching. The subject was an episode in the life of King Ramakamheng the Great, one of the Thai kings of the Sukhotai period (thirteenth century). This King is one of the heroes of Thailand. He developed his country's administration, religion and especially home and industrial pottery-making.

After the teacher had described certain events in the life of the King, several small children came forward dressed in the costume of the period. One boy wearing a black jacket with a gold belt, a long white robe trimmed at the sleeves with gold, an enormous black and gold hat and pink striped trousers, who represented the King, seated himself on a school chair which served him as a throne. His prime minister, played by another small boy, and dressed with similar magnificence, came forward on his knees to receive the commands of the King.

'We have given justice in our government,' piped the little King, 'and if there are any abuses people can address themselves to me. The provinces are inspected by our own chosen men, who are our eyes and our ears. . . . Let us do this work with all our hearts so that in the future it may provide a livelihood for our people.'

Then two even smaller boys appeared, dressed in green jackets and black skull-caps. They represented Chinese craftsmen whom King Ramakamheng introduced into Thailand to teach his people the art of ceramics. These boys then handed out modelling clay, and, to the accompaniment of singing, the children set about making pots, vases and dishes under the guidance of the two 'Chinese' potters.

The whole idea, of course, was to turn what would probably have been a dull lesson in history into something alive and interesting, something in which the children could take an active part.

My last evening in Bangkok was spent at the Silpakorn Theatre, the Thai equivalent of a National Theatre. Here students of the Institute of Fine Arts present episodes from the country's classical drama, based on the ancient Hindu epic *The Ramayana* which in Thailand is called *The Ramakien*. It was a masked play, called in Thailand the *Khon*. Almost all the actors wore masks, and mimed their parts, the voices being spoken or sung by a chorus off-stage. The costumes were magnificent, scarlets and greens and yellows spangled with gold; towering gold head-dresses, gold embroidery, golden ornaments, all scintillating in the brilliant stage lighting. The play, which was more of a ballet than a drama, took a leisurely course, watched by the attentive Siamese audience which knew every line of the verse, every note of the music, every movement of the dance. For more than three-and-a-half hours I was dazzled by the colour, bewitched by the grace of the dancers, fascinated by the music. The effect was such that when eventually I left the theatre and threaded my way through the clamorous traffic of Bangkok I felt confused and bewildered.

When I said to a Thai friend that night, 'as a Buddhist you have as your ideal the attainment of serenity of soul, inner peace', he agreed. 'Then,' I asked him, 'how do you expect to attain serenity of

Thailand is anxious to accept the best of Western ideas and techniques. But the country is equally determined to maintain its deep-rooted cultural traditions such as the teaching of the graceful classical dances

soul by bringing in Western ideas, Western hustle. Western machinery, automobiles, refrigerators and so on? The play which I saw tonight,' I continued, 'was a superb work of art, the product of a culture much older than ours, something supremely civilized and worthwhile. Surely you don't want to exchange that for canned music and Western films? It seems to me that you are on the wrong track. Sometimes I think that instead of the West bringing technical assistance to the East, the East should be bringing spiritual assistance to the West!'

I said this to test his reactions, adding that the Thais whom I had met seemed a very happy people, generous to strangers, contented, smiling, serene, even if some of them were relatively poor. His answer was interesting, and did much to strengthen my faith in what the United Nations are attempting to do in Thailand.

'It is true,' he replied, after some reflection, 'that not all the things which the West has brought to Thailand are good things, although many Thais like them. But you should remember the good things too. Take health for example. Those people you saw in the country, and here in Bangkok, living on the canals, bathing in the same water that they have to use for

other purposes, including drinking, yet they are happy, it is true. But only if they are well.'

He paused and then added: 'Have you thought of the thousands who die each year from malaria, typhoid and other preventable diseases?'

He went on to speak with high praise of the work of the World Health Organization team operating in northern Thailand, and reminded me that a huge area had been cleared of that dreadful disease, yaws, by the use of penicillin injections. 'As for your fears that the culture of Thailand may be destroyed by Western innovations,' he said, 'I don't think there is much fear of that. You will never turn the Thais into Westerners. Our religion and culture are too deeply rooted for that. No! I think that in the end we shall take the best which the West has to offer, and leave the rest to you.'

10 Influences of great men: Tagore and Gandhi

Introduction

In every age great men arise who are affected not only by their own and related cultures, but who in their turn influence people far beyond the confines of their own countries. The East has produced many great men. The examples selected in this chapter are two twentieth-century Indians—the poet Rabindranath Tagore who was also philosopher, educator, novelist and painter and Mahatma Gandhi one of the outstanding figures of this age who led his people to independence using only the method of non-violent resistance —a method which had and has repercussions throughout the world. His greatness came from the spirit in search of truth, his influence and unparalleled leadership from his universal love and faith in mankind. He drew his strength from what he called 'soul force', an inner strength. Belief in 'soul-force' and non-violence cannot be sustained without an abiding faith in the innate goodness of all one's fellow human beings.

Gandhi is one of the great figures of the twentieth century, unique in many ways; but perhaps his most outstanding contribution lay in his supreme achievement of applying and transforming the principle of non-violent resistance into a successful instrument for achieving liberty, justice and peace. In his hands it became not just a personal discipline but a social technique to resolve conflicts and for community or national emancipation. He opened up before the world a new way of life, the path of peace, a method of combating in a creative and constructive way aggression and exploitation—whether it was fighting for the rights of Indians in South Africa, for the rights of untouchables or for the national independence of India. His constant references to the world beyond India prove that he felt his beliefs and techniques were equally applicable to the rest of the world. The Gandhian strategy of social dissent, though not new historically, gained special significance as it has come to be more widely adopted in recent times. The Gandhian technique, employed where bargaining was not possible, was pacific but involved active sacrifices. Non-violent resistance meant also the readiness of the participant to sacrifice his life for his principles. In recent years some people in other countries in the West have adopted this practice; the struggle in the United States for Civil Rights is fashioned on the Gandhian technique.

A study of Gandhi's writings and

Gandhi

Tagore

speeches makes it clear that One World and World Peace were inherent in his philosophy of life. When Gandhi was fighting for the rights of the Indians in the Transvaal, Tolstoy in one of the letters he wrote to Gandhi referred to the purity of the means he had adopted to fight the evil of racial injustice in South Africa and said that what he was doing was of world significance.

Gandhi will always be remembered as perhaps the first non-violent liberator of a nation. He made the Indian masses feel a new sense of dignity. He taught them that in their endurance and patience were hidden enormous reserves of strength which not even the most powerful imperialism could overcome. By precept and example he infused in the Indian people a new consciousness of strength and self-respect. Gandhi realized that violence can provoke only greater violence. Hatred cannot be overcome by hatred. It is love alone that can triumph over hate and violence. His method of fighting an alien imperialism was therefore not by methods of violence, but by an appeal to its own conscience. His conception of non-violent non-cooperation was not only superb strategy for an unarmed nation, it was also the declaration of a new political faith based on man's innate goodness and rationality.

Gandhi's life was rooted in India's religious tradition with its emphasis on a passionate search for truth, a profound reverence for life, the ideal of non-attachment and the readiness to sacrifice all for the knowledge of God. Gandhi himself said 'thanks to the tradition of our ancient seers, sages and saints, if there is a heritage that India can share with the world, it is this gospel of forgiveness and faith which is her proud possession.'

Rabindranath Tagore is perhaps the only Asian poet whose genius was recognized all over the world during his own lifetime. Honours were heaped on him by learned societies and humble institutions alike.

Tagore was called the Sentinel of the East and the Poet Laureate of Asia. His writings have been translated into almost all the major languages of the world. His book of poems *Gitanjali* (song offerings) was published in 1913 and he was awarded the Nobel Prize for literature—the first time an Asian had been so honoured.

Poems, novels and plays translated into English by the author and into other languages often by illustrious writers, presented 'the mind of India' to a whole generation of Occidentals.

By his own countrymen, too, he was considered a profound sage whose words were worth the closest attention. His observations on the relation between Indian thought and Western civilization exercised undeniable influence. The East he said, must accept industrialization and technical progress but he considered that it was the role of the Orient to show that certain pernicious influences could be avoided. He insisted that above all the basic spirituality of Eastern thought should be kept intact. He believed therefore that education had a primary role to play in this evolution and its fundamental object was 'not merely to give us information but make our life in harmony with all existence'.

He converted his school Santineketan (the Abode of Peace) into a world university called 'Vishva Bharati' so that it became not only a centre of Indian culture, but of world culture. With a deep faith in the cultural federation of different races and cultures of the world, he devoted himself in his writings and thinking to the cause of understanding and friendly co-operation with the whole world.

'Humanity is torn by suffering and suspicion,' he wrote 'by disharmony which has wrought havoc in the very midst of our life on earth. It is for us in the Brotherhood of Letters to rescue humanity from the misery of unnatural relationships. To whatever land we may belong, this must be our common mission on this plane of united effort to achieve goodwill between man and man, establish a secure foundation of fellowship which will save humanity from suicidal war.'

Tagore saw his people in India and in Asia achieving this goodwill and establishing a solid foundation of fellowship, not by attempting to wipe out their differences, which he believed neither possible nor desirable, but by accepting the belief 'unity not in spite of the differences but through them. Let all human races retain their own individual personalities and yet come together not into a uniformity that is dead but into a unity that is living.'

All his life Tagore showed no mercy towards nationalism, which he termed 'that dominant intellectual abstraction', but he offered a glimpse of hope of a world transfigured 'when the diverse races and the nations have evolved their perfected distinct characteristics but all attached to the stem of humanity by a bond of love.'

Gandhi and Tagore differed greatly in physical appearance and personal habits, and in general outlook—at several moments of crisis in India's political history, the two disagreed over the course of action to be taken. But these were on the surface; their deeper affinity transcended all occasional barriers—their recognition of the important role of education, their belief not in narrow nationalism but internationalism, their belief in the basic spirituality of Eastern thought and their belief and faith in human dignity bound these two great men together—the man whom Churchill once described as the 'naked fakir' and the aristocratic poet.

Some aspects of the thoughts and lives of these two men are considered in the extracts which follow.

Mahatma Gandhi

Mahatma Gandhi was assassinated by a Hindu fanatic on 30 January 1948 and his tragic death shocked the world. Below is an extract from an extempore speech delivered by Professor Sarvepalli Radhakrishnan (then Vice Chairman of Unesco Executive Board and later President of India) at Unesco House.

'There are many famous men, many important men, big in their own way, big in their own space and time, but they are small in stature compared to Mahatma Gandhi. His mastery over himself, his courage and consistency of life, his profound sincerity of spirit, his abounding, all-embracing charity and that strong conviction that he had, and shared with other great ones of history, that martyrdom of the body is nothing compared to the refinement of the soul. All these great qualities show, if I may say so, his essentially religious genius: the impact of religion on life, the impact of the values of eternity on the shifting problems of the world of time.

'The kind of religion Mahatma Gandhi professed is one to which even the most sceptical, even the most intellectual highbrows could pay allegiance. "There are people who call God truth. I say Truth is God. There are men in the world who have denied God, but there are no men who have denied Truth. I am a believer in Truth. That is God for me".'

'You may always take it that the prophets of the spirit, by simply standing outside history, mould history. They leave the greatest impression on history simply because they have this quality of detachment from any kind of allegiance to earthly possessions themselves. Gandhi belonged to that type. He had no attraction for the material things of life so far as his personal life was concerned, though he was anxious to make the material conditions of life better for large numbers of men.

'Freedom for him was not merely a political fact, it was a social reality. He was anxious that India should be converted from social corruption and from communal strife, and that the people raise themselves in their own esteem, discover their own dignity in their own conscience, in the depths of their own souls.

'He felt that while August 15th was a day of triumph so far as political problems were concerned, it was a day of humiliation because the country was then enslaved by petty communal passions.

'I met Gandhi early in December 1947 and when I was discussing the political situation with him, he said: "Either I heal the differences or I die in the process." He died in the process.

'And yet if there is any message that he has left behind, it is the message that we can cure these ills only by the methods of peace and reconciliation.

'Whatever we may think about Gandhi's part in the liberation of India, his essential object was not so much the liberation of India as the liberation of the world. He was trying to use India as an experiment by which he would be able to suggest to the world other ways by which differences could be adjusted and settled.

'There are people who tell us: non-violence is the dream of the wise, violence is the history of man. We know the results which such battles have achieved. But there is another battle steadily going on in the hearts of men: a battle for human decency, for human dignity, for the removal of physical strife which constricts human life, for preparing the world for a condition of warlessness. That is the battle which is going on, and so far as that battle is concerned there has not been a greater fighter than Gandhi himself.

'It is one thing to bring about changes in the social architecture of the world. We can go about establishing world organizations, but no world organization can thrive unless that spirit is there: that spirit, that love is stronger than hate: that understanding is much better than lack of understanding; and if Gandhi stood out for any ideal, it was for this ideal of developing unity of religion, unity of peoples, unity of cultural thought, and for preparing the world for a world culture, a world conscience. This world conscience is the spiritual counterpart of the material world community. These world organizations cannot be established unless the spirit for which Gandhi stood is there to inspire them.

'He has met with the fate which awaits all those who are ahead of their time; the victim of misunderstanding, reaction, hatred and violent death.

'We made Socrates drink death, we nailed Jesus to the cross, we lighted the faggots which burned the martyrs, and Gandhi has not escaped that fate. And yet his life has a kind of classical completeness about it.

'Here he was, laying down his life, facing unreason, hatred, anger, dissension, and at the last moment with the name of God on his lips, and with love and forgiveness in his heart. Thus as he crumpled down, with blood streaming from his lips, he lifted up both his hands and greeted the murderer who was there facing him. You cannot conceive of a death more noble, less hateful than that.

'His body is reduced to ashes, which are scattered on the waters, but the spirit in him is a light from above which will penetrate far into space and time, and inspire countless generations.'

The speeches and writings of Gandhi

Sarvepalli Radhakrishnan
A great teacher appears once in a while. Several centuries may pass by without the advent of such a one. That by which he is known is his life. He first lives and then tells others how they may live likewise. Such a teacher was Gandhi. The following selections from his speeches and writings will give the reader some idea of the workings of Gandhi's mind, the growth of his thoughts and the practical techniques which he adopted.

Gandhi's religion was a rational and ethical one. He would not accept any belief which did not appeal to his reason or any injunction which did not commend to his conscience.

If we believe in God, not merely with our intellect but with our whole being, we will love all mankind without any distinction of race or class, nation or religion. We will work for the unity of mankind. 'I have known no distinction between relatives and strangers, countrymen and foreigners, white and coloured, Hindus and Indians of other faiths whether Mussulmans, Parsees, Christians or Jews. I may say that my heart has been incapable of making any such distinctions.'

This view leads naturally to the adoption of non-violence as the best means for solving all problems, national and international. Gandhi affirmed that he was not a visionary but a practical idealist. Non-violence is meant not merely for saints and sages but for the common people also.

Gandhi was the first in human history to extend the principle of non-violence from the individual to the social and political plane. He entered politics for the purpose of experimenting with non-violence and establishing its validity.

In the struggle for India's independence, he insisted that we should adopt civilized methods of non-violence and suffering. His stand for the freedom of India was not based on any hatred for Britain. We must hate the sin but not the sinner. 'For me patriotism is the same as humanity. I am patriotic because I am human and humane. I will not hurt England or Germany to serve India.' He believed that he rendered a service to the British in helping them to do the right thing by India. The result was not only the liberation of the Indian people but an increase in the moral resources of mankind.

In the present nuclear context, if we wish to save the world, we should adopt the principles of non-violence.

In the present predicament when we are not able to adjust ourselves to the new conditions which science has brought about, it is not easy to adopt the principles of non-violence, truth and understanding. But on that ground we should not give up the effort. While the obstinacy of the political leaders puts fear into our hearts, the common sense and conscience of the peoples of the world give us hope.

We live in an age which is aware of its own defeat and moral coarsening, an age in which old certainties are breaking down, the familiar patterns are tilting and cracking. It is our pride that one of the greatest figures of history lived in our generation, walked with us, spoke to us, taught us the way of civilized living. Plato said long ago: 'There always are in the world a few inspired men whose acquaintance is beyond price.'

Gandhi's words

'My notion of *democracy* is that under it the weakest should have the same opportunity as the strongest. That can never happen except through non-violence.'

'The golden rule of conduct is *mutual toleration*, seeing that we will never all think alike and we shall see Truth in fragment and from different angles of vision. Conscience is not the same thing for all. Whilst, therefore, it is a good guide for individual conduct, imposition of that conduct upon all will be an insufferable interference with everybody's freedom of conscience.'

'Even the most despotic government cannot stand except for the consent of the governed, which consent is often forcibly procured by the despot. Immediately the subject ceases to fear the despotic force, his power is gone.'

'I do not want my house to be walled in on all sides and my windows to be stuffed. I want the cultures of all lands to be blown about my house as freely as possible. But I refuse to be blown off my feet by any. I would have our young men and women with literary tastes to learn as much of English and other world languages as they like, and then expect them to give the benefits of their learning to India and to the world.'

'I would develop in the child his hands, his brain and his soul. The hands have almost atrophied. The soul has been altogether ignored.'

'To call *woman* the weaker sex is a libel, it is man's injustice to woman. If by strength is meant brute strength then indeed, is woman less brute than man. If by strength is meant moral power, then woman is immeasurably man's superior. Has she not greater intuition, is she not more self-sacrificing, has she not greater powers of endurance, has she not greater courage? Without her man could not be. If non-violence is the law of our being, the future is with woman. . . . Who can make a more effective appeal to the heart than woman?'

'I have nothing new to teach the world. Truth and non-violence are as old as the hills.'

'God has created different faiths just as

He has the votaries thereof. How can I even secretly harbour the thought that my neighbour's faith is inferior to mine and wish that he should give up his faith and embrace mine? As a true and loyal friend, I can only wish and pray that he may live and grow perfect in his own faith. In God's house there are many mansions and they are equally holy.'

NON-VIOLENCE

'*Non-violence* is the greatest force at the disposal of mankind. It is mightier than the mightiest weapon of destruction devised by the ingenuity of man.'

'My experience, daily growing stronger and richer, tells me that there is no peace for individuals or for nations without practising Truth and Non-violence to the uttermost extent possible for man. The policy of retaliation has never succeeded.'

'I can no more preach non-violence to a coward than I can tempt a blind man to enjoy healthy scenes. Non-violence is the summit of bravery. And in my own experience, I have had no difficulty in demonstrating to men trained in the school of violence the superiority of non-violence. As a coward, which I was for years, I harboured violence. I began to prize non-violence only when I began to shed cowardice.'

'I am not a visionary. I claim to be a practical idealist. Religion of non-violence is not merely for the *rishis* and saints. It is meant for the common people as well.'

'Passive resistance is a method of securing rights by personal suffering; it is the reverse of resistance by arms. When I refuse to do a thing that is repugnant to my conscience, I use soul-force. For instance, the government of the day has passed a law which is applicable to me. I do not like it. If by using violence I force the government to repeal the law, I am employing what may be termed body-force. If I do not obey the law and accept the penalty for its breach, I use soul-force. It involves sacrifice of self.'

'The accumulated experience of the past thirty years, the first eight of which were in South Africa, fills me with the greatest hope that in the adoption of non-violence lies the future of India and the world. It is the most harmless and yet equally effective way of dealing with the political and economic wrongs of the down-trodden portion of humanity. I

have known from early youth that non-violence is not a cloistered virtue to be practised by the individual for the peace and final salvation, but it is a rule of conduct for society if it is to live consistently with human dignity and make progress towards the attainment of peace for which it has been yearning for ages past.'

'Non-violence in its dynamic condition means conscious suffering. It does not mean meek submission to the will of the evil-doer, but it means the putting of one's whole soul against the will of the tyrant. Working under this law of our being, it is possible for a single individual to defy the whole might of an unjust empire to save his honour, his religion, his soul, and lay the foundation for that empire's fall or its regeneration.'

'I must continue to argue till I convert opponents or I own defeat. For my mission is to convert every Indian, even Englishmen and finally the world, to non-violence for regulating mutual relations whether political, economic, social or religious.'

'Passive resistance is regarded as the weapon of the weak, but the resistance for which I had to coin a new name altogether is the weapon of the strongest. I had to coin a new word to signify what I meant. But its matchless beauty lies in the fact that, though it is the weapon of the strongest, it can be wielded by the weak in body, by the aged, and even by the children if they have stout hearts. And since resistance in Satyāgraha is offered through self-suffering, it is a weapon pre-eminently open to women.'

Rabindranath Tagore

PHILOSOPHER, EDUCATOR, NOVELIST, POET AND PAINTER

Satyajit Ray

Rabindranath Tagore has left behind him a heritage of words and music and poetry and ideas and ideals, that has the power to move us today and in the years to come. He wrote over three thousand songs and poems. His short stories are gems of prose composition. In these he depicted the lives of common people with sympathetic insight, revealing their problems and portraying their courage under suffering. His plays and novels give a masterly analysis of the historical and social forces which gave shape to India's literature.

The Tagore family had an impressive

lineage; it dated back to the first group of learned Brahmins that came from Kanauj and settled in Bengal in the eighth century. Tagore's grandfather, Dwarkanath, was one of the most brilliant and colourful figures of the nineteenth century. The talented family into which Tagore was born in 1861 proved a potent factor in the flowering of his genius. His grandfather went to England in defiance of contemporary conventions. His father was a leader of revolt against orthodoxy in his championship of the Brahmo faith and among Rabindranath's brothers and sisters were a scholar, a poet, a musician and the first woman to edit a literary journal in India. It was a household which hummed with activity.

At the age of seven Rabindranath was sent to school, he went to four schools and hated them all. He was only thirteen when his first book of poems, *Kabikahini*, came out. When he was sixteen his brother brought out a literary magazine called *Bharati*, and Rabindranath found an admirable platform for his literary activities. His essays included pieces on European poets like Dante and Petrarch.

In the summer of 1879 Rabindranath went to England. While there he became acquainted with Western music. Some of the tunes he had learnt found their way into his enchanting opera, *Valmiki-Pratibha*. There were other tunes, however, which had their origin in classical Indian *ragas*, used for the first time in an operatic context.

A year later Rabindranath published *Sandhya-Sangeet* and this was the beginning of his pre-eminence among the rising writers of the day. Shortly after his marriage at the age of twenty-two, he went to look after the family estates and found himself in the very heart of rural Bengal, in the area of the river Padma.

With a worldly wisdom unusual in a poet but characteristic of the Tagores, Rabindranath in later life set out in a practical way to improve the lot of the poor peasants of his estates and his own gain from this intimate contact with the fundamental aspects of life and nature, and the influence of this contact on his own life and work are beyond measure.

Living mostly in his boat and watching the life through the window, a whole new world of sights and sounds and feelings opened up before him. It was a world in which the moods of people and the moods of nature were inextricably interwoven.

The people found room in a succession of great short stories, and nature in an outpouring of exquisite songs and poems. Dominant was the mood of the rains, exultant and terrible.

In 1901 Rabindranath decided to take over some property belonging to his father in Bolpur. This property had been handed over by the board of trustees and the board specified that the place was to be used for meditation. A temple of worship had been built and close by was a place for meditation, Santiniketan, the Abode of Peace. Rabindranath had been worrying about the education of his children and he decided to start an experimental educational institution in Santiniketan. It was to be a school but not like the schools that had been the nightmare of his own childhood. It was to be like the forest hermitages of classical India.

In December 1903 the decision of the Governor General to split Bengal into two provinces was published. The idea was to create a separate province with a Muslim majority, which would induce a rift between the two main religious groups and thus avert the possible growth of a united front against the Government.

But in proposing the partition, Curzon merely fanned the flame of patriotism that had been smouldering in the minds of certain visionaries all though the period of the renaissance in Bengal. These men now came to the fore and led the millions to rise in protest. The series of stirring patriotic songs which Rabindranath composed for the occasion were sung in processions in the streets of Calcutta with the poet himself in the lead.

After the partition of Bengal in 1905 Rabindranath turned to other activities— teaching at his school, editing journals and engaging himself in almost every conceivable form of literary activity. That his own countrymen now regarded him as their leading man of letters was proved by his fiftieth birthday celebrations in Calcutta. Sponsored by the Bengal Academy of Letters and attended by thousands, it was a unique literary manifestation in India. But to the outside world Rabindranath was still an unknown name.

In 1912 Rabindranath visited England to study the educational methods of the West and also to acquaint the West with his work at Santiniketan. Purely by chance he showed some of his work to William Rothenstein who had met the poet on an earlier visit to India. Rothenstein was so impressed that he sent a copy of the translation to W B Yeats, who said, 'I know of no man in my time who has done anything in the English language to equal these lyrics. Even as I read them in these literal English translations, they are exquisite in style and thought.'

The *Gitanjali* was published in England in the same year, and the Nobel Prize came in 1913, and a knighthood in 1915. Touring the United States and Japan in 1916, Rabindranath made eloquent appeals for peace. He felt that world peace could only be achieved through intellectual cooperation between nations. 'The call has come to every individual in the present age to prepare himself for the dawn of a new era, when man shall discover his soul in the spiritual unity of all human beings.'

In December 1918 the school at Santiniketan was given a new name *Vishya Bharati*, 'the World University'. In the difficult period of political upheaval in India after the war and particularly after the massacre at Jallianwallahbagh when the British General Dyer opened fire on a peaceful crowd, Rabindranath Tagore addressed a letter to the Viceroy, Lord Chelmsford, condemning the Government for the killing at Jallianwallahbagh and asked to be relieved of his knighthood.

The next ten years of Rabindranath's life were filled with ceaseless activity. The urge to travel, and the necessity to collect funds for his university, took him to all parts of the world and the West and much of the East, welcomed him with open arms.

Wherever he went, he spread the message of peace and stressed the importance of intellectual cooperation between nations. He said: 'We ought to know that isolation of life and culture is not a thing of which any nation can be proud. In the human world, giving is exchanging, it is not one-sided.'

His great humanist ideas found an echo in the best minds of Europe, and some became his close friends.

In the meantime, the institution of Santiniketan had come a long way from its modest beginnings. Its scope for studies had greatly increased. There was Kalabhawan for the study of painting, under masters like Nandalal Bose, who was himself a pupil of Abanindranath, a nephew of the poet. The Sangeet Bhawan which neglected no branch of Indian music had also grown under Dinendranath, another of the poet's nephews. Special provisions had been made for conducting oriental studies, and scholars came from abroad and stayed to lecture for study and research.

But there were some Europeans who did even more than that. C F Andrews, a missionary who had met the poet in England came to the Ashram in its early days – drawn by the poet's personality – and stayed on till his death, working with a selfless devotion to the poet and his cause that few Indians could equal.

The poet's last European tour began with a visit to Oxford where he delivered the series of Hibbert lectures which were called *The Religion of Man*. It was at this time that Rabindranath went to the Soviet Union for the first time. On the eve of his departure from Moscow he told his hosts: 'You have recognized the truth that in extirpating all social evils one has to go to the root, and the only way to it is through education.'

In 1931 the leading citizens of Calcutta united in an appeal to observe the poet's seventieth birthday. The sponsors of the *Golden Book of Tagore* which was a testimony to the love and reverence that the intellectuals of the world bore for the poet consisted of three Europeans and two Indians; there was Romain Rolland from France, Albert Einstein from Germany and the poet Kostes Palamas from Greece. The Indian sponsors were the scientist Jagadish Chandra Bose, and Mahatma Gandhi.

At the age of seventy Rabindranath found a new outlet for his creative urge in the form of painting.

The last years of the poet's life were spent largely in his beloved Santiniketan. In his writings he was now producing some of his most mature, original and striking works and these included text books and nonsense rhymes for children, not an unusual occupation for someone who had loved and understood children all his life and done so much to mould them for a better future.

On the occasion of his eightieth birthday celebrations, in 1941, Rabindranath composed a message – his last message to the world. It was called 'Crisis in Civilization'. In the course of the message Rabindranath said: 'I had at one time believed that the springs of civilization could issue out of the heart of Europe. But today, when I am about to leave the world, that faith has deserted me. I look around

and see the crumbling ruins of a proud civilization strewn like a vast heap of futility. And yet, I shall not commit the previous sin of losing faith in Man. I shall await for the day when the holocaust will end and the air will be rendered clean with the spirit of service and sacrifice. Perhaps that dawn will come from this horizon, from the East, where the sun rises. On that day will unvanquished Man retrench his path of conquest, surmounting all barriers, to win back his lost human heritage.'

'The enchantment of lines'

Sandy Koffler

At the age of sixty-seven, Tagore felt an irresistible urge for a new form of expression. A latent genius long asleep within him suddenly revealed itself, and the venerable sage of India became a painter. For twelve years he devoted his energy to drawing and painting, little by little abandoning his writer's pen. When he died in 1941 at the age of eighty, he had produced nearly 2,000 works of art, of extraordinary design and strange rhythmic beauty.

The poet turned to painting when he discovered that his hand was moving automatically across the pages of his manuscripts, transforming the scratches and erasures into designs. 'I have fallen under the enchantment of lines,' he explained.

Rabindranath's scratches and erasures took the form of thin horizontal threads which he enclosed in an outline something like a cartouche.

His first exhibition, held in the Galerie Pigalle in Paris in 1930, created a sensation not only in the French capital but in India where his own countrymen were astounded to learn that their beloved poet was also a painter. The same year a few examples of his works were shown in London, Berlin and New York. His first exhibition in India came in February 1932, when 265 of his drawings, paintings and engravings were displayed to the public in Calcutta, followed the next year by another exhibition in Bombay. In 1946 four of his paintings were included in an international exhibition of modern art organized by Unesco in Paris.

Nevertheless, to the world at large, Rabindranath Tagore the Painter still remains practically unknown.

Although he used all kinds of paints and

produced coloured chalk drawings, pastels and later dry-points and etchings, Tagore's preferred medium was liquid colour. He used any ink at hand, usually ordinary fountain-pen ink. When this was not available, he crushed flower petals and used them as pigments. To obtain a glossy effect he chose different kinds of oils, particularly coconut oil and mustard oil. He rarely used a brush (when he did it was a home-made version) and disdained the artist's palette. Instead, he worked with cloth soaked in colour, the back of a fountain pen, his thumb, a stick or, more often, a knife.

Tagore was associated with the most celebrated painters and artists of the world for over half a century. In the course of his many voyages to foreign lands he acquired a profound firsthand knowledge of both Oriental and Western art. On a visit to Japan, for instance, he once left on a weekend trip to see a private art collection in Yokohama and stayed on for three months to make a minute study of the technique and styles of Japanese and Chinese painting. So deep was his interest in art that in 1920 he even founded an art school at Santiniketan.

Yet, despite all this, Tagore's art is peculiarly his own, without ties to either the past or the present. Rabindranath followed no set rules; his works are the spontaneous creations which sprang from his fertile imagination, simple, yet disconcerting, original, totally sincere and idealistic. Like his poetry they are deeply thought-provoking and shrouded in mystery, the outpouring of a man enamoured of pure beauty, form and colour. 'My morning was full of songs,' Tagore said, 'let sunset days be full of colour.'

Santiniketan

'ABODE OF PEACE'

Guy Wint

By its very nature Santiniketan is a criticism of the orthodox Indian universities. It is a protest against their size, against their soullessness, against the ugliness of many of their buildings, against the gradual falling away from the old invaluable Indian tradition of the devoted relationship of pupil and teacher. Rabindranath Tagore regarded education as an art, and also he thought that education proceeds best through art – and religion as understood by the poet and the artist.

Tagore painted most of his works on paper using inks or flower petals as pigments. He rarely gave them titles, though he called them 'my versification in lines'. *Left:* Exhausted pilgrim. *Right:* Mother and child. *Below left:* Tagore wrote: 'The black and white threads weave the destiny of man into a mystery of entanglements'

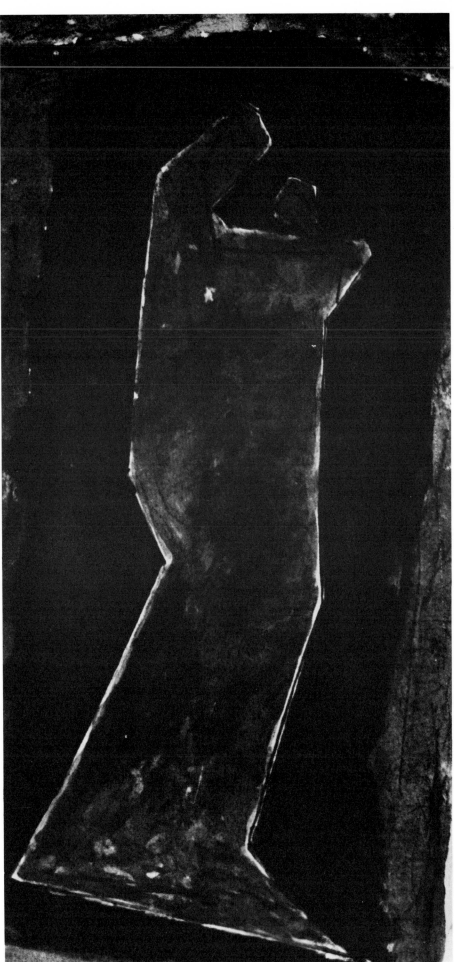

The guiding principle of Santiniketan is described in a celebrated pronouncement by Rabindranath. 'The highest education', he wrote, 'is that which does not merely give us information but makes our life in harmony with all existence. . . . Let us have access to the life that goes beyond death and rises, above all circumstances, let us find our God, let us live for that ultimate truth which emancipates us from the bondage of the dust and gives us the wealth, not of things but of inner light, not of power but of love.'

At Santiniketan, all the subjects which were taught in the Western-style universities could be studied, but the method of study was to be Indian, or at least Indian as interpreted by Rabindranath Tagore. The lecture room and the examination hall did not dominate; instead the teacher

Above: Here Mahatma Gandhi is received by Tagore at Santiniketan in 1940

taught the pupil through a personal relation. The imagination was cultivated as well as criticism. And in addition many subjects not taught in the Western-style universities were offered at Santiniketan, among them Indian dancing and music and contemporary Indian poetry. The result, it was claimed, was a better balanced personality. Those educated at Santiniketan felt themselves nurtured in an Indian tradition—through a live, developing tradition, not an ossified one.

Reading Tagore on education it is impossible not to be reminded again and again of Plato; and walking through Santiniketan it is easy to feel that one is visiting an academy not of the modern world but of Periclean Athens. In Santiniketan there is the same mixture of humanism and theism as in Plato; there is

the combined worship of beauty and exactness of thought. The dominant impressions which the visitor brings away are of an elegance alike of spirit and of externals, of simplicity, of decent and graceful leisure, and of abundant youth, but youth which is anything but raw or callow.

Some visitors have of course felt that such an institution was too precious for the strenuous and earthy contemporary India, with all its urgent problems of social and economic reform. Perhaps in its earlier days the criticism was partly fair. Even Gandhi was inclined to share the doubt. But Santiniketan has moved with the times and has been adaptable. That is a sign of its strength.

Soon after India became independent, Santiniketan was reorganized. It has been

incorporated as a statutory full-fledged university, with a much wider curriculum, offering courses to meet the needs of the new India. But emphatically it has not lost its special nature, or become a replica of other universities. It has preserved its autonomy, its traditions, its spirit and its special customs, its insistence on the living personal relation of teachers and pupils, its cultivation of the harmonious corporate life.

Today Santiniketan is at once school, university, research institution and international centre. The school is coeducational; boys and girls live in separate hostels but share the same class-rooms. kitchens and playgrounds. In the university, nearly all the ordinary subjects may be studied; but, following a tradition established by Rabindranath, students are encouraged to combine 'light-bearing' subjects (those inviting study for their own sake) with 'fruit-bearing ones' (those which have practical usefulness). 'Fruit-bearing' is very much in the centre of the research programme of the institution. At the neighbouring centre Sriniketan, some of the most stimulating work in modern India has been done on the sociology of peasant life and on methods of rural education. The man or woman who obtains part of his education in the College of Music and Dance is urged in due course to move over to Sriniketan and study his countrymen working at their humbler tasks.

Because of its international reputation, Santiniketan soon attracted scholars from the outside world. It became, and has remained, one of the most cosmopolitan places in Asia. This has been reflected in journals and annals, which are published by the institution.

One of its most interesting ventures at the moment is the systematic training of teachers intended for the villages. More will probably be heard of this in the future; it is a development which would certainly have delighted Rabindranath Tagore's friend, Mahatma Gandhi.

11 The women of new Asia

Introduction

A silent revolution has taken place in the last fifty years in the role played in society by the women of Asia. While the women of the West had to struggle dramatically to obtain their emancipation, the trail blazed by the gallant Suffragettes paved the way for the later emancipation of women in Asia. In India, for example, women like Annie Besant and Margaret Cousins in association with Indian women like Rajkumari Amrit Kaur, Dr Muthulakshmi Reddy, Mrs Sarojini Naidu, Lady Sivaswami Iyer and others, helped in the struggle for women's rights; Margaret Cousins organized the Woman's India Association in 1917. What is perhaps a little ironic is that women in India today enjoy greater freedom than their Western sisters because they receive equal pay for equal work!

Despite all this, even today the average Westerner's image of the Asian woman is something essentially feminine and exotic, confined merely to the house and not competing in careers which, till quite recently, even in the West, have been regarded as male preserves. It therefore comes as a surprise to realize that the world's first woman Prime Minister was an Asian—Mrs Bandaranaika of Ceylon, who was elected to the post in July 1960 and held it till 1965. India, too, has a woman Prime Minister, Mrs Indira Gandhi, re-elected for a second term in March 1967. This slim and outwardly frail-looking woman is certainly no mere figurehead and has undertaken a task that would have daunted many a brave man. For India, apart from being the largest democracy in the world, has had to face the serious impact of two successive droughts on her food production in addition to the many other difficulties which beset all developing countries on their road to economic development. Indira Gandhi can best be described as a child of Mahatma Gandhi's Indian revolution. She was only four when her father (India's first Prime Minister, Jawaharlal Nehru) was taken to prison for the first time in the non-co-operation movement. Shortly after her marriage, in connection with the Quit India Movement launched following the arrest of Gandhi and of the entire Congress Working Committee, she and her husband were sent to prison where she spent nearly a year. Indira, who has two sons, takes the duties of motherhood seriously and has not let her political responsibilities come in the way of her responsibilities to her children.

Indira Gandhi's own life illustrates very clearly the type of problems met by the women of New Asia. When first elected as Prime Minister after the tragic death of her predecessor Lal Bahadur Shastri she said: 'I do not regard myself as a woman. I am a person with a job. In the Indian Constitution all citizens are equal, regardless of sex, religion, language and state. And therefore I am just an Indian citizen and the first servant of the land.'

It is true that a woman's place in Muslim society has traditionally been strictly in the home. But a new wind of social change sweeping through Muslim countries is giving more women the chance to train for careers and professions. What does the average Westerner think of when he hears the words 'Muslim women of Asia'? More likely than not he conjures up a vision of princesses straight out of One Thousand and One Nights, clad in diaphanous veils and spending their lives nibbling sweetmeats while confined in harems guarded by great silent eunuchs. How far this legend is from the truth today is brought out in the article on Muslim Women in Pakistan and Indonesia where some eighty million Muslim women live.

Nearly fifty years ago, a sweeping revolution under the leadership and impelling drive of Kemal Ataturk gave birth to the modern Turkey. The spectacular changes in the status of Turkish women which it brought about have since become a goal to inspire those working for the emancipation of women in many other countries. A brief sketch on Ataturk and the emancipation of women shows how the position of Turkish women changed in a relatively short period.

In India, too, where from ancient times onwards men have played a dominant role, women have occupied places of honour in society and even wielded power in times of stress as well as of peace. We have only to look to ancient Hindu mythology, or to history, to provide such examples. During the Indian revolution of 1857 the gallant Rani of Jhansi, led her troops into battle against the British. What is perhaps even more significant is the fact that India's foremost feminists have been men. In their different ways, the early nineteenth-century reformer, Ram Mohan Roy, and later Mahatma Gandhi, Karve and Jawaharlal Nehru, encouraged women to take part in the country's life and activities. All three were passionately interested in

the need for proper educational facilities for women. Ram Mohan Roy fought hard to abolish 'Suttee' the practice whereby Hindu wives immolated themselves on the funeral pyres of their husbands. Nehru once said: 'I have long held that a country's progress can be measured by the status and progress of the women of the country.' He played an active role in pushing through the Hindu Code Bill which gave women complete equality with men as far as marriage and succession rights were concerned.

In India the process of feminine emancipation was activated above all by Mahatma Gandhi calling upon India's women to participate in the movement for independence, and to go to jail in their thousands. The most famous woman leader of the Nationalist Movement was Sarojini Naidu, who was elected a President of the Indian National Congress. In 1930, during the famous Salt March led by Gandhi, when Gandhi was arrested it was she who took charge. She was indeed a remarkable woman. In 1917 she led a deputation to the Secretary of State for India to try and establish equal political status for women. After independence she became Governor of Uttar Pradesh. She was also a talented poetess whose poems, written in English, won great praise from well-known English critics.

In India the idea of women working actively alongside men in various spheres of political life is not novel. In 1936 Mrs Vijaya Lakshmi Pandit became the first woman minister, and after independence she held such posts as President of the United Nations General Assembly, Ambassador to Moscow and Indian High Commissioner in London. It is not strange to find women as Cabinet Ministers, Ambassadors, Governors, Mayors and Sheriffs in India.

It is worthy of note that Indian women in general are playing an active role in several professions and fields of life. They have prepared themselves for this through education and training. The number of competent and qualified women teachers is rapidly increasing at all levels of education.

In the medical profession and in nursing, qualified women are making a valuable contribution. In the field of social work and community development women are playing the leading role. Even in administration and in law women are working alongside men, and many of them have

Five women of the new Asia
Mrs Bandaranaike

Mrs Indira Gandhi

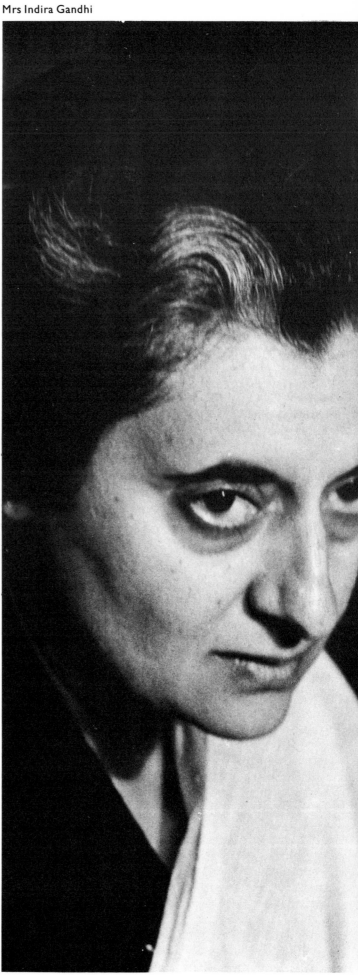

Mrs Vijaya Lakshmi Pandit

Mrs Sarojini Naidu

Madame Sun Yat Sen

risen high and held important positions. A few enterprising women have entered professions such as engineering and architecture and have given a good account of themselves. More and more avenues of work are being opened to women and it is found that those who take advantage of them, competing on equal terms with men, acquit themselves creditably.

In Burma women from time immemorial have had equality with men. At one time there was probably polyandry (the form of polygamy in which the woman has several husbands). Marriage is an equal contract, civil and not religious. Divorce is by consent. All property is shared equally between husbands and wives. Most of the trading is done by women, and in the case of market traders, the housekeeping is often done by the husband. In Burma an ever increasing number of women and young girls are volunteering to train as doctors, nurses, social workers and midwives, thanks to the energetic efforts of Daw Khin Kyi (widow of the statesman who negotiated the treaty with Britain which gave Burma independence, but was later assassinated), who became Director of Burma's Mother and Child Welfare Department.

Descriptions are included of what emancipation has meant in the lives of women in a selected number of Eastern countries—Pakistan, Indonesia, Turkey, Ceylon, Burma and Thailand. These articles (which are part of the material gathered by Unesco in a collection of studies entitled *Women in the New Asia: the changing role of men and women in south and south-east Asia*) enable a more realistic appraisal to be made of the past, present and future of millions of women in Asia.

Mrs Barbara Ward in her introductory essay has pointed out that these studies 'may help us to emerge a little from the cocoon of our preconceptions, including our own culturally derived stereotypes about what are truly "masculine" and what "feminine" social roles—and also about what are really "Eastern" and what "Western" patterns of living'.

New horizons for Asia's Muslim women

Anne-Marie Hussein
Political rights have been granted to Muslim women without a struggle. Faithful to the traditions of Islam, the modern states of Indonesia and Pakistan, from the moment they came into being, recognized the political independence of their

Muslim girls and boys mix freely at Gadjah Mada University in Djakarta, Indonesia, during a break in class schedule

women. They also took steps to ensure that women should by law remain the equals of men in their working life. Pakistani and Indonesian women have the vote, and may stand as candidates in any kind of election. In Indonesia it is not unusual for women to be members of municipal and departmental councils, and there have been several women Cabinet Members.

The Pakistan Government has taken special steps to encourage women to enter into public life and affairs, fearing perhaps that they might otherwise be prevented by shyness or inexperience from assuming their share in the direction of community affairs. In theory the same equality holds true for working women. Nearly all civil service posts are open to them, and salaries must be exactly the same as for men.

This rosy picture of women's rights does not hold true, however, for the condition in which the majority of the women of Indonesia and Pakistan found themselves at the beginning of the century, and in which many of them still find themselves today. For we must always bear in mind that one of the chief consequences of colonization was the moulding of the community in such a way as to arrest and paralyze its normal evolution. In such circumstances the role of woman became insignificant, and a spiderweb of customs prevented her from exercising even the most trivial rights, which, theoretically, at least, were hers.

Women were still respected as mothers, but childbearing was regarded as virtually their only function, and it occupied the greater part of their time and energy. A woman took no part in activities outside the family circle, and even there, her situation was often precarious. She was married at a very young age, without being consulted, to an unknown suitor chosen for social or economic reasons.

The situation of a woman today in both Indonesia and Pakistan depends largely on the class of the community to which she belongs. Peasant women in the villages cannot indulge in the luxury of a quiet, idle life. They work in the fields side by side with the men. They go to market, sell their produce, and some of the very poorest of them work as servants in private homes or shops. One should bear in mind in this respect that both Indonesia and Pakistan are mainly agricultural countries, and farmers form the majority class. Woman's importance in a village family is

singularly illustrated by a custom widespread among Indonesian peasants. When a young man cannot afford to pay the traditional bride-price, he enters the bride's family and pays his debt by working for his in-laws.

It is not women belonging to the wealthier classes who are most faithful to the old traditions, for they were the first to admit the liberal ideas. One result produced in these rich families a generation of daughters who scornfully refused to interest themselves in purely domestic subjects and embarked instead on more intellectual studies. Their studies were seldom carried very far since marriage soon intervened. The fact that increasing numbers of girls are attending coeducational schools and universities is evidence of a gradual change.

Ataturk and the emancipation of women

Afet Afetinan

Turkish women of the Ottoman era (fourteenth to early twentieth century), especially those in the cities, spent their lives in the complete seclusion of the harem. Their occupation consisted mainly of doing or supervising the housework, looking after the children or embroidering. Their social life was restricted to family gatherings.

In the nineteenth century there was a movement towards western ways of life which led to considerable changes in education, art and science, as well as an evolution in social life. As a result, some progressive ideas had already been implanted in women's minds by the end of the century.

Already before 1869 the Government decided to open primary and secondary schools for girls, but because the teachers in such schools would necessarily be male and because girls of eleven to thirteen years of age were considered as having reached an age when they should be segregated from men, public opinion would not tolerate the idea. In 1870 a school was opened in Istanbul to train women teachers for the primary and secondary girls' schools. Although initially most of the teachers in this school were men, by 1900 women were in the majority and hence the number of women with a modern education likewise increased.

The years 1908–18 were marked by two developments: enrolment in girls' schools

progressively increased, and certain men even ventured to go out in the company of their wives. During the war the first faculty for girls attached to the University of Istanbul was opened (1914). In 1921 the Arts Faculty agreed to coeducational attendance at lectures.

The passive resistance with which women, from the beginning of the twentieth century, opposed veiling and the withholding of the right to go out freely, to ride in the same carriage as their husbands and to sit next to them, eventually triumphed over the fanaticism of public opinion.

In the modern and secular state which was created in 1923, Turkish women had at last attained the rights enjoyed by women in other modern states. The republican constitution of Turkey made elementary education for boys and girls compulsory, but because of the shortage of teachers and school buildings as well as an anticipated 'birth explosion', its application remains partly theoretical. Turkey's high percentage of illiteracy, at present about 60 per cent, is thus likely to remain so for some time. It has to be emphasized that between the sexes it is largely the women who remain illiterate.

All faculties of the Istanbul University started opening their doors to female students from 1921 on and many teacher-training schools, *lycées*, and other institutes were opened for the benefit of girls. In addition, many of the existing schools introduced coeducation. In 1928 the adoption of the Latin alphabet made learning much easier and as a result there was an immediate increase in the number of literate persons.

Once women began to study in colleges and universities many of them entered a variety of professions and trades. But this was not always an easy matter, as was seen in the case of the medical profession. However, a small minority approved and supported women in their struggle. Encouraged by this support, seven girl students enrolled at the faculty of medicine of Istanbul University in September 1922. Because, in terms of dress, women were still bound by the old customs these first women medical students wore their veils while attending lectures with men and continued to do so until 1925, when Kemal Ataturk urged the adoption of European dress.

The first women medical students completed their studies in 1927 and, after a

111

When attending lectures with men, veils were worn by the first women students who enrolled at the Faculty of Medicine in Istanbul. This practice continued until Kemal Ataturk in 1925 urged the adoption of European dress

year's internship, received their diplomas as fully qualified doctors. These and other women doctors who had studied in Europe or America worked only as general practitioners. When some of them wanted to become specialists, however, most of their male colleagues declared that despite their attainments as students, women would not be successful as practising doctors. In time, the difficulties were overcome and women who have specialized in different branches of medicine have once again proved their capabilities.

Teaching was the first profession open to women in Turkey. Today women are found in virtually every profession. The engineer who supervised the building of the Ataturk Memorial mausoleum in Ankara, for instance, was a woman, Sabiha Gütayman. The chief architect of the Evkaf (religious trusts) in Istanbul is also a woman, Cahide Tamar. The famous Rumeli Fort in Istanbul was restored by three women architects.

On the stage, women have likewise distinguished themselves.

The first woman joined the Turkish bar in Ankara in 1928. Today, in Turkey, men and women are equal in the eyes of the law. The many social reforms introduced during the presidency of Kemal Ataturk (1923–38) always took account of women's position; many legal rights and duties were freely conceded to them.

The Turkish Civil Code, in terms of civil rights, did away with all the legal differences between men and women. However, the remnants of social mores still persist in the remote rural areas.

Thus, Turkish women managed within a quarter of a century to overcome a fanatical opposition and thereby set an example to other women of the Muslim world. The man responsible for the reforms in Turkey was Kemal Ataturk, who believed in preparing both the people around him and also public opinion before introducing anything new.

Ceylon: silent victory

Subada Siriwardena

Women in Ceylon have equal opportunities for employment in any profession or occupation, and even the portals of the Ceylon Administrative Service which replaced the earlier Ceylon Civil Service, are now open to women. At the same time it must be said that though Ceylon's women themselves and men's attitudes towards them have changed, this still applies only to a few men, and relatively few women are actually able to avail themselves of the opportunities open to them. The position of women has changed, but only for a few. The old ideal is still popularly accepted, that is, that of getting married and being a successful wife and mother.

It is true that working-class men and those of the lower middle-class, where incomes are insufficient to make ends meet, do want their wives to add to the family income by going out to work, but once they become economically well-off they too would wish to keep them safe at home.

As a result most fathers decide to give their girls only a secondary education and stop their schooling after that or even earlier. But nowadays, there is a large influx of girls to secondary and higher education. At the university level there is as large a proportion of women—as of men —following various courses of study.

Most of the women of the present generation who are educated are asserting their rights silently, but effectively, and have found themselves in paths of employment which were never trod by women before. One of these is Minette de Silva, Ceylon's first woman architect. Thus today we have women who are highly qualified teachers, university lecturers, doctors, lawyers, librarians and Members of Parliament and recently (1960) even a woman Prime Minister.

Girls are today going to foreign universities at their own expense or through scholarships sponsored by Unesco and the International Federation of University Women, etc. They go for courses ranging from university academic courses to courses in home science, nursing and beauty culture. Many educated women are engaged in social service work, running creches, female adult education, poor relief work, etc. The Lanca Mahila Samitiya is a women's association for such voluntary work.

I was born on 12 December 1928. Both my father's parents were illiterate but well-to-do farmers, and father acquired a government scholarship to Oxford. He was head of the Department of Indo-Aryan Languages at the University of Ceylon for some time. Both my mother's parents were literate, and were also rather well-to-do farmers. She was an uncertified Sinhalese teacher when she was

Minetta de Silva, Ceylon's first woman architect, seen here with some examples of her work, which has included a broad range of architectural designs from private homes and large scale housing projects to open air theatres and low-cost school buildings for Ceylon. Her buildings reflect her search for a synthesis of traditional and modern design—a regional modern architecture. She embodies, as an integral part of the construction, the skills of local craftsmen and artists, as can be seen in the tiled wall

given in marriage at the age of twenty-four to my father, who was in his forties at the time. The parents had decided for her and she had simply to consent. My father did not wish her to go out to work, and with reluctance she had to give up her job. Within one year after marriage I was born.

On my father's death, which occurred when I was eleven years old, the burden of bringing up the family fell on my mother's shoulders. More than anything else she strove to meet my father's last wish on his death bed—to give us children a good education.

By the time I was fourteen my mother had trained me to cook and sew and look after the younger ones. We were all sent to both Christian and Buddhist English schools. Later my brother and I both graduated at the University of Ceylon, but my sister gave up school after a few years.

I was given in marriage in 1956 at the age of twenty-seven to my husband, who was thirty at the time. The marriage was arranged by my parents, but subject to my consent. My husband is a Food and Drugs Inspector, educated in Ceylon and England.

Immediately after graduation I took to the teaching profession. My husband soon understood my desire to continue to learn and as he was convinced that I would not assume undue independence he allowed, and indeed encouraged, me to start reading for the M.A. in Education. I travel daily to the university in my own car, which I drive myself. My husband takes pride in my work, even in the face of some criticism from his colleagues.

But although I have a certain amount of independence which most women in Ceylon do not enjoy, this does not mean that I have deviated much from the ideal pattern of the wife and mother. My position at home follows very much the traditional pattern. My husband decides all important matters, and often it is acceptable to me. He commands and I obey. Except on scholarly matters it is not for me to argue with him. I have to accept the fact that he knows best and that this is all for my own good. I never go out or do anything outside the precincts of the home without his permission. But we do discuss important matters together, although the tendency is for him to decide finally. I feel quite happy and secure in this manner.

We hope to give our daughter the best education available in this country, and later even in England if she turns out to be enterprising and interested. We shall leave it to her whether or not to choose a career, or what career to choose. Whether she has a career or not, we wish to see her happily married to an intelligent, educated, good-natured, well-mannered and understanding Sinhalese Buddhist. Provided these characteristics are there we do not mind her making the choice of the young man without allowing us to arrange her marriage.

Burma: family in transition

Ni Ni Gyi

That her granddaughter in short sleeves and high-heeled sandals should be at a cocktail party with a glass in her hand (even though it be orange or tomato juice) is hardly a picture that my grandmother Daw Mein Ka Lay would have imagined in her wildest dreams half a century ago. We have certainly come a long way since the *ya-hta-lone*, the Burmese horse and buggy days. In her time Ma Mein Ka Lay, as my grandmother was called, was dedicated to the home and spent all her time at household chores, and would never go out at night except maybe to a pagoda festival, and then only in the company of the whole family.

Thus it is evident that even the staid and conservative Burmese culture which had always boasted of being impervious to the influence of 'foreign matter' is showing signs of thawing.

In my childhood the family was made up of my grandmother, father, mother, my sisters, an aunt (my mother's cousin) and cousin who was really a poor relative living with us.

The family system was very strong and absolute respect and obedience were shown all along the line. My grandmother, being the oldest in the household, formed the apex of authority and respect, and she was followed by father, mother, aunt and cousin down to the children, from the eldest to the youngest. Burmese children from childhood are instilled with the idea of absolute reverence for the following in the order given: Lord Buddha, his teachings, the clergy, parents and teachers. This is the reason why implicit obedience is accorded the parents.

The attitude is somewhat changed now;

the trend is towards more rational obedience, and relations between my mother and ourselves are on a more informal plane. If my mother makes a certain decision, we are able to explain things to her and even disagree with her and she takes it in the best light. In fact, when I accompanied my husband on a world tour in 1955 my mother was very much against it, but I was able to make her understand my point of view and even got her blessing for the trip.

My grandmother went to a lay school where she studied the three Rs and scriptures as well. The reason for the girls going to a lay school was that it was not proper for the monks to teach girls. By the time my mother went to school, Rangoon could boast of a modern school called the Empress Victoria Buddhist Girls' School, and my mother and aunt were proud to be its pupils and to learn English there. At that time my maternal grandmother's idea was to give them enough 'modern education' to enable them to read English newspapers and she made them leave school after middle grade. It was strongly felt that a full education was only for the men.

The philosophy with regard to education had greatly changed when we reached school age. My father, in particular, had a very practical philosophy. Since he had no sons he was determined to give his daughters the best education he could. He thus sent us as boarders to a convent renowned for its high standard of education. My grandfather was at first very much against the idea of our going to an English school where we wore only European clothes and were given English names.

In our generation two of the daughters got the benefit of foreign education. One of my sisters went to study in England before the war. The idea of a young unmarried girl going abroad was not looked on with favour. Quite a few of our elderly relatives criticized my parents for letting a young girl go alone to a strange country, where she might be exposed to the 'wild ways of Western civilization'. When I went to study in the United States as a state scholar a decade later opinion had changed considerably and my going abroad met with complete approval from everyone.

My grandmother wore white cotton jackets (almost Chinese style) complete with cloth buttons, fixed her hair up with one or several combs on the top and walked sedately so that not even her ankles showed. Her tight sleeves came down to her wrist and her *longyi* to her ankles, and her hair for formal occasions was done up like a cake on her head.

The above style of dress still prevailed until the end of the war. However, the postwar fashion is to wear short or three-quarter sleeves and now the present generation of teenagers and young girls go in for sleeveless jackets, brassieres, short knee-length skirts and high-heeled sandals.

One feature of our generation which was not common in the time of my mother and grandmother is the emergence of the career woman. Burmese women have always been noted for their shrewd business acumen and their ability to stand on their own as village chiefs, and have even sat on the throne at different stages of Burmese history, but their taking to regular careers is a new phenomenon.

The rising cost and standards of postwar living have made it necessary to have two incomes in order to live well.

In my grandmother's and mother's day, the position was reversed. The husband took pride in the fact that he was the sole 'rice-winner' and that his wife could afford the luxury of staying home. We find that the modern career woman-cum-housewife is heavily burdened with social obligations after office hours. In addition to her own professional social contacts, she is also expected to keep up with her husband's.

Throughout Burmese history, the position of Burmese women has always been on a par with that of men. However, apart from the days when women ruled the country, the Burmese women have not taken any great interest in politics. There is no great political consciousness such as is to be found in some other countries. Accordingly, there is no Burmese counterpart of the political stature of Mrs Pandit, Madame Sun Yat Sen or Mrs Roosevelt.

Thailand

'I AM NO LONGER THE HIND LEGS OF AN ELEPHANT'

Pramuan Dickinson

When I asked my parents' approval of my decision to get married, my mother said: 'If your grandmother were still alive she would be shocked by this.' This was because I had decided to marry a young man from a place far from our community, and our hemisphere—in Canada. It was so un-

usual that a strong protest was to be expected, at least, at first. 'But the world has been changed a great deal,' said my father, 'how can one resist such a great change?'

My father was right. The world has been changing a great deal from my grandmother's days to our present time. My grandmother married a man from the same community, but whom she had never met before. My mother became a little acquainted with my father before they married, but he came from a place in Central Thailand far from her community. This was something of a shock because my father spoke a different dialect and no one in the family had ever heard of the village he came from.

In my grandmother's day it was unusual for women, especially unmarried girls, to travel very far from home. My grandmother, like all girls of her age, was educated at home only. She was taught by her mother to work in the household—cooking, spinning, weaving and sewing. My grandmother did not learn to read and write because it was thought not proper for girls to do so.

When my grandmother's fifth child was about ten years old, a school for girls was set up in the community, and she was sent to it. My mother was too old to go, so she continued to study at home until she married my father who helped her to learn both reading and writing.

In my generation education was compulsory up to the fourth grade. Boys still had a better chance because they could stay at monasteries in Bangkok. Only rich people could afford to send their daughters to expensive boarding schools, but every year the Government granted some scholarships to both boys and girls to study in the field of education. This was the only chance for girls of poor families to go to school in Bangkok, and only provided that they were very bright. At present it is quite different. Girls have many more opportunities for education. They may now choose careers as teachers, doctors, lawyers and many other professions.

I was sent to a well-known boarding school for girls. I was the first girl of the family to come out of the home to a school so far away. I was to go even further later on when I was given a Unesco fellowship to study at the University of Toronto, in Canada, where I met the man who became my husband.

Looking back at the family history, I can see a tremendous change in the expectations about women's roles in the family. My grandmother used to tell me how she was selected as a wife. One day as she was weaving, an elderly lady whom she knew dropped by and watched her closely as she worked. It dawned on my grandmother that the lady had a son who was just at the right age to get married. My grandmother was right. A few days later, her mother told her that the lady had asked for her to be married to her son.

I told my grandmother that I would have been angry because nobody seemed to care what the girl herself might feel, and also that the girl should have the right to select her husband. My grandmother laughed and said: 'Grandchild, we girls at that time did not bother very much talking or even thinking about "rights" as you do now, but we were still very happy. There is an old saying, "A woman is the hind legs of an elephant". That means that you are to be the follower only, and I had done my duty as a good follower. That's all.'

In my mother's day, the majority of women still stayed at home. Very few had independent careers. Wage-earners were almost all men. There was only one woman in the local town who had a job as a teacher. Another woman, a nurse, worked in Bangkok.

At present, it is not unusual for women to earn their own living. Most young wives and mothers take jobs outside their homes. All my female cousins of my age are now wage-earners. Families have become smaller than those in my mother's day. Most families can no longer take in all the distant relatives as dependents, in the household. In most cases where mothers work, servants must be hired to help in the home.

Within three generations, roles expected of men and women, boys and girls, have been tremendously modified by the great change of the world. And the rate of change has increased rapidly. I believe there was little difference between the social life of my grandmother and her own mother. But in the case of my mother and myself, one can see a big gap between the two generations, and the change is still going on very rapidly.

12 Economic and social problems

Introduction

While the cultural contributions of the East have been great it is necessary to know about the changing economic conditions as well, the problems that face these countries and the attempts that they are making to raise the living standards of their people. It is difficult for those who live in so-called affluent societies to have any idea of the poverty and privations that face these people and the growing gap in the living standards of the rich and poor countries. In the rich countries one farmer can feed twenty-three people. In most of the poorer countries in the East one farmer can barely feed himself. While the privileged one-third of the world's population earns about one thousand dollars each year, in the poor countries in the East they earn about one hundred dollars each year. Many of these countries tend to have widespread under-employment, illiteracy, poor housing, low nutrition and health standards and an acute shortage of educated people and teachers—formidable problems for anyone to face.

Paul Hoffman of the United Nations said some years ago: 'Poverty and hunger were just words to me until I saw poverty and hunger in the Far East. Then and only then did I understand Gandhi's description of the life of an Indian peasant as "an eternal compulsory fast" and today with exploding populations, in order to win the fight against poverty, many countries are going to have to run fast, just to stand still. And the problem is aggravated as peasants move from poverty in the country to unemployment in the cities. What the people of these countries need is insurance against disaster as they move to modernize their agriculture and industry; help from their own governments and help through external aid.'

The potentially rich resources of the ex-colonial countries in the East have not been developed and this is the reason for the poverty of their people. As one country after another in the East became independent, it started on plans for economic development to raise the living standards of its people. For it is a recognized fact that economic development is the means by which material hardships can be reduced and by which poverty can be attacked at its root.

Industrialization is essential to economic progress. It is the indispensable tool in the struggle to raise living standards among the less fortunate of the world's people. Economic development must go hand in hand with the production of more food and the improvement of health, the spread of education and the promotion of social welfare and human rights. It will help to put more money into the pockets of the people who need it. Without the increase in spending power the people in the East as in other under-developed countries cannot know freedom from misery and want. It is an essential step towards a world free from hunger. The economies of countries which depend on one or two primary commodities must be diversified to absorb the shocks and uncertainties of world trade. Capital must be forthcoming for investment in roads, railways, harbours, airfields, factories, hospitals, schools and training colleges as well as industries.

The technological revolution which has transformed the West and helped to raise living standards has now to be transferred to the East to help to raise living standards and eradicate poverty and its inherent evils. One of the problems is that it has to be transferred to an environment which is not yet ready to assimilate it. Therefore the very technology that is needed for development brings problems in its wake.

The nations of the East which seek to develop their economies today face all the old dilemmas of rapid transition—how to modernize static farming, how to squeeze savings from a poor pre-industrial society, how to produce those industries which actually produce a surplus, how to finance the new skills needed to produce more capital before the capital exists to divert to the schools. But they face even tougher problems—the population explosion, urbanization beyond control, trade patterns which work to their disadvantage and inappropriate technology.

Indeed one of the ironies of the population explosion in the East is that it is not so much a question of increasing births but the result of more efficient 'death control'. More effective measures of improving health, eradicating diseases, lowering rates of infant mortality etc. have meant that in countries in the East there is an increase in population before other factors in the community—food production, educational development, savings, industrial development—have become really dynamic. The result is that population is now outstripping the growth in all these facilities. The only way to deal with the problem is with a two-pronged approach—the positive method of increasing production with the aid of modern technology and the negative method of population control.

The greatest potential resources of any country are its human resources—trained men for administration, education, public health, medicine and industry. Within the context, the need, the passion for education is turning into an irresistible clamour in the East sparked by the triple cry for national development, national freedom and the dignity of man. Without scientists, engineers and technicians at all levels no country can call itself free. In the East there is now a new talisman—education. There is no question of forcing education on unwilling or bewildered people. They want it and will walk miles to get it—all over the countries in the East children are hypnotized by the word school. Mothers start riots when the local politician fails in his promise for a school by the autumn. Education has become a precious latch-key, the sure escape from the prison of poverty.

The articles which follow attempt to give an idea of some of the problems which face countries in the East—the problems of poverty, hunger and disease. Nothing illustrates more clearly the urgent need for the modernization of agriculture and the development of industry, than the descriptions of famine in India. Industry is needed to reduce the dependence on the monsoon by providing large-scale irrigation facilities, by providing fertilizers to increase the yield of the land and by absorbing the excess manpower which will come off the land as a result of the modern methods of agriculture. In recent years so much has been heard about the poverty in the East and the impression has been given that development in these countries is static. But progress has been made, though some of it has been swallowed up by the population explosion. Shortage of space has meant that it has not been possible to include descriptions of the very real progress that has been made in building up the industrial base in these countries—the modern steel works, chemical plants and atomic power stations, the hydroelectric stations, the new transport facilities, or the plans for agricultural development. Some idea of new developments can be seen in the article on the new capital of Pakistan and the imaginative project of the Great Asian Highway. The struggle against malaria illustrates the determined drive to improve health and the five articles on schools in different parts of the East capture some of the enthusiasm for education which is regarded as one of the main keys to freedom and development.

Great famines of history

Although we know that famines ravaged Egypt during the reigns of the Pharoahs and the later Ptolemy dynasty, we are not sure exactly when they took place or how many victims they claimed. The first of the great famines of European history of whose facts we can be absolutely certain was the one at Rome in 436 BC, when thousands of starving people were driven by desperation to throw themselves into the Tiber.

We know too that during the first centuries of the Christian era many parts of the world were visited by the grim spectre of famine and in 879 there occurred the 'universal famine', a terrible calamity which was repeated nearly three centuries later in 1162.

India, because of its almost entire dependence upon monsoon rains, is probably more liable than any other country to crop failures which may deepen into famine. Thus, down the centuries, hunger has stalked across it. Between AD 1022 and 1033 great famines occurred there in which entire provinces were depopulated. During the second half of the fourteenth century there were great famines when millions starved to death and not even the King, Togluk, could obtain the necessities for his household.

Famine afflicted various areas of France during the Middle Ages, and the food shortage in England became so serious in 1586 that the government of Queen Elizabeth was forced to pass a number of laws for the relief of want which were eventually (1601) codified in the famous statute on which the English Poor Law system became based.

The Great Famine of Bengal (1769–70) carried off one-third of the population (10 million people), and twenty years later there occurred the Doji Bara, or 'skull famine', so called because the people died in such numbers that they could not be buried.

France under Louis XVI experienced a terrible shortage and mismanagement of food supplies. Famine gripped Ireland in 1846 and 1847 due to the failure of the potato crop. In the second half of the nineteenth century, famine struck in many places: Algeria (300,000 deaths) 1868; Rajputana, India (1½ million) 1869; Madras, Bombay and Mysore (5 million) 1877 and 1888; North China (9½ million) 1877–78; eighteen provinces of Russia (2 million) 1891–92; India (1 million) 1899–1901. Even in the twentieth century, India has still not been freed from the scourge of famine.

The year of the famine

Melville Hardiment

For most of us a famine is a news item, a row of statistics, a collecting box label. In the West it is difficult to grasp the concrete reality of famine, without firsthand experience.

I know a little what it is like to be in a famine. I once saw one.

Imagine a fertile province in India where I once lived, with its cultivated fields, tiny villages and thriving cities. As the hot weather progresses, the rivers and streams dry up and become children's playgrounds. Work is carried out only in the early mornings and in the cool of the evenings, and people sleep away the heat of the middays and afternoons.

The river beds crack and the banks of the streams crumble, but that is usual and life goes on as ever. There is water in the village well and each morning and evening the women of the village gather to draw up their supplies and gossip. It is a large, bricklined well, twelve feet in diameter, and protected by a low wall. It is all of one hundred feet deep, and a row of projecting bricks form a circular staircase right down to the water level. The depth of water can be calculated by counting the number of bricks showing above the water.

That is how it was the year of the famine. As the hot weather neared its end we began to wonder whether the monsoon would be late or early. It was the normal topic for that time of the year. The monsoon is the season of the rains that sweep across India in a curved path from the Bay of Bengal and drop their last pourings over the Arabian Ocean. Sometimes the rains do not come. That spells famine in India.

Gradually that year it became evident that the monsoon would be late. When the time came to plant the thin rice shoots in the paddy fields the rains were very late indeed, and we men, who normally met at the barber's shop in the village square, began to visit the emptying well along with the women.

The swelling sun gleamed and glittered like a huge brass bedknob. We kept constant watch for the first tiny ball of cloud that would herald the break in the weather and relief from the eternal heat and flies. All that long and arid season however, the sun and sky remained hard and immaculate.

By then the women had all begun to talk of the emptying larders. The rice chatties were depleted and maize was scarce. Some of the shops in the bazaar no longer opened and their closed shutters were a sign of what was to come. And so, each day at the well, where far too many steps were now showing, we loudly proclaimed our faith in the imminence of the monsoon. 'It's bound to arrive tomorrow' we told each other. But it never came.

Distrust and aggression crept into our midst. Each family began to be very secretive about food. And one evening I suddenly realized that the famine was among us. It had very swiftly and secretly infiltrated into the village without us noticing. That is the awful facility of a famine.

I discovered the famine one evening while I was out for a walk. I always walked along the banks of our river, where the cracked fissures lay on the hard, baked surface of the bed like immense, black starfish. I passed the burning ghats where the Hindus burned their dead, and that evening there were six funeral pyres, and clustered around each were young parents. The young and the very old are invariably the first casualties. There had been no cholera, or smallpox or typhoid that year, so I knew these must be victims of hunger.

From that moment life took on a new meaning. Shops no longer opened at all, and the wealthier shopkeepers left. There was a spate of rumours about the monsoon and its approach, and about government grain supplies on the way. But the food chatties were scraped clean and every tiny store of food hoarded and guarded. We all began to walk about in a trance, and as the days passed there was soon just a foot or so of muddy liquid at the bottom of the well. It became impossible to think, or even feel anything. The funeral pyres increased in number each evening.

Then the first refugees from villages to

There was water in the village well, and each morning and evening the women gathered there to draw up their supplies and gossip. But as the weeks passed the water level dropped until there was just a foot or so of muddy liquid

When famine strikes the first victims are usually the very young and the very old. They were innumerable among refugees

the east of us hurried through in family groups, each group carrying the young and bundles of household effects and belongings that they had already begun to cast away by the time they had reached us. By then too, they were in a desperate state, and the men of our village had to fight with some of the stronger of them, who tried to take what water we had left.

And then in ones and twos and threes and fours, our families packed up similar bundles of possessions and joined the scrambling stream of refugees trekking westwards to the hills and deep jungles of Hazaribagh and the hoped-for land of promise that lay just beyond, but which always remained just beyond the next range of hills, and which we never did find. The old and the infirm we left behind. It was what they would have wanted had we given them a choice, but there was no choice and they lay there on their charpoys in the gloomy interiors of the abandoned houses, until death came to deliver them.

Of the 917 people in our village, there were only 486 there next year to meet at the well and wait for the monsoon. But that year it did come.

The rains
that did not come

Millions of people in India were faced in 1966–67 with a grave shortage of food, and even starvation, because of the rains that did not come the year before. The Indian farmer is utterly dependent on the monsoon rains that normally fall from July to September.

In 1965–66 the monsoon rains started at the usual time, but they soon tapered off and then stopped. The failure of the rains was of such proportions that the Indian government described it in an official white paper as 'a natural calamity of a magnitude unknown in recent times'.

Some ten million tons of rice, corn, millet and pulses perished in the parched earth around Rajasthan, Gujarat, Maharashtra, Madhya, Pradesh, Mysore and parts of Andhra and Orissa. In September and October the rains which should have given life to the crops for harvest the following spring also failed. This meant a probable loss of a further two to three million tons of food.

In 1964–65 India produced eighty-eight million tons of food grains and imported a

further six and a half million tons, bringing food available for the year to ninety-four million tons. In 1965–66 the country was able to grow only seventy six million tons and, with population increasing by twelve million a year, she would need more than ninety six million tons to maintain the level of subsistence of the year before which could by no means be described as lavish.

Even taking into account government stocks of a little over two million tons and about the same quantity of private stocks, the government of India soon realized that the country's needs would be between eleven and fourteen million tons short. In any country such a proportionate shortfall would have been critical. In India, vast both in area and population, it could be disastrous.

The precariousness of this situation has long been obvious to many people, not least to the Indian government.

For a time during the 1950s agricultural production in India was increasing by about 3 per cent per year, but recently the increase has slowed down.

If agricultural production has stagnated, the growth of population has not. India's population is today increasing by 2·4 per cent per year – more than twelve million people every year bringing into the world with them a need for two million more tons of food grains. In the late 1960s India's population reached 500 million.

The net result has been that for several years, small improvements which have been made in India's diet have been owed to heavy food imports. The Indian farmer has merely kept step with the rising population – until the 1965/66 season.

The government took immediate practical steps to meet the deteriorating situation. Rationing was introduced.

On his return to Rome after a month's tour of India, the Director General of the Food and Agriculture Organization spoke of the Indian government's gratitude for the spontaneous manifestation of goodwill towards her throughout the world. He said: 'The fact that actual famine has not occurred and starvation deaths are so far not evident should not be construed as the government having raised a false alarm. On the contrary there is real shortage of food over a widely dispersed area and the government have acted with commendable foresight in taking preventive measures at an early stage. Even now, difficult months lie ahead, and much

will depend on the speed with which foreign supplies will reach India before the monsoons break in July.'

The present food crisis has shown how precarious is the balance between subsistence and starvation. One bad harvest can upset this balance and bring a severe crisis. The government of India is fully conscious of this and has decided to accord the highest priority to agriculture in its fourth five year plan.

Iran

MOBILE BRIGADES STRIKE
AT A VILLAGE SCOURGE

The world malaria eradication campaign is based on the mosquito's habit of resting on interior walls after he has fed on someone's blood, and on the possibility of spraying those walls with residual insecticides that will kill most of the mosquitoes settling on them over a period of several months. In this way, the chain of infection can be interrupted (the mosquito becomes infected by biting an infected person and passes on the disease by biting a healthy person). The accompanying photograph shows a member of a malaria eradication team working in Iran taking a mosquito from a wall which was sprayed with DDT insecticide ten days previously. The insect will be studied in the Kaserun Malaria Centre where research is being made into mosquito resistance to insecticides. The other photograph shows Iranians watching an anti-malaria team at work in their village.

Malaria strikes first at a country's most precious resource, its young children, and the disease is actually held responsible for 10 to 15 per cent of infant mortality.

Buddhist priests
and modern science

A 'MIRACLE'
IN THE HUMMING SWAMP

Ritchie Calder

The malaria team sprayed with DDT the priceless mosaics on the walls at the temple of 'the Reclining Buddha of the Humming Swamp'. Priests in their saffron coloured togas, their heads and eyebrows close-shaven, stood by in silent approval. Above them glowed the golden smile of the recumbent Buddha, 65 feet long and sheathed from head to foot in gold leaf, an image so big that they had to build the temple round it.

Today the Humming Swamp does not hum so much. When we went out with Dr Bhatia, the Indian entomologist from the World Health Organisation (WHO) and his team of mosquito hunters, we dipped in vain into the water-grasses of the irrigation streams. In a day's search it was impossible to find a single *Anopheles Minimus*, the midget mosquito which had kept northern Thailand malaria ridden for generations. And we could have searched in vain through the whole of Serapai, the district which three years ago WHO in conjunction with the Thai Government and Unicef chose as a demonstration area for malaria control.

Here indeed was a modern miracle, a miracle for which the Buddhist priests can rightly claim a large share of the credit. The Miracle of the Humming Swamp is a lesson for the whole world. Modern science has played its indispensable part, but equally indispensable was the co-operation of the Buddhist priests who, throughout the whole area, instructed the faithful to work with the WHO inter-national experts, with the Government authorities and with the diligent Thai doctors.

I have a great respect for the Chief Abbot who received me in the great Temple of the Golden Buddha. When I thanked him for the example he had given by instructing the priesthood to co-operate with WHO which supplied the experts and Unicef which supplied the DDT and the equipment, he demurred.

Why, he said, should he or the priests be thanked for obeying the injunctions of the Lord Buddha and working for the living wellbeing of the people? Science and religion were as one when they strove for the good life.

This was reiterated by the Governor of Chiengmai who, like his predecessor who launched the project three years ago, has been the friend and active helper of the international team. He was proud that in his province there had been this project which had benefited his people and which in a few years would mean that all Thailand would be delivered from malaria, but which had also brought doctors from other countries for training. These doctors (with WHO fellowships) would apply in their own countries lessons learned at Chiengmai.

When Dr Sambasivan arrived in the spring of 1949 he had to plan a campaign which would be economical in DDT and in

Above and *below*: anti-malaria team at work in Iran

121

manpower, because it had to be scaled to the resources which Thailand could afford in extending the lessons of the project to the whole country – financial, but also medical resources. Thailand is short of doctors.

First it was necessary to choose a workable area. He selected Chiengmai in northern Thailand, in the hills behind which lies Burma. This was an endemic malaria area. That is, malaria was constantly present in 60 to 70 per cent of the population, not flaring up into sudden and deadly epidemics, but robbing the people of health and fitness and liable, like a sleeping volcano of disease, to erupt.

Second, they had to find the mosquito responsible for malaria in this part of the world. There were thirty types of mosquito in the area, any one of which might be the villain.

They were lucky. The very first day, Dr M D Bhatia, who had joined the mission from the Malarial Institute of India, and his assistants, found the spores of human malaria in the salivary gland of the thirteenth mosquito they examined – the *Anopheles minimus*.

Third, they had to study its habits. They found that, unlike certain other mosquitoes which favour stagnant water, it bred only in running, fresh water. This was lucky because the experts could define its area of operations. It belonged chiefly to irrigation channels fast fed from the hills and could not survive in the sluggish canals of the lowlands.

Fourth, they had to find its bases for attack on humans. They systematically examined the peasant huts – built on stilts, with plaited mat walls and thatched with attap, a broad, brown leaf, tobaccolike. After studying the habits of 15,000 specimens, they satisfied themselves that it rarely rested higher than 8 feet from the floor – an economy when it came to spraying – that it lurked in the walls and in hanging clothes, and that it was mainly active between 9 in the evening and 4 in the morning.

They decided to attack its 'airstrips' – the walls and hangings of the houses. The homes of 40,000 people were involved but, with the help of the priests and the village headmen they set about it systematically. All over the area one sees huts with letters and numbers and dates painted on them 'A/16 DDT 21/4/50', meaning the village, the number of the

house and the date of the first spraying. So thoroughly was this done that the DDT sign is now the postal address of the householders.

At the end of the first year, the Thai members of the team led by Dr Udom and Dr Vimol were entirely capable of handling the scheme and the international members retreated to the role of advisers. This tactful move strengthened rather than lessened their authority.

All this time Unicef had been providing the DDT sprayers and vehicles for the pilot project, matched in cost by the Government's provision of staff.

They extended the Serapei project to five times as many people, 200,000, and at the same time trained and advised the personnel which the Thai Government installed and financed in the adjoining area of Hangdong. This scheme was also so successful that it was extended five times.

Yet another scheme was started in central Thailand, covering a population of 50,000. In this case half the cost of the materials was born by WHO directly.

The pilot projects also provided training facilities for the American and Thai staffs who were to work the ECA schemes in conjunction with the Thai Government. This provision of direct American aid has taken the place of the WHO/Unicef contributions and, following through the plans prepared by the WHO experts, aims to clear Thailand of malaria within three years. Thus the protection already given to 600,000 people will be extended to another 4 million.

By killing the mosquito with the lingering poison of DDT, the Chiengmai methods broke the cycle of malaria. And they killed off the species. In a search of 5,000 man-hours not an *A-minimus* has been found. The disease faded out.

This parable of health began with the Kathin and it ended with the Kathin.

The Kathin is the festival which goes on for weeks in celebration of the end of the Buddhist Lent and the beginning of the Buddhist Spring. With the last of the Monsoon, the thousands of young Thais who have entered the monasteries for a term of spiritual service – and practically every Thai does – emerge and exchange their humble yellow robes for civilian garb. The permanent priests receive from the faithful their new robes. And everyone makes merry.

It was at the Kathin that the Chief Abbot

had first enjoined the people to cooperate with WHO, and when we reminded the Governor of Chiengmai, Udom Bunya-prasop, of this he immediately said we must join in the Kathin. He ordered a procession complete with the Corps of Court Dancers and the Busabok, the triumphal car which the people drag with ropes through the streets.

The beautiful dancers of the Court, with their vivid robes and flowered headdresses and their golden finger-nails, six inches long, danced barefoot in the streets. Every turn of the foot, every gyration of the body, every movement of the hand is the exquisite dumb-alphabet of age-old legend. And the procession moved through Chiengmai to Wat Suan Dawk the principal temple.

Only once a year does the Golden Buddha, the most precious image in all North Thailand, emerge from the dim recesses of his temple. For this occasion, the Chief Abbot gave a special dispensation with priestly rites, the golden image was carried down the temple steps and enthroned on the lawn before the pagoda. People prostrated themselves before it. The Dancers danced before it.

Tradition and modern science met in common thanksgiving.

The stairway of the giants

Paul Almasy

In diverse lands and throughout history man, the settler and the farmer, has often challenged a hostile Nature, transforming desert, jungle or steppe to draw his sustenance from the soil. Yet rarely has he ever changed a landscape as profoundly as in the Bontok Valley on the Philippines' island of Luzon.

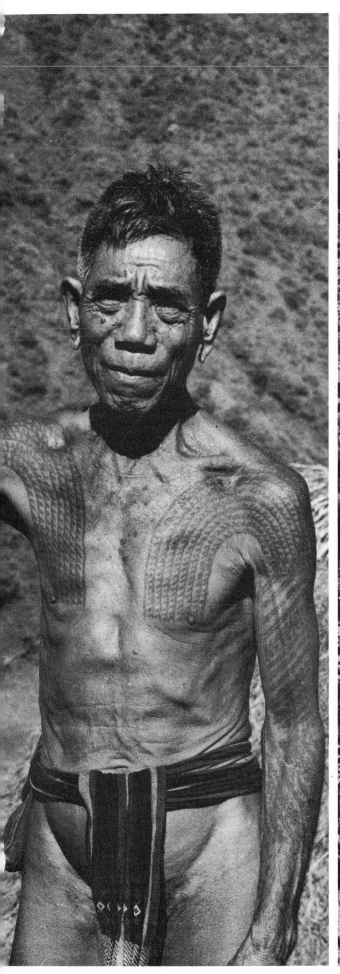

9

Here, in the heart of a wild mountain range, the famous terraced ricefields of the Ifugaos, spreading over several hundred square miles, are a green and living testament to the ingenuity of this people in devising agricultural techniques –a masterpiece of human patience and endurance.

Describing this region is impossible– only pictures can give an idea of the scope of this achievement–one of history's most remarkable examples of agricultural development. In the Banaue Valley alone, terraces cover 400 square kilometres and the walls supporting them total some 15,000 miles in length. Archaeologists and historians who have studied the Bontok ricefields estimate that the islanders must have worked from 1,500 to 2,000 years to build the terraces and their systems of irrigation. There are terraced ricefields in China, Japan and Indonesia, but these ricefields of the Ifugaos in the Luzon mountains are by far the biggest in the world, with the highest and the best-constructed stone walls.

It is believed that a small tribe which emigrated from Indonesia taught the Ifugaos how to construct ricefields in terraces. This must have happened some 4,000 years ago. Remains studied by specialists suggest that the Upper Bantok Valley took on its presentday aspect only at the beginning of the Christian era.

We know very little about the Ifugaos who, 4,000 years ago, took on this gigantic task which the people of the Philippines call the 'eighth wonder of the world'. They probably came from the Asian mainland and they reached Luzon while seeking a new land in which to settle, or after fleeing from a powerful enemy.

Today the Upper Bontok Valley and the neighbouring valleys are inhabited by various tribes, one of them still known as the 'Ifugaos'. Their neighbours are the Bontoks and the Kalingas. All these mountaineers are exceptionally gifted farmers and they maintain the terraces of their ancestors with great technical skill. They are continually improving irrigation systems and ways of growing rice and raising livestock (their two main occupations).

There is no better proof of their ingenuity than the scarecrows they construct to protect their seeds from the birds. These scarecrows resemble those found in other lands, but are kept perpetually moving, operated by the brooks and the many little streams in the region.

A mechanism as ingenious as it is simple transmits the energy of the streams to the scarecrows through a system of cords. In some cases, the moving scarecrows may be as far as 800 yards from the water.

While the Kalinga ricefields are not as spectacular as those of the Ifugaos and the Bontoks, they are remarkably well maintained. The homes and villages of these mountaineers are among the cleanest and best kept in the world. Yet it is not uncommon to hear certain city-dwellers refer to these tribesmen as 'savages'. It is a pejorative and unjustified label for people who are among Asia's most highly skilled farmers and who have been able to create and to preserve such gigantic works of engineering.

Islamabad

A NEW CAPITAL FOR PAKISTAN

In the north of West Pakistan, on a site formerly occupied by six small villages, a great modern city has been born: Islamabad, the new capital of Pakistan. It is situated about twelve miles from the present provisional capital at Rawalpindi and some 750 miles from Pakistan's former capital, Karachi. Work began in 1961, and today Islamabad is a bustling city of 50,000 people. The first primary school was opened in 1963, and the secondary school for girls already has 500 pupils. Over 3,250 houses have been built, 700 are now being constructed and a further 2,400 will be built. Pakistan House, a six-storeyed hotel with 275 rooms has been built primarily to provide living facilities for members of the Pakistan National Assembly. Designed by the Italian architect, Gio Ponti, its main colour scheme is green and white–the colours of Pakistan's flag–symbolizing peace and prosperity. A simple and graceful building, it offers a blend of traditional and modern architectural features. Half the planned streets are open to traffic. The city will eventually have about 100 roads and foot bridges and 100 miles of roads of all grades. Islamabad can fairly claim to be one of today's most striking architectural and town-planning achievements. It has not merely been planned as the administrative centre of a nation but also as a symbol of its way of life, its history and traditions and the image of its hopes for prosperity and social stability.

The Great Asian Highway

M S Ahmad

A great highway network, often following the caravan routes of antiquity, will soon span the continent of Asia from Turkey and Iraq to Singapore and Saigon. Known as the Great Asian Highway it is being built by the international cooperation of some twenty countries working within the framework of the United Nations. When completed it will offer the motorist an opportunity for new contact with the people of Asia by driving across 35,000 miles (55,000 km) of international roads.

This is a bold and imaginative project to endow southern Asia with an up-to-date international highway system. The backbone of the undertaking will be the great network of old caravan routes which have survived the ravages of time although some date back to as much as 1,000 years before the Christian Era. It is over these caravan routes that Marco Polo and other travellers like Fa-Hsien and Ibn Batuta explored the lands of the East, that the armies of Gengis Khan, Alexander the Great and Tamerlane marched on their road to conquest, and that the silk, jade and spices of the Orient were transported by the traders of the past.

The development of trade routes was by no means easy. Asia is made up of vast plains, some fertile others totally desert, mountain ranges which include some of the highest in the world, and rivers, mighty and long and often turbulent. The trade routes naturally sought out the mountain passes (most of them still in use) and followed the rivers.

Today, however, many of these land routes have fallen into disuse and cannot possibly meet the needs of the developing countries of south Asia. The creation of a vast network of international highways, linking up the existing roads and raising these to the standards needed for motorized traffic has thus become an urgent, priority problem.

The idea of linking Asian countries through a network of international highways was born in November 1958 at the Highways Sub-Committee of Ecafe, the United Nations Economic Commission for Asia and the Far East. The proposal was to establish an international highway system linking existing main roads all the way between Vietnam and Iran, and then bringing them up to a minimum standard.

The Asian Highway will be reminiscent of the ancient caravan routes between Europe, the Middle East and Africa, and

Top: highest tunnel. The highest road tunnel in the world is now being completed in Afghanistan. It will carry the Asian Highway through the Hindu Kush range at an altitude of 10,000 feet (3,200 metres). This shows the construction of the approach road to the Jalang tunnel, 8,200 feet long (2,750 metres) that will shorten the existing road by 120 miles (190 kilometres)

Centre: longest bridge. The bridge completely spanning the horizon is Asia's longest: 10,000 feet (3,300 metres). It has been built across the River Sone in India about 375 miles (600 kilometres) from Calcutta. Seven major bridges will be built for the Asian Highway in East Pakistan

Bottom: smartest vehicle. Colourfully decorated motor lorries like this one in Pakistan are a common sight on the roads of Asia. The custom of smartening-up the carriages with ornate designs and symbols also exists in the Middle East, and is a centuries-old practice in Sicily as regards ordinary carts

will produce great economic advantages. It will provide movement within each country and facilitate overland international trade; many of Asia's traditional commodities such as rice, rubber, cotton, timber, fuel and minerals, which now move between countries by circuitous sea routes could be moved more economically by road and be independent of rising ocean freight rates.

Besides developing trade, the Asian Highway will stimulate tourist traffic within Asia and enable lower income groups to enjoy the wonders of this great continent. Tourists will be able to journey by road to places of historical interest and visit the many pilgrim centres, now almost inaccessible except at very great expense. The opening of the international road will be welcomed by millions of Buddhist, Hindu and Muslim pilgrims.

The Asian Highway will also open new vistas for the hundreds of thousands of small villages in the densely populated areas of the region.

Road transport will continue to provide a major means of inland transport. It provides direct and indirect employment and thus contributes to economic and social advance. When eventually completed, the Asian Highway system will serve an area of about 2½ million square miles (6½ million sq. km) with a population of over 700 million people.

Gaps forming a very small percentage of the total length in the Asian Highway will

GREEN LIGHT FOR EDUCATION

Georges Fradier

have to be filled, major bridges built and many routes upgraded.

In the case of land-locked Afghanistan, Laos and Nepal, the terrain and economic conditions are such that only an international highway system can provide cheap and adequate access to neighbouring countries and the ports for external trade.

It is gratifying to note the enthusiasm and zeal with which governments are trying to implement the project. The roads of the Asian Highway have to a large extent been included in national high priority road programmes.

However, even though progress has been commendable, much work remains to be done owing to technical and financial difficulties, and some gaps have still to be filled, amounting to about 1,130 miles (1,816 km) But these are small gaps, considering that the total length is about 14,300 miles (22,940 km).

The Asian Highway project is undoubtedly a grand concept, and it has created great expectations as its materialization will be of great help in building an edifice of human brotherhood and peace, besides serving economic, social and cultural purposes. The years that have elapsed since 1959 are not a long period for the fulfilment of this international road network, and substantial strides have already been made. Nevertheless, this progress will have to be sustained and everything done to hasten the day when streams of cars and trucks will flow along the roads linking the various capitals, trading posts, cultural and historical sites of the regions.

It will be some years before the Asian Highway is finished, but the plans have to be made now and work taken in hand according to the economic requirements and resources of each country.

Once the roads have been linked from country to country, efforts will be turned to the progressive modernization of the network as a whole. Thus the countries of southern Asia, once largely isolated from the outside world, will be able to develop their trade, will get to know their neighbours better, and will also share fully in the economic and social progress of a continent which has now turned resolutely towards the future.

A dramatic change is taking place in the Middle East today as countries adopt modern techniques to attack the roots of ignorance and poverty.

One thing struck me above everything else. The apathy and resignation which was said to be widespread among the people of the Middle East is completely gone today, particularly amongst the younger generation. Everywhere the battle has been joined against poverty, against inequality and, more precisely, against their deep basic causes. Each nation, without exception, has its plan for modernization and re-equipment. Everywhere new land is being conquered for cultivation, new industries are springing up and new roads and hospitals, new laboratories and new schools are being built. Sweeping land reforms are taking place alongside significant administrative changes and amazing improvements in the social structure. Everywhere the 'unchanging East' is changing.

This desire for progress, for new techniques and new ideas, has seized not only statesmen and other top-level leaders but every section of the population in the Middle East. Today, from Afghanistan to the banks of the Nile, the common slogan is 'Our future depends on our schools', and the green light is being given to educational improvement.

In the past ten years literally thousands of new schools have been built in the countries of the Middle East. Primary schools, destined first for those regions where hardly any existed before; secondary and technical schools, industrial training centres; universities; engineering institutes as well as new libraries and laboratories have been created. Education, these countries have discovered, can no longer remain the slow percolation process of the past, starting at the top social stratum and only rarely getting down to the broad mass at the base. Today the ordinary people who need education most can no longer afford to wait. They want education at all levels and they want it now.

Afghanistan has launched a vigorous campaign against illiteracy, has revised its teacher training and recruiting methods, and in the past few years has also opened a number of new secondary schools. In 1950 the Afghan Institute of Technology was founded in Kabul, the capital, and it has now graduated civil and electrical engineers, mining and automobile technicians;

courses are open for civil aviation technicians too.

Iran's problems are different. It can be proud of its secondary schools, engineering colleges and its fine university, but it is handicapped by a lack of skilled supervisors and foremen to man its industries. The traditional methods of the copper engraver's shop or the goldsmith's workroom cannot be applied in operating a mine, a seaport, a railroad or an oil refinery.

So today Iran is giving technical education the biggest green light. All children (aged eleven to thirteen) in the last two classes of primary school will henceforth spend 50 per cent of their time on manual work—at work benches in city schools, at school farms in the villages. Each rural school will have its own fields for cultivation and experimentation and special watering systems for market gardens. Each city school will have its workshop complete with tools and equipment.

Within the next five years some 3,000 of these new classes will be giving practical instruction to over 90,000 children. Iran's revolutionary programme, to cost about 300 million rials (about $65 million), is one which many technically advanced countries might well envy today.

In the Lebanon educators are busily revising the school textbooks using scientifically exact criteria, and are now applying psychological tests to teacher trainees and primary and secondary school children in order to select better qualified teachers and provide vocational guidance for young people.

Syria is known mostly for its magnificent architecture of antiquity and its picturesque villages. But Syria is also a country of new factories, new dams and new schools. Since 1946, some 337 primary and 48 secondary schools have been built, new colleges have been founded (Faculties of Letters, Science, Engineering, Education in Damascus and Aleppo) and building is still going on. Within the past seven years this tiny nation of three million inhabitants has ended the teacher shortage in primary, secondary and vocational schools. The next goal is to train enough qualified teachers in higher technology and advanced science.

Baghdad, the capital of Iraq, is a city whose name once ranked high in the history of science. 'It will once again become a great centre of science,' say the people of Iraq. A few years ago the idea would have

New knowledge is being gained here by Iraq's future science teachers in the spacious laboratories of Baghdad's college of arts and sciences. Three years ago Baghdad had no laboratories

A school farm and a garden now provide practical lessons in the benefits of new farming methods. A club for young farmers and cooperatives is also in action here

seemed simply absurd. Baghdad had no laboratories, no science faculty, not even a scientific library. Iraq's chemists, physicists and biologists are usually graduates of British, American or German universities.

Today, students who want to study science at college are no longer obliged to go abroad. Baghdad now has an excellent school of engineering, a medical school and a newly created College of Arts and Sciences which will ultimately form part of the future University of Iraq. The departments of chemistry, physics and mathematics are only three years old but the standards and quality of instruction are already on a par with other long-established college faculties in other countries.

Egypt has not had the same problem of creating a higher educational system overnight. Its very modern universities in Cairo and Alexandria attract students from many countries, and the celebrated Al-Azhar University, once restricted to theological teaching, is now a new centre of modern learning.

Today Egypt is expanding technical education to meet the expected acceleration of industrial development. Training is being geared to research in the sciences, and particularly research in industrial chemistry. But for the man in the street in Egypt, 'scientific research' means the Desert Institute at Heliopolis, north of Cairo. It is becoming the national centre for specialized research on soil, climate,

desert flora and fauna, desert chemistry and geology.

All the countries of the Middle East, thus, are on the move. Their educational problems in practically every case are now directly linked with technical and economic development plans.

A university town built by a country doctor

In 1942 Manipal was a village with a few hundred inhabitants on the outskirts of the town of Udipi in the state of Mysore, southern India, hardly distinguishable from scores of similar hamlets in the region. Today, Manipal is a town of nearly 10,000 inhabitants. It has a medical school, an engineering college, a college of arts, letters and science, a college of commerce, a school of music, three elementary schools and a secondary school. How did this obscure village become a thriving town and a vigorous educational and cultural centre?

The transformation of Manipal has come about through the vision and determination of a country doctor named T M A Pai who sparked a remarkable community enterprise in education and science. Dr Pai, who was born in a village not far from Manipal sixty-seven years ago, studied at the University of Madras and after obtaining his medical degree returned to practise in his native village.

As he went his rounds, Dr Pai mused on many problems, but the one that pre-

occupied him most of all was India's lack of schools, not only schools to train other doctors like himself, but schools for engineers, technicians and teachers of all kinds. 'Knowledge is power' was his guiding maxim.

In his own area there were no facilities for higher education and he knew that any promising young men and women were without the means to continue their education at Mangalore or Madras. How could he help them?

The answer came in 1940 when, after discussing the problem with leading citizens of Udipi, he decided to create an educational cooperative to give the area the schools it needed. Two years later, in 1942, his courageous project came into being with the foundation of the Academy of General Education at Manipal. The first aims of the Academy were to make available technical and commercial education by supporting or building schools and colleges. A vigorous drive was undertaken to enlist support and donations from all sections of the community.

The project started modestly enough with a few vocational courses but soon expanded to include two primary, a higher elementary and a secondary school. By 1949 Dr Pai was able to enter the field of higher education with the establishment of an Arts and Science College, later named the Mahatma Gandhi Memorial College to honour the memory of the great Indian leader.

Four years later, in 1953, he astounded

educationalists by setting up India's first privately sponsored medical college, the Kasturba Medical College, named after the wife of Mahatma Gandhi. This was one of Dr Pai's most significant achievements. He and his friends had been moved by the plight of the many young men for whom there were no places in existing colleges in India, so they launched the Kasturba Medical College on a cooperative basis, asking the parents of the students who would benefit from its tuition to contribute equal amounts to the project. Sixty-seven per cent of the first class graduated as doctors in 1959.

In 1960 a large teaching hospital was added to the College. This has provided clinical facilities for the students and has helped to relieve some of the region's urgent medical problems.

Today the Academy has 800 medical students, 700 at the Polytechnic School, 1,200 at the College of Arts, Letters and Science, 200 at the School of Commerce. The primary schools founded by Dr Pai have 900 boys and girls, the secondary school 550 and the School of Music 350.

Dr Pai's achievement is a triumph of educational planning and educational financing from cooperative sources, for today the Academy's resources amount to £250,000 ($700,000). Most men would be satisfied to see their hopes and dreams realized on such a lavish scale. But Dr Pai is still looking far ahead. Today he is giving Manipal a large modern library of which the Academy's present library will be the nucleus. 'I believe', he said recently 'that it is the duty of everyone to give everything he can to help the development of education'.

A new university is born

AT ASSIUT THE ANCIENT CAPITAL OF UPPER EGYPT

S A Huzayyin

In 1957 the United Arab Republic established a new university at Assiut in Upper Egypt. Prior to 1952, the United Arab Republic had three modern universities together with Al-Azhar, the traditional theological university of the Muslim World. These, however, were not enough to meet the needs of the developing country. They were also all concentrated in the north in the two single large cities of the country, Cairo and Alexandria.

This meant that in the provinces of the south the young people were deprived of

At its foundation the university of Assiut gave priority to science and engineering faculties. Already 500 science and engineering students have graduated to join those now carrying out development programmes in Upper Egypt. These are the buildings of the science faculty

an equal opportunity to attend university. Only the well-to-do could afford the long journey and the costly life of the far cities. Some 800 kilometres extending along the narrow strip of the Nile valley south of Cairo had no higher educational services.

The idea of establishing a university in Assiut, the capital city of the region of Upper Egypt, goes back to 1949. But the effective step to bring the project into existence was taken in 1955. After two years of planning and preparation, two faculties for science and engineering were inaugurated in 1957. In Upper Egypt, the High Dam of Aswan was to be built and schemes for industrial as well as agricultural development had to follow. We had to think of the need for technicians to carry out the vast programmes which were to change the face of this ancient land. This meant the need for faculties of science, engineering, agriculture, medicine, veterinary medicine, business administration, etc.

In 1958 a third faculty, agriculture, was added. In 1960 the faculty of medicine was inaugurated and in 1961 new departments of pharmacy were added. In the same year a new faculty of veterinary medicine was established. In 1962 the faculty of commerce and business administration was added. In following years new faculties for dentistry and for arts (humanities), will complete the picture of the university. (It is a plan which has been carefully prepared and which will take some ten to twelve years to implement in full.)

At Assiut there were no buildings available as a permanent campus for the new university. A good secondary school building was taken as temporary headquarters.

Of course for an agricultural country as densely populated as ours, it was a pity that the university should take such space from the arable land. But it was planned that once the faculty of agriculture was established, it should undertake a project of reclamation covering at least four times as much of desert land in the vicinity. The reclaimed land would then be handed over to landless peasants in the area according to agrarian reform laws. This will not only afford good training opportunities for our students; it will also show the local community that the university did not deprive them of good arable land. It will also help integrate more intimately the work of the university with the efforts being made in the area to raise the standard of living of the people.

It is estimated that the total cost of the campus will be in the neighbourhood of eight million Egyptian pounds. The programme started late in 1958 with the building of large workshops for engineering (and where most of our furniture and some of our scientific apparatus is now being manufactured) and part of our recreation grounds. It is hoped that by 1968–69 the whole campus will be completed. It will accommodate some 12,000 students (attending eight or nine faculties), and eventually 16,000 students.

The question of style of buildings was

also carefully considered. The idea of a classical style was discarded. We are building a university in the second half of the twentieth century, and feel that it should reflect its time and age.

Equipping a scientific department with apparatus needs very careful planning to avoid waste and make one's funds go as far as possible. It also implies other difficulties connected with obtaining hard currency. Another problem we faced was that we had to get our equipment from different countries, East and West. This entailed a special training of technicians and, in some instances, the sending of technicians abroad, or receiving the help of foreign technicians for short terms at Assiut. One other problem which we had to tackle was the repair of instruments. But the workshops of the university were of invaluable help in this respect.

As for books, we began collecting some during the two years of planning before we went to Assiut in 1957. We started with a nucleus of more than 50,000 volumes for our library. But we found real difficulty in getting back-numbers of scientific periodicals. The university is setting up its own press to publish a *Bulletin of Science and Technology*, as well as text books prepared by the staff and sold to students at cost price.

Staffing of the scientific departments was probably the most difficult of all our problems. Fortunately, when the idea of the university was first conceived in 1949, some fifty graduates from the other universities were sent abroad for Ph.D. work in the various disciplines. They represented the nucleus of our first faculties. The staff of the university was then regularly added to year by year from returning members of missions or by other recruitment for leading posts. Gradually we also received a small number of visiting professors from other countries, mostly through cultural exchange agreements.

Ours was to be essentially a provincial university. It was decided that our places should be allocated primarily to students taking their secondary school certificate from schools in the five southern provinces of the country. This meant that the new university would alleviate pressure on the universities in Cairo and Alexandria.

Entry into all universities in the United Arab Republic is based on open competition between students finishing their secondary education. In addition to the numbers accepted from the country, 10 per cent of the total is allocated to students from different Arab and other countries. At present girls make up 8 to 10 per cent of our enrolment, but the percentage is steadily rising.

The establishing of our university in Upper Egypt has provided a new opportunity for girls in this part of the country to obtain a university education. At present nearly 80 per cent of our students are from the five southern provinces of the country.

As in most other countries, our youth justly feel that we are becoming an engineering society. So most of our boys (and many of our girls) prefer to join the engineering faculty. Next in preference are the faculties of medicine (and pharmacy) and science.

Life in the campus is gradually taking shape. Ours will be one of the rather rare examples of a complete campus, comprising both academic buildings and living accommodation for a section of the staff and student population. At the same time, recreational amenities are gradually being added.

Extramural activities and extension services include Assiut and the whole region north and south of it. The faculty of agriculture gives advice and guidance to peasants and farm groups. The hospital is designed to serve the whole region and to be a centre for health services and research. Even the workshops of the faculty of engineering are in the service of any citizen who wishes to avail himself of their services at cost price. The university of Assiut is gradually building up its status as a provincial institution in the service of the community and the whole neighbourhood.

Yet even this new university is not limited in its services to the area in which it is located. It is in our tradition in this land to consider ourselves as an integral part of the Arab people as a whole. In addition to the percentage of seats reserved for students from Arab and other neighbouring countries, these students are accorded every care to facilitate their stay with us. Already students from more than ten countries, coming from as far as Malaya, are studying in this small university. The numbers of students and the countries from which they come are gradually increasing. This is a welcome feature of our university education.

The little world of Asia's teachers

A visit to a few 'ordinary' schools in the East inspires not only sympathy for the teachers, but also admiration for these poorly but neatly dressed men and women, who are at their schools from an early hour each day. Two things about the average school strike one immediately: it is too small for its purpose and it is forbiddingly austere. It may be a straw hut built by the village council or a group of small mud houses or, more often, a 'modern' building of bricks and cement, which means it is even less attractive with its treeless courtyard and its dusty school garden.

A glance around the classroom offers a neat but bleak perspective of benches, a dais and a single window. There is nothing to relieve the bare walls; not even a map or a picture. But the teacher is not likely to be conscious of this emptiness; his own home is just as austere, and even the best furnished living-room in the neighbourhood probably has nothing but a calendar or a religious print by way of ornament. A classroom with a blackboard, a few chalks and a sponge is relatively well-off.

The teacher has probably never heard of visual and audio-visual aids to teaching. If you mention these things to him, he will probably nod and smilingly tell you that they are not yet available in that part of the world. Here, in fact, even the basic equipment—maps, wall charts and large sheets of drawing paper—are all difficult to come by, if indeed the school has any sort of paper other than perhaps the portrait of the Chief of State which hangs in the headmaster's office. A radio? Yes! one would be useful, but there is no mains electricity so it would have to be a battery set. And anyway there is no one to look after it or to repair it if needs be.

And here are the children—a hundred or so, apparently of all ages between seven and fourteen, squeeze themselves on to the narrow benches. How still and well-behaved they are; just as quiet in the stifling summer heat as they are in the Monsoon season or in the chill cold of winter.

They work hard on the whole, the teacher tells you, or at any rate they are eager to learn, but after a few hours they get tired and their attention wanders. 'The trouble is,' he adds, 'that some of them don't get enough to eat. They come from poor families. If only we could help to feed them.' (School canteens are practically non-existent in Asia. Among the

Above: bathtime for the children of a fisherman in the Philippines; but when they are older will there be schools for them to go to? The education authorities are making a sustained effort to replace the 85 per cent of schools which were destroyed during the last war. To meet any sudden increases in enrolment or when typhoons·have°damaged school buildings they also build 'temporary' school houses of light materials such as softwood and bamboo

Below: preparing a silk screen for the production of charts at a teaching aids centre in Bandung

exceptions: Ceylon, where each child receives a cup of milk and a bread roll each day; Korea, where in many schools children are given powdered milk, supplied, as in Ceylon, by American funds; the Philippines, where a cheap meal is available; Madras State, where subsidies enable school committees to serve meals, an experiment which the State developed until 30 per cent of schoolchildren were getting one meal a day in 1966.)

As to the children's health, all the teacher can tell you about it is that on the whole it is good—as good as can be expected. There are no files to supply further information and no doctor to look after the children, although nearly all the countries are trying to expand their medical services.

The next thing that strikes you are the obvious differences in size and apparent maturity among the children in the classroom. You are not mistaken; they are of all ages. Some are perhaps brighter than others and each year they go on to a higher class until they finish the school programme. But these are not the majority.

'There are always some who stay in the class for another year,' says the teacher; 'that is something that really plagues us in this school.' It is also the constant headache in many other primary schools throughout Asia. Far too many children stay for one, two or even three years in the first class, eventually struggle into a more advanced one, then become discouraged and give up.

The teacher will sometimes admit that the lessons he gives, as well as those of his colleagues could, in principle, be improved. (An inspector will tell you how difficult it is to overcome the placid resistance of teachers who have been trained according to old-fashioned methods.) But to improve teaching takes time.

The school programme is packed with subjects; nothing has been forgotten. First come languages (generally at least two have to be learned and in some countries as many as five). Then come arithmetic, history, geography, object lessons and elementary science; next the arts and manual work, such as agriculture; drawing, singing, dancing, sports and gymnastics; and what some countries consider a basic subject—religion or civics and ethics. 'It is a great deal for one man to cope with,' says the teacher. It is also a great deal for the children to cope with,

and they too are likely to lose themselves in this labyrinth of subjects, loosely related to each other and still less related to the local life.

Nowadays, however, some countries do encourage the use of active methods: 'projects' or practical tasks are carried out in the community schools of the Philippines, 'coordinated education' in India's new schools, and 'interest centres' form part of the programme in some Laotian schools. Usually the good pupils learn everything by heart, and unfortunately they are not alone in thinking that this is the best way of passing examinations.

Again, the teacher himself has only a handful of books and his pupils have to make do with the unique textbook which serves them throughout one year—a textbook sometimes shared by two or three children. One reason for this terrible shortage is that during the past ten years it has been necessary to translate into national or local languages books which were only available previously in English, French or Dutch. Another is that Asia is short of paper. Finally, however cheap the textbooks may be, there are always people and communities for whom they are too dear.

The educational picture of Asia is changing too rapidly for it to be summed up briefly. The important fact which stands out is that the peoples and governments are resolute in their determination to vanquish the many obstacles to educational progress. A veritable revolution lies ahead for the underequipped countries and their largely illiterate populations.

In India, for example, educational projects are drawn up by the governments of the different States and coordinated in an overall plan by the Ministry of Education. India's Third Five-Year Plan (1961–66) aimed at making primary education compulsory for all children from six to eleven and at increasing the school population to 54 million. The final goal for India is free and compulsory primary education up to the age of fourteen. In Pakistan, the government has set up a National Education Commission which recently published a complete report on education at all levels.

Plans have also been drawn up by ministries or planning councils and commissions in Afghanistan, Burma, Cambodia, Ceylon, Korea, Iran and Vietnam.

In some countries, recently created planning and statistical departments are still not properly equipped for their job. But the need to plan methodically the extension and reform of primary education is now universally recognized. This was apparent when representatives of Asian states recently met at Karachi at the Unesco-sponsored conference which produced a work plan designed to ensure 'universal, free and compulsory education in Asia'.

The first of the fifteen objectives in this remarkable programme is to ensure at least seven year primary education for all children within the next twenty years. It is a tremendous task and must be carried out stage by stage. Thus, the second aim is to raise the number of primary school pupils to 14 per cent in 1970, to 17 per cent in 1975 and, eventually, to 20 per cent in 1980.

Five objectives concern teachers: there should be one teacher for thirty-five pupils. All teachers should have a good secondary education plus at least two years' professional training. Within five years enough training colleges and special courses are to be established to produce the qualified teachers which the development programme requires. Teacher training colleges will have specialized instructors in the proportion of one for fifteen student teachers. In its budgetary provision, the plan envisages the increasing of recurring expenditures to 12 dollars per pupil in 1970, to 16 in 1975 and to 20 in 1980.

Sigota goes off to the bamboo school

Ritchie Calder

Sigota is a jungle schoolgirl, aged twelve. She is the eldest of four children, three girls and a baby boy, who share house with their father, mother, both sets of grandparents and 200 other people.

They are Dyaks, or headhunters, except that they do not hunt heads any more, and are much more peaceable than the nations who regard them as uncivilized, and much more moral than some of those who deplore the fact that they are pagans.

Sigota lives in the tree-tops. Her home is a 'longhouse', built on stilts which support a platform of bamboo slats bigger than a football field, with a hut stretching all the length—just one long room with

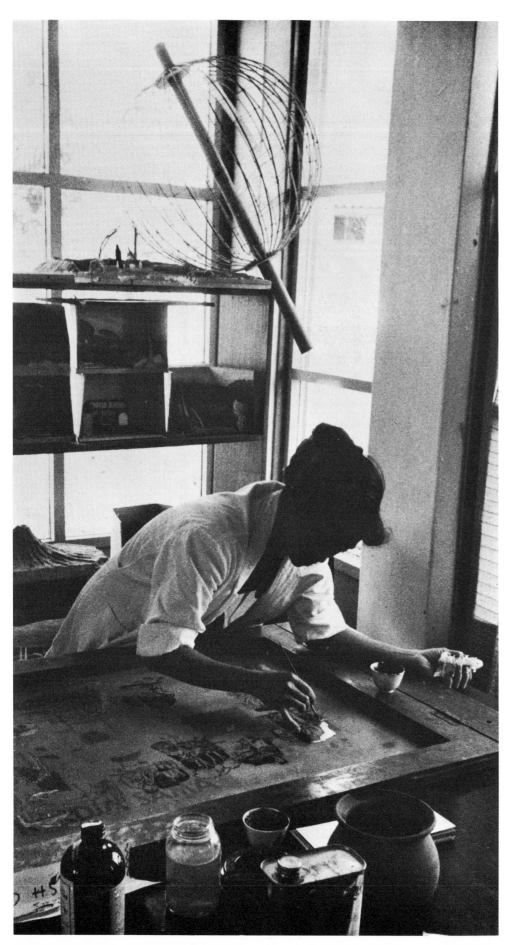

plaited screens of banana leaves partly separating each family. Maybe a longhouse may seem curious to people outside Borneo, but a city tenement or an American skyscraper would seem just as curious to Sigota. It depends upon whether you think of a longhouse as horizontal or vertical.

Yes, Sigota is a schoolgirl. She was working since seven this morning but at seven in the evening, with the crescent moon just making the darkness visible, she, together with Sengos (both of them in bright sarongs and ornaments in their hair), and Bait, a schoolboy friend of twelve, and a dozen other 'schoolchildren', some of whom were over twenty years old, joined a procession of hurricane lamps and flashlamps.

They went downstairs to school which is a thatched open hut in a clearing beyond the longhouse. The blackboard was lit by a hurricane lamp which periodically dimmed out behind a screen of moths. Each pupil had a tiny wick lamp in front of him by which he had to read his books and tot up his sums.

They began to read in unison 'Ay man saw a tiger . . .', 'I cennut towch the top of the coconut tree . . .', 'My father went to mercut today'.

Sigota is a star pupil. Solo she recited 'My mother is tired. I am sorry.'

Proudly the teacher in white pyjamas showed to me his certificate accrediting Ibrahim bin Mantali, aged forty-five, as a temporary teacher. It stated that he had passed standard four in Malay and standard three in English.

He may not have had much schooling himself, but he has brought literacy to these jungle Dyaks. And Sigota and Bait and their friends want to learn, even if it means going to school in jungle darkness, alive with strange sounds – including the echoes of the ABC.

With its 90,000,000 inhabitants spread out over the world's largest group of islands, Indonesia needs to train a vast army of teachers
Above: a student in handicrafts class at a teacher training college

Index